# The Scars of War

**Asian Voices**
**A Subseries of Asian/Pacific Perspectives**
Series Editor: Mark Selden

*Identity and Resistance in Okinawa*
    by Matthew Alden
*Tales of Tibet: Sky Burials, Prayer Wheels, and Wind Horses*
    edited and translated by Herbert Batt, foreword by Tsering Shakya
*Voicing Concerns: Contemporary Chinese Critical Inquiry*
    edited by Gloria Davies, conclusion by Geremie Barmé
*Peasants, Rebels, Women, and Outcastes: The Underside of Modern Japan*
    by Mikiso Hane
*Comfort Woman: A Filipina's Story of Prostitution and Slavery under the Japanese Military*
    by Maria Rosa Henson, introduction by Yuki Tanaka
*Japan's Past, Japan's Future: One Historian's Odyssey*
    by Ienaga Saburō, translated and introduced by Richard H. Minear
*Sisters and Lovers: Women and Desire in Bali*
    by Megan Jennaway
*Moral Politics in a South Chinese Village: Responsibility, Reciprocity, and Resistance*
    by Hok Bun Ku
*Queer Japan from the Pacific War to the Internet Age*
    by Mark McLelland
*Behind the Silence: Chinese Voices on Abortion*
    by Nie Jing-Bao
*Rowing the Eternal Sea: The Life of a Minamata Fisherman*
    by Oiwa Keibo, narrated by Ogata Masato, translated by Karen Colligan-Taylor
*Growing Up Untouchable in India: A Dalit Autobiography*
    by Vasant Moon, translated by Gail Omvedt, introduction by Eleanor Zelliot
*Exodus to North Korea: Shadows from Japan's Cold War*
    by Tessa Morris-Suzuki
*Red Is Not the Only Color: Contemporary Chinese Fiction on Love and Sex between Women, Collected Stories*
    edited by Patricia Sieber
*Sweet and Sour: Life-Worlds of Taipei Women Entrepreneurs*
    by Scott Simon
*Dear General MacArthur: Letters from the Japanese during the American Occupation*
    by Sodei Rinjirō, edited by John Junkerman, translated by Shizue Matsuda, foreword by John W. Dower
*A Thousand Miles of Dreams: The Journeys of Two Chinese Sisters*
    By Sasha Su-Ling Welland
*Unbroken Spirits: Nineteen Years in South Korea's Gulag*
    by Suh Sung, translated by Jean Inglis, foreword by James Palais

# The Scars of War

*Tokyo during World War II:*
*Writings of Takeyama Michio*

Edited and Translated by
Richard H. Minear

*ROWMAN & LITTLEFIELD PUBLISHERS, INC.*
Lanham • Boulder • New York • Toronto • Plymouth, UK

ROWMAN & LITTLEFIELD PUBLISHERS, INC.

Published in the United States of America
by Rowman & Littlefield Publishers, Inc.
A wholly owned subsidary of The Rowman & Littlefield Publishing Group, Inc.
4501 Forbes Boulevard, Suite 200, Lanham, Maryland 20706
www.rowmanlittlefield.com

Estover Road,
Plymouth PL6 7PY,
United Kingdom

British Library Cataloguing in Publication Information Available

**Library of Congress Cataloging-in-Publication Data**

Takeyama, Michio, 1903-1984.
  The scars of War : Tokyo during World War II : writings of Takeyama Michio / edited
and translated by Richard H. Minear.
    p. cm.
  Translation of selections from Japanese.
  Includes index.
  ISBN-13: 978-0-7425-5479-5 (cloth : alk. paper)
  ISBN-10: 0-7425-5479-1 (cloth : alk. paper)
  ISBN-13: 978-0-7425-5480-1 (pbk. : alk. paper)
  ISBN-10: 0-7425-5480-5 (pbk. : alk. paper)
  1. World War, 1939-1945--Japan. 2. Japan--History--Allied occupation, 1945-1952. I.
Minear, Richard H. II. Title.

D754.J3T275 2007
940.53'52135092--dc22
[B]
                                                2007000386

Printed in the United States of America

⊗™ The paper used in this publication meets the minimum requirements of American
National Standard for Information Sciences—Permanence of Paper for Printed Library
Materials, ANSI/NISO Z39.48-1992.

For Paul S. Minear,
in memory

# Contents

Foreword    ix

Illustrations    xii

Introduction    Takeyama Michio, 1903–1984    1

The Writings

Part I.    The War    29

Ichikō in 1944 (1946)    31

The End of the War (1953)    43

White Pine and Rose (1947)    53

Scars (1949)    71

Part II.    Crisis and Challenge    97

Germany: A New Middle Ages? (1940)    99

The Younger Generation (1945)    115

Part III.    The Tokyo Trial    123

The Trial of Mr. Hyde (1946)    125

Letter to Judge Röling (1949)    139

Part IV.　　Turn to the Right　　151

The Student Incident: Observations and
Reflections (1950)　　153

Those Who Refuse to Enter the Gate: Thoughts on
One Contemporary Frame of Mind (1951)　　173

Index　　199

About the Editor　　207

# Foreword

For more than half of my graduate training in the 1960s, I was the recipient, via the National Defense Education Act of 1958, of financial support from the U.S. government. That training involved the study of both Japanese and Chinese languages. Early in my career as a historian of Japan, I tended to think of language as a tool for the more serious business of monographic research. That was the philosophy behind the NDEA: study languages to know your potential enemies, decode the threatening world, be of use to national defense. In that post-Sputnik world such usefulness justified federal support.

Later I came to see how blinkered that view was. Language is a tool, yes, but it is also a treasure chest, the repository of the wisdom of a culture, an instrument of exquisite nuance, a living thing. So I came to think of translation not as a technical skill in pursuit of other ends but as a high calling in itself. Perhaps it is *only* by translating that we come really to understand the document at issue.

Those of us with language competence, whatever our primary fields, owe it to our fields and, yes, to the society that supports us, to spend part of our time translating—not recondite texts, in the first instance, although their translation has its uses, but prose and poetry that can speak to nonspecialist readers, whether those readers are found in college and precollege classrooms or in public libraries.

Our professions prize specialized scholarship, and translation usually doesn't qualify. Discretion, the better part of valor, suggests that we get tenure first. That is the route I took, not with calculation but because I was slow in unlearning that part of my graduate training. Yet how many of us who surmount the hurdle of tenure produce scholarly research that is worth as much as any one of the monuments of the culture we study? Even today, too few such monuments are available in competent English translation; major works remain unavailable. And if one of our criteria in selecting what to translate is usefulness—in the classroom, in the public arena, in undermining the insularity of an increasingly insular U.S. society—then it is not only major works that merit translation. It goes without saying that we should translate and retranslate winners of the Nobel Prize for Literature. But diaries of ordinary men and women, documents of protest, popular songs, TV shows—in translation all these serve important functions, functions that specialized research does not serve.

I've moved in these comments from intrinsic value to usefulness, so let me return to intrinsic value, value in this case to the translator. I find translation both impossible and rewarding. It's not simply that I'm accomplishing something that others haven't done or can't do. It's that I'm gaining from the experience of immersing myself so thoroughly in the frame of mind and the patterns of speech of another human being. Even when I disagree on important issues with the author, I gain from association with the works I translate. The primary beneficiary of the translation is the translator.

If I have fallen short either in understanding Takeyama Michio's thoughts or in recreating them in English, it is my fault, not the fault of those who have assisted me. This project got its start when Steve Ericson invited me to write an introduction to his translation of Ushimura Kei's *Beyond the "Judgment of Civilization"* (2001). Ushimura's fifth chapter, "Takeyama Michio and the Tokyo Trial," led me to Takeyama's "The Trial of Mr. Hyde"; Ushimura sent me a photocopy, and that essay became my first Takeyama translation. In the years since, I have incurred many other debts, including to the W. E. B. DuBois Library of the University of Massachusetts, the Harvard-Yenching Library, the Prange Collection at the University of Maryland, and the Archives of the University of Chicago. Whenever I visit a library and depart with notes, photocopies, or books on loan, I feel like a thief making off with treasure. These repositories make it possible for scholars to do their work.

Individuals who have rendered particular assistance include Sakai Hajime, emeritus professor of physics at the University of Massachusetts, who helped me understand both Takeyama's prose and wartime Japan, which he experienced; Sharon Domier, invaluable East Asian reference librarian; my History Department colleagues Steve Platt and Sigrid Schmalzer; and, for brief inquiries, colleagues here and across the country. Mark Selden helped with both comments and connections. As has been the case throughout my career, I have benefited from the careful reading and comments of my two most faithful readers, my parents, Paul and Gladys Minear, centenarians both; Dad died in February, less than a week after discussing this foreword with me.

Largest of all my debts are those to Takeyama Yasuko, widow of Takeyama Michio, for permission to translate these essays, and to Hirakawa Sukehiro, professor emeritus of Tokyo University and son-in-law of Takeyama Michio. Professor Hirakawa checked my translations very carefully and suggested many improvements. Of course, neither of them is responsible in any way for my editorial comments. In fact, Professor Hirakawa has taken sharp exception to the comments he has seen. My interpretation of Takeyama is mine alone, and the valuable cooperation I have received from Professor Hirakawa in no way indicates that he endorses my views.

For permission to reproduce images I thank Fukutake Shoten, Kōdansha, and the Prange Collection at the University of Maryland; for permission to quote archival material, the University of Chicago. Don Sluter created the maps; Edgar Sabogal and Donna Meisse scanned the photographs. For subventions to support publication I thank Audrey Altstadt, chair of the History Department; Lee Edwards, dean of Humanities and Fine Arts; and Paul Kostecki, associate dean of the Graduate School at the University of Massachusetts. At Rowman & Littlefield Jessica Gribble was in charge; Erica Nikolaidis was production editor and Veronica Jurgena, copy editor.

Amherst, Massachusetts
February 2007

Richard H. Minear

Note: All Japanese names are in Japanese order: surname, then given name.

EASTERN JAPAN

Japan

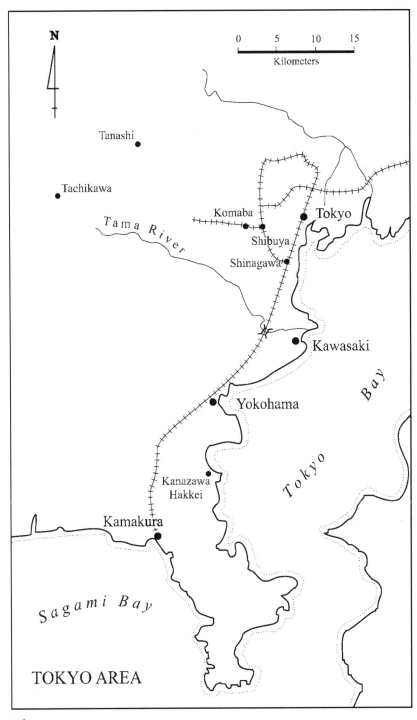

TOKYO AREA

Tokyo

Figure 1. Komaba campus: the main gate, seen from the railroad tracks, with the main building and its clock tower (ca. 1936). Courtesy Kōdansha.

Figure 2.    Students walking from campus to Shibuya, two wearing capes. Courtesy Kōdansha.

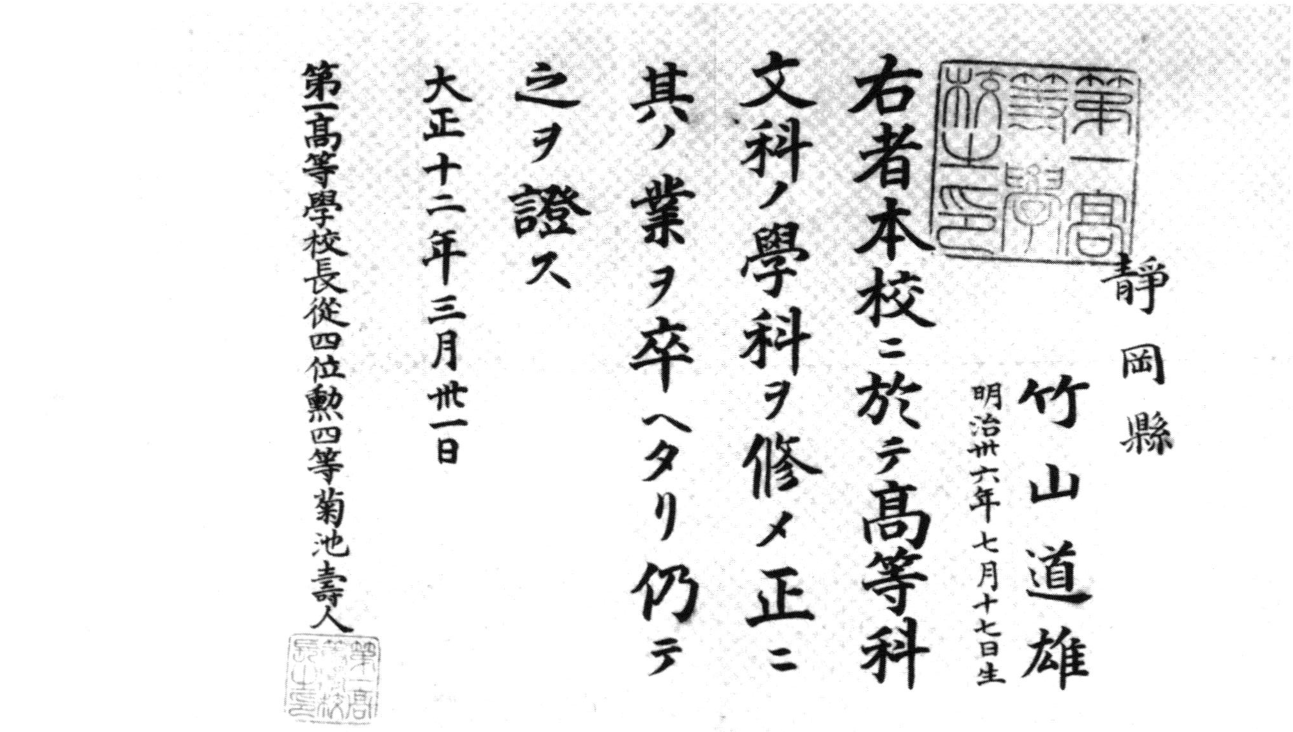
静岡縣
竹山道雄
明治卅六年七月十七日生
右者本校ニ於テ高等科
文科ノ學科ヲ修メ正ニ
其ノ業ヲ卒ヘタリ仍テ
之ヲ證ス
大正十二年三月卅一日
第一高等學校長従四位勲四等菊池壽人

Figure 3. Takeyama Michio's certificate of graduation from Ichikō. Takeyama is listed as from Shizuoka Prefecture, born July 17, 1903 (Meiji 36); he majored in humanities. The graduation date is March 31, 1923 (Taishō 12); headmaster Kikuchi's name appears just above the smaller school seal. Courtesy Kōdansha.

Figure 4.   Takeyama during his time (1923–1926) at Tokyo Imperial University. Courtesy Fukutake Shoten.

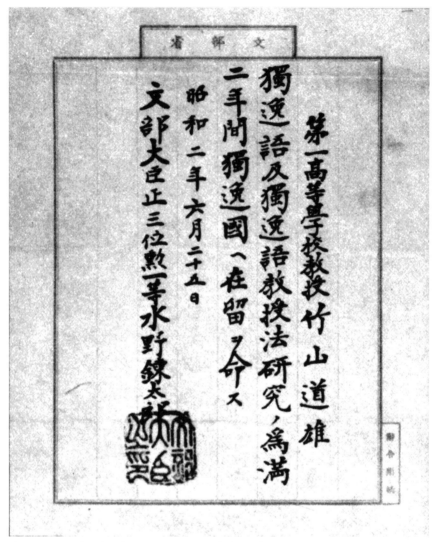

Figure 5. Notice dated June 25, 1927, ordering Takeyama Michio, teacher at Ichikō, to Germany for two full years of study of German language and pedagogy. The signature is that of Minister of Education Mizuno Rentarō; his name is just above the seal. Courtesy Kōdansha.

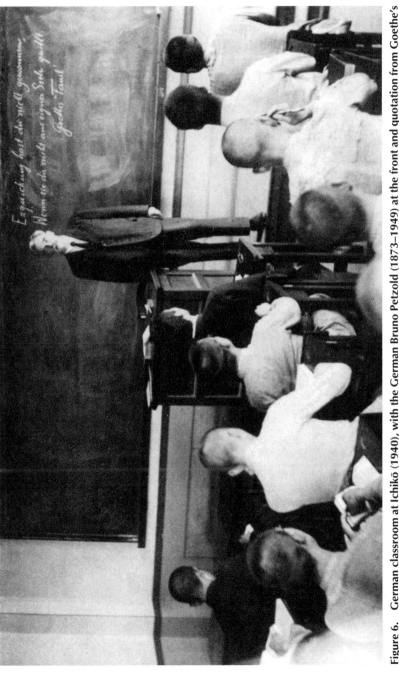

Figure 6.   German classroom at Ichikō (1940), with the German Bruno Petzold (1873–1949) at the front and quotation from Goethe's *Faust* on the blackboard. Courtesy Kōdansha.

Figure 7. Ichikō faculty during the term of Headmaster Abe. Abe is in the front row, fifth from left; Takeyama is in the second row, third from right (two in from the military officer). Courtesy Kōdansha.

Figure 8.  Wartime dorm assembly. Headmaster Abe, in puttees, stands at center table facing the student speaker. Courtesy Kōdansha.

Figure 9.   Students studying by candlelight (dorm lights went out at 10 p.m.). Courtesy Kōdansha.

Figure 10.   Ceremony for Ichikō students heading for work assignment, textbooks in knapsacks. Courtesy Kōdansha.

Figure 11.   Wartime inspection. Military officers are on the left, Ichikō students on the right. Courtesy Kōdansha.

Figure 12. Party to send off an Ichikō student who has been called up. Courtesy Kōdansha.

Figure 13. Takeyama (front row, third from right) and colleagues with Ichikō students headed for war. Courtesy Fukutake Shoten.

**Figure 14.** Young Washio, *kamikaze* pilot. Courtesy Kōdansha.

Figure 15. Wartime memorial service for Ichikō dead. Their portraits stand in front. Courtesy Kōdansha.

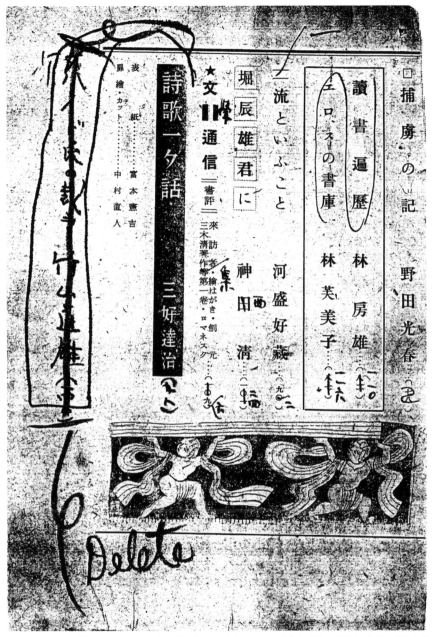

Figure 16. Table of contents for the journal issue in which "The Trial of Mr. Hyde" was set to appear. The censor has ordered its deletion. Courtesy Prange Collection, University of Maryland.

ケ *HOLD*

ハイド氏の裁き

竹山道雄

ある日、私は賊犯裁判を傍聴に行つた。

この日は特別な審理が行はれてゐたので、入場券もいらず、所持品の檢査もなかつた。法廷の内は、その構成が大へん複雑で、はじめてここに入つた私には勝手が分らなかつた。高い段の上に坐つてゐる裁判官たち、その下の谷のところに置いてある卓の前にこもごもに立つて發言する檢事と辯護士、それからずつと遠くの天井に近いところの硝子箱の中にゐる通譯たち――。このやうに、諸方から發せられる言葉が二重の國語になつてイヤホーンを通じて傳はつてくるので、しばらくはけつきりとした焦點がつかめなかつた。そして、場内に盈つた晩秋の日ざしが流れてゐたが、それがときどき目も眩めくほどに明るくなり、またくらく翳つたりした。

傍聴席から見下すと、各國の旗を飾つた前に、血色のいいMPがきちんと立つて人形のやうに配置されてゐる。かつての將軍たちや重臣たちが三十人ほど、蒼黒い顔を妙につやつやと光らせて坐つてゐる。あちらこちらに赤と白の電燈がしきりに明滅してゐる。タイプライターが蝉の唸りのやうに鳴りつづけてゐる。にりめぐらす電線を通じてさまざまな傳令が……たえず交されてゐる。これらのものが、私にはまるで夢の中にゐるやうな氣がするのであつた。

この日に論告されてゐたのは、まだ新聞にも報道されたことのない人であつた。その顔もついぞ寫眞でも見たことがなかつた。この被告は東條大將のすぐ後の、かつて大川博士が狂態を演じたあとの空席に坐つて、傲然とあたりを睥睨してゐた。

その樣子はすさまじかつた。全被告席を壓倒してゐた。他の被告たちもみな落ちついて、考への狹い人間のもつ威嚴といつたやうなものをもつて、一種の凄味を發散してゐる人たちではあつたが、この未知の被告に比べては影がうすかつた。その獰猛兇惡な風貌

Figure 17.   The first page of "The Trial of Mr. Hyde," with censor's "Hold" order. Courtesy Prange Collection, University of Maryland.

Figure 18.   Takeyama circa 1950. Courtesy Fukutake Shoten.

Figure 19.    Takeyama in his old age. Courtesy Fukutake Shoten.

~

# Introduction: Takeyama Michio, 1903–1984

*Richard H. Minear*

What was life like for civilians in Japan during World War II? How did the war affect jobs, food, attitudes? What happened to family life? The government controlled what people knew about the war, but how effective was that censorship? Were civilians fanatical or resigned? What did they think of the military government and of the American enemy? In the last months of the war, when American firebombing destroyed on average more than half of the sixty largest cities, how did they cope? What was *life* like?

Sixty years after the end of the Pacific War there is still little material in English about the Japanese experience on the home front. There are a few accounts in the form of fiction; there are oral histories recorded decades later. This dearth of firsthand material stands in striking contrast to the wealth of material in English on politics, war strategy, battle histories, and battle memoirs. Yet without some sense of what life was like on the home front, we cannot begin to understand the Japanese experience of World War II.

Teacher, writer, translator, Takeyama Michio was a civilian in Tokyo during World War II. Through his family he had connections to important politicians, and he taught at the elite preparatory school Ichikō. So he was in contact with Japan's movers and shakers past, present, and future, and he shared their experiences. Soon after the war, when memories were fresh, he wrote eloquently of the deprivations of wartime living, the anguish of seeing students depart for the front or for *kamikaze* service, friction between civilians and the military, the determination to keep on despite everything, and the lessons the war taught him. His essays bring alive for us the months

1

and years of the Pacific War as they affected him and the students under his charge at a time of national crisis. Takeyama's essays paint a poignant picture of the home front experiences of a man of intelligence, conscience, and candor. He was not a Japanese everyman, but his essays are eloquent evidence about life on the Japanese home front.

In 1970 an American associate, Ivan P. Hall, composed a biographical statement about Takeyama. Hall wrote that Takeyama

> belongs to the first rank of modern masters of Japanese literary style. His place in contemporary letters is assured not only by his many prize-winning novels, essays and other works, but also by his embodiment as its last living member of one of the great schools of early twentieth-century Japanese literary humanism. His consistent loyalty to his own principles over the decades of turbulent political and social change has earned him a reputation for great intellectual honesty and moral integrity, and has commanded the respect of friend and foe alike.
>
> His whole life . . . has been dedicated to the education and inspiration of young men roughly seventeen to twenty years of age, on whom Professor Takeyama—more in the manner of a prep school master than of a university academician—has left the imprint of his personality, as well as of his mind. His former pupils, now in their thirties and forties, are to be found in some of the most promising academic, journalistic and literary positions in Japan. . . . As a man of principle, and of authority, who not only has helped to keep the flame of liberalism and humanism burning in Japan, but who also has done much to introduce the best in Western culture to his own countrymen, Professor Takeyama has behind him a distinguished career every step of which has reflected the same ideals and purposes as those for which the IACF strives."[1]

As do many eulogists, Hall exaggerates: Takeyama's place in "contemporary letters" is not assured; nearly forty years after Hall wrote, Takeyama is far from a household name. But much of his life was "dedicated to the education and inspiration of young men," he did introduce much European culture to Japan, and his former students did rise to great prominence. I will have more to say about the circumstances that gave rise to Hall's tribute.

Takeyama wrote in many forms—novels, essays, travel accounts—and about many topics. Among the most important of these topics was the Asia-Pacific War, the focus of dozens of essays and two books, one fiction and one nonfiction. It was the novel *Harp of Burma* that made Takeyama famous; published in serial form in a children's magazine in 1947 and 1948, it appeared in book form in 1948. Noted director Ichikawa Kon made it into a movie not once, but twice: in black and white in 1956 and in color in 1985. Both films were popular successes. And in 1986 there appeared an *anime* version. But the essays I have chosen for translation here depict the war's impact in personal terms on Takeyama and those around him. This volume presents translations of ten works Takeyama wrote between 1940 and 1955; these are the first English translations of all ten works. Beyond their depiction of the scars of war, these writings chart the development of Takeyama's thinking, from sharp critic of Nazi Germany in 1940 to Cold War warrior in the 1950s. In Japan at the time, neither stand was popular. Takeyama stood against the tide, not once but twice. In speaking out against Nazi Germany in 1940, he flew in the face of the government's decision to ally Japan with Germany; in speaking out against the "progressives" of the postwar era, he challenged the dominant academic trend of the early postwar era. But if the former required a certain amount of personal courage, the latter placed Takeyama in alliance with most postwar Japanese governments and with important forces outside Japan. A fascinating recent book, *A Postwar History Centering on 'Harp of Burma'* (2004) makes a very useful start at telling Takeyama's story, dealing as it does with much more of Takeyama's life and work than *Harp of Burma*; but even in Japanese there is no full-scale biography.[2]

## Biography

Takeyama Michio was born in 1903. Since the Meiji Restoration of 1868, the Japanese national government had pursued a Westernizing course. It had abolished the class system, ending the legal privileges of the samurai class, from which Takeyama's forebears came. Through an ambitious program of industrial development and military reform, the government had developed Japan's wealth and power. It had established a constitution (1889) and a national parliament, the Diet. The first session of the Diet had met thirteen years before Takeyama's birth, and his paternal grandfather had been one of its members. (In that election only males over twenty-five who paid substantial taxes could vote, so the total electorate numbered only 400,000.) Less than ten years before his birth, Japan had defeated China in the Sino-Japanese War (1894–1895); one year after his birth came the outbreak of the Russo-Japanese War (1904–1905), which ended also in Japanese triumph. The old order was passing.

Takeyama's heritage was a distinguished one.[3] Okada Ryōichirō, the grandfather elected to the first two Imperial Diets, was a Shizuoka landowner. His grandmother's family, the Takeyama, had provided critical service to Tokugawa Ieyasu during the wars of unification in 1600; she herself was the daughter of the founder of the Hamamatsu Bank. Their second son, adopted out into a family without a male heir, was Ichiki Kitokurō, one of the most distinguished

politicians of the early twentieth century. Their third son became the husband
of a Takeyama daughter, whose family name he assumed. This couple had
seven children; Takeyama Michio was their third child and second son.

Takeyama's father was quite conventional. Of him, Takeyama wrote, "My
father was a progressive, rational bourgeois who reached maturity in mid-
Meiji and saw no point at all in the traditional training," that is, in a Confucian education. But Takeyama's uncle by marriage, Uchida Shūhei, who
died in 1944 at the age of eighty-seven, was an eccentric, and he is the title
character of the essay, "The Last Confucian."⁴ In this 1953 essay Takeyama
shows his sympathy with the "weird" uncle, for like him, Takeyama was
unconventional: "Among relatives who were all officials and entrepreneurs,
I was the exception, the only one to enter the Faculty of Letters [of Tokyo
Imperial University] and cause my father to lament, 'I've lost a son.'" The
uncle's sympathies were with Takeyama, who learned later from his mother
that the last Confucian had told her, "Of your children, he alone may become a real human being. Take care of him."

Travel outside Japan was one leitmotif of Takeyama's life. From 1907 to
1913 he lived in colonial Korea, where his father headed the Seoul branch
of a major Japanese bank. As an adult he studied in Germany and traveled
widely in Europe, China, South Asia, and Southeast Asia. Skipping a grade
in his late teens, he entered Tokyo's First Higher School (Ichikō) in 1920.
Then came Tokyo Imperial University, from 1923 to 1926. There he specialized in German language and literature.

Takeyama never had difficulty with the academic side of school, but
he underwent other experiences that affected him profoundly. When the
family moved from Seoul to Hamamatsu in 1913 (Takeyama was ten), he
experienced bullying. Brainy, slight of stature, and a newcomer, he made a
natural target. In 1915 he broke his right leg above the knee, and the doctors
inserted a piece of ivory to help repair the damage. In 1916, a close classmate
died on a school excursion. In 1923, his first year at Tokyo Imperial University, the great Kanto earthquake struck. It did not damage Takeyama's home,
but it shocked Takeyama, who prowled the disaster area.

All Ichikō graduates were bound for one of Japan's prestigious public universities. That Takeyama was bound for Tokyo Imperial University was taken
for granted. But Takeyama's father had expected him to enroll in the Law
Faculty. Instead, without telling his father, he enrolled in the Letters Faculty,
first in aesthetics, soon thereafter in German. He wrote his thesis on a prose
tragedy, *Maria Magdalena* (1844), by the nineteenth-century German poet
Christian Friedrich Hebbel. While at the university, Takeyama traveled to
Taiwan, then under Japan's colonial rule, and to Hokkaido.

Immediately upon graduation at age twenty-three, he began teaching German language and culture at Ichikō. A year later he traveled to Europe for the first time, via Egypt, to study for three years in Weimar Berlin. The contrasts of Weimar wealth and poverty shocked him. He made several excursions to Paris, a city he found more to his liking, and with the aid of Berlitz and Alliance Française he polished his French. He also visited Spain, Italy, Great Britain, and Greece. Here is his own account, composed in 1949:

> From the reality of Europe I got a truly unexpected impression. Especially as concerned Germany: I marveled, is this the revered and lofty country and people? The Berlin of 1928 and 1929 was a wasteland. I sensed everywhere the unmistakable symptoms of a decadent age. I thought to myself, "The level of the people is really low. " Having now experienced conditions after a lost war, I understand it entirely, but back then I had no idea at all of society, and I was thrown all of a sudden into that swamplike modern city and was shocked: "How can such things be?" Berlin was the most flourishing intellectual center, and there I saw splendid people; but in terms of the whole, I wanted to cover my eyes before the shallow, inferior vitalism that was the public mood. I think I understand how Nazism arose on that foundation.[5]

In 1931 and again in 1938 he traveled to China. In 1940 he published "Germany: A New Middle Ages?", an essay sharply critical of Nazi Germany; it is translated in this volume. When during the war the Ministry of Education decreed an end to academic instruction in the French language, Takeyama helped to keep one French course alive at his own school.

Takeyama married in 1939; children arrived in 1942 and 1943. In May of 1942, five months after Pearl Harbor, his first book appeared. *Warrior of Light and Love* has a martial-sounding title, suitable at first glance to the militarism of the war years. Indeed, most Japanese writers assisted the war effort. But Takeyama's subject is the life of Albert Schweitzer. His target audience is teenagers, and Takeyama "hope[s] that those in the first years of youth can take away something of the personality and actions of Schweitzer," whom he describes late in the book as combining "a warrior's courage and a saint's meekness." He asks the indulgence of his young readers for the fact that Schweitzer's early life lacks drama and concedes that "an author who has no grounding in religion cannot hope to convey accurately the life of this person whose every act arises from religious conviction." He closes by citing two late letters in which Schweitzer laments the fact that the outbreak of war in Europe has brought physical hardship to his mission in Lambarene and forced him to change his plans, which included a trip to the United States and a return via Japan. It is hardly a subject or treatment that Japan's wartime authorities would welcome, nor is it—350 pages long—an easy book for young readers.[6] He also produced translations of major European writers—Albert Schweitzer, Thomas Mann, Friedrich Nietzsche, and Henrik Ibsen—along with literary criticism and occasional pieces.

After the war Takeyama taught five more years. Ichikō survived only until 1950. In that year the government reformed the educational system on the American model: six years of primary school, three of junior high, and three of high school, followed by college; in this process Ichikō became Tokyo University's General Studies division. Takeyama taught there in 1950–1951 before resigning. His second book appeared in 1947, as did the serialized *Harp of Burma*. In 1948 *Harp of Burma* appeared in book form, and in 1949 and 1950 won prestigious prizes. In 1955 Ichikawa Kon's film version (released as *The Burmese Harp* in English) won the San Giorgio Prize at the Venice Film Festival and enjoyed enormous popularity at home; in 1985 Ichikawa did a remake, this time in color, once again to popular acclaim.

In the early postwar years very few Japanese intellectuals traveled as widely or as often as Takeyama. Most lacked the finances, the connections, or both. At first under PEN Club auspices, later with financing from the Congress for Cultural Freedom (CCF), he resumed his travels: Burma and East Pakistan and India (1955); Europe (thirteen months, 1955–1956); Taiwan (1958); Europe (seven months, 1959–1960); Moscow (1961); Europe (1964); South Korea (1965); Malaysia, the Philippines, Hong Kong (1966); Portugal and Spain (1966); Turkey (1969); the south of France (1972); and Europe (1975). He never did visit the United States.

Takeyama helped to found and edit the journal *Jiyū* [Freedom] and was active in it for nearly two decades, from 1949 to 1967. During those same years he became a figure of contention. The Left attacked him; he did his own attacking. "Those Who Refuse to Enter the Gate" (1951) shows Takeyama at his polemical best; it is the final translation in this volume. In 1965 he wrote a series of essays attacking the role of the Catholic Church in the European Holocaust. In 1968, when protests erupted over the planned visit to Japan of the USS *Enterprise*, which carried nuclear weapons, he spoke out in favor of allowing the vessel to enter the harbor of Sasebo. In a country that still held Hiroshima and Nagasaki fresh in memory, that was a bold stance. Takeyama died in 1984 at the age of 81.

## Ichikō

Takeyama's life and thought are bound up inextricably with Ichikō. As its name indicates, Ichikō is first (the *ichi* of Ichikō) of Japan's higher schools.

Ichikō was a public institution that prepared its graduates for public institutions, but the closest analogues in the United States and the United Kingdom are private schools, Andover and Exeter, Eton and Harrow, that prepared their students for top universities, Harvard and Yale (private), Oxford and Cambridge (public). An extraordinary percentage of Japan's twentieth-century elite were graduates of Ichikō. They included five of ten civilian prime ministers between 1921 and 1945 and two early postwar prime ministers.[7] To quote the Ichikō commemorative volume, the list of leading bureaucrats is "broad and deep, virtually innumerable."[8] One study estimates that one-quarter of Japan's top-level bureaucrats and 40 percent of Japan's ambassadors and ministers were Ichikō graduates.[9] Intellectuals and writers abounded. Ichikō even produced people of the Left.[10] On the faculty at various times were such stellar figures as Nitobe Inazō, Uchimura Kanzō (driven to resign in 1891 over his refusal to bow to the Imperial Rescript on Education), Natsume Sōseki, Yanaihara Tadao, and Takeyama. Yanaihara, like Takeyama, was also an Ichikō graduate.

In 1920, at the age of seventeen, Takeyama entered Ichikō; he graduated in 1923. In 1926, at the age of twenty-three, he was appointed a lecturer at Ichikō. After three years of study in Europe, he returned to Ichikō and remained on its faculty until its dissolution in 1950. He was then forty-seven and had spent fully half his life there, first as student, then as teacher. As Takeyama himself wrote late in life: "I graduated from the school, taught at the school, and was there until the school's demise at the hands of the school reform. I never really experienced the stormy seas of the broader society. School employment meant low salary and long hours in the classroom, but there was a good bit of time to loaf. The air in the faculty lounge was very good, so it was my intention to spend my whole life as a higher school teacher in an (old-style) higher school. But then came the war, and the world changed, and it became impossible to be as easygoing as before."[11]

Ichikō was at the very apex of preuniversity education in Japan. Far fewer than 1 percent of the boys who entered Japan's schools (at age six) made it to public or private universities (ages twenty to twenty-three). In 1908, for example, 5.4 million boys and girls were enrolled in elementary schools, and only 7,500 in universities. Those proportions held steady into the late 1920s.[12]

Before 1918 there were eight higher schools in Japan, named not by location but in order of establishment: First, in Tokyo; Second, in Sendai; Third, in Kyoto; and so on. At first there were three imperial universities: Tokyo Imperial University, Kyoto Imperial University, and Hokkaido Imperial University. In the decade after 1918, the imperial university system expanded greatly, and with it the higher schools, which quadrupled in number; but the original eight retained their prestige.

Ichikō students were selected for ability. No one got in without excelling on the entrance examination. But the exam was only one of the hurdles. Candidates had to have "acceptable manners, health, and demeanor." Speech impediments, physical deformities, or behavioral quirks could be disqualifying. Ichikō students lived in on-campus dormitories (by contrast, university students lived in rooming houses), so Ichikō and the other higher schools were actually "all-male boarding academies" financed largely by the national government. Of Ichikō in the 1890s, Donald Roden has written: "Ichikō, Eton, and St. Paul's were more striking in their similarities than in their differences. In each case the school resembled a cloister purposefully set apart from a society in transformation; a surrogate family where an all-male faculty assumed both paternal and maternal responsibility; a training-ground for future leaders to acquire the affectations of gentlemanly character."[13]

In 1920, the year Takeyama entered, the Ichikō faculty numbered sixty-four, including thirty-three full faculty, five assistants, twenty-one adjuncts, and five "foreign lecturers." There were 1,122 students. The entering class numbered 363, culled from 3,628 applicants. Six years later, when Takeyama returned to teach immediately after graduating from Tokyo Imperial University, the numbers had changed only slightly: adjuncts were up thirteen, and admissions were 380, culled from a significantly larger applicant pool of 4,971.[14]

The higher school experience left few students unaffected. Dormitory living featured rituals, including "storms"—attacks on underclassmen in the dorms, in which half-naked upperclassmen kicked and beat the victims and soaked them (and their rooms) with water. Dorm life featured grunge living—"higher school barbarism" was the phrase: students bathed only infrequently, wore old and battered clothing, and pissed from dorm windows. The latter practice was termed "dorm rain"; Roden calls it "the ultimate expression of higher school primitivism," of adolescents "rejoicing in their own filth." He speaks of "roach-infested hallways, dust-covered windows, and fetid lavatories." Counterpart schools in the United Kingdom and the United States saw similar practices.[15]

Still, higher school was often described as "an isolated castle of freedom,"[16] a "utopian oasis of manliness"; Roden speaks of a "pedagogy of seclusion."[17] In Japan as elsewhere, these schools marked off "adolescence as an institutional moratorium between childhood and adulthood."[18] Here is Ichikō's school song:

From our vantage atop Mukōga Hill
We the stalwarts of the five dormitories,
Our ambitions soaring to the sky,
Gaze down upon a vulgar world
Which revels over moonlight reflections
Of cherry blossoms in its saké cups
And which is addicted to the dreams of ordinary life.[19]

Hill versus plain, elite versus plebeian, the refined versus the vulgar—such was the Ichikō self-image. In his reminiscences about the year 1944, Takeyama calls Ichikō a "Magic Mountain," a reference to the isolated community in Thomas Mann's great novel.

The 1937–1938 Ichikō handbook gives a near-complete picture of Ichikō that year.[20] The faculty included fifty-five professors, one of whom was Takeyama. There were nine adjuncts, including seven foreigners: Bruno Petzold and another German teacher, a Frenchman, and four with English surnames. There were six assistant professors and thirty-three lecturers. Where the faculty had earned degrees abroad, that fact was listed: two from Paris, one from Cambridge, one from Fribourg, one from the University of Chicago, one from Kenyon College (an MA). Nine faculty were army officers, ranging in rank from second lieutenant up to lieutenant colonel; most of the military men taught physical education and physical training.

The 916 students were divided by year, by specialty (letters or sciences), and then into subgroups of about thirty. Four hundred forty-six were in letters; 470 in sciences. Two hundred sixty-one students came from Tokyo Prefecture. Hyogo Prefecture (which includes Kobe) supplied thirty-three, and Kanagawa (near Tokyo), thirty-two; Kyoto, eighteen; Hokkaido, ten; Chosen (Korea), two. Korea had been Japanese since 1910. Taiwan had been Japanese since 1895, and the list includes a column for Taiwan, but in that year there were no students from Taiwan. In addition, there was a special group: fifty-seven students from China and thirty-seven from Manchukuo, Japan's puppet state.

Language training played a major role for all Ichikō students. Cohorts of about thirty students were separated along language lines: among the seniors, there were five "English" cohorts, three "German" cohorts, one "French" cohort, and one "foreign languages" cohort. The curriculum centered on Western languages (roughly one-third of class hours) and the liberal arts—the European and American liberal arts. Most higher school students could "read English and one other foreign language, abilities which would give them access to the untranslated bulk of Western socialist literature when their interests turned in that direction."[21] This explains why in his lecture of July

1945 ("The Younger Generation," translated here), Takeyama could refer in passing to Romain Rolland, Jean Cocteau, and Erich Maria Remarque and expect his listeners to understand his meaning.

Classroom instruction was important but far from all-important. Staying away from classes was virtually a "student privilege." Building character took precedence, and Ichikō "rarely expelled a single student for academic reasons." Roden writes: "Grades had little if any meaning . . . expulsion for academic reasons was virtually an impossibility, and passage to the university was assured."[22] Higher school graduates might not get their first choice of national university or of specialization, but they would be admitted to one of the national universities, which functioned as graduate schools do today in the United States—three years of professional training.

Japan's higher schools of the 1920s were closer to today's American colleges, albeit with far less of the professionalism and diversity. The higher schools were smaller than the universities (Ichikō graduated 320 in 1931);[23] they were less career-oriented; the students were in their late teens, not their early twenties. Dormitory living, uniforms, self-government, rowdiness, school songs—in Japan these characterized higher school life, not university life. One commentator saw in the higher schools "the energy and sentimentality of youth, as well as a certain decadence. Whether relaxing or studying, on the whole there was a certain gut-level feeling of 'living life to the hilt.'"[24]

The Ichikō spirit would reappear in Takeyama's *Harp of Burma*, where the military unit—Ichikō students on an outing?—sings its way through Burma. Here is one passage:

During the past three days we had sung all the songs we knew, except for *Hanyu no yado*. Each song had its special memories, and now that we were leaving we sang all of them with deep emotion. But the one that moved us the most was *Miyako no sora*—"The Sky over the Capital."

*Miyako no sora* is the school song of the First Higher School of Tokyo, the one its students sang in farewell to classmates who had to leave to go to war. One after another they went away, as if beckoned by some invisible hand, and it seems that for a time the song echoed through the school grounds morning and night. We learned it from an alumnus of this school, when his company happened to be stationed in the same town that we were. It was a fine tune for sending off young men, a tune with a bright, gay rhythm and yet a poignant sadness to it. Even now I can hear it whenever I close my eyes. As I listen, it awakens vivid memories of those days. If the Japanese people had sung more fine songs like *Miyako no sora* during the war, instead of cheap patriotic songs, everyone might have survived with greater dignity.[25]

Ichikō shaped Takeyama as student, teacher, author.

It was while he was on the Ichikō faculty that Takeyama broke into print on the national scene. In an April 1940 essay on Nazi Germany, Takeyama expressed in stark form his disdain for the Nazis. This is how Takeyama concluded: "The symptoms of illness of modern society that were predicted sixty or seventy years ago by Nietzsche and warned of by many other thinkers are today everywhere visible and have changed into new forms. It has been realized most clearly and deeply in Germany. . . . But if we limit the issue to the single point of 'freedom of thought,' if the British-French side wins, at least for our lifetime, it will be preserved in some form. If Germany wins, it will be fundamentally and instantly stolen from us."[26] Takeyama wrote this a scant five years after Minobe Tatsukichi (1873–1948) had been forced to resign from the House of Peers because of his theory that the emperor was an organ of the state. Until then that theory had enjoyed wide acceptance, but in the 1930s it ran afoul of right-wing fundamentalists who charged Minobe with lèse-majesté.

During the war Takeyama accompanied one group of students to work at a factory in Hitachi. In an essay of June 1943 that appeared in the Ichikō school journal, he described the conditions there:

Now I'm at the labor site in Hitachi, writing this essay in haste late at night. Beginning just last night, alerts were issued, and the rumor is that enemy planes have bombed Kitakyushu at last [the first bombing raids on Kyushu occurred in June and July 1944]. Tonight's class took place in a *tatami* room on the second floor of one of the factory outbuildings atop the hill, with blackout curtains drawn; we read the first chapter of Goethe's autobiography, the section where the young Goethe captures the rays of the dawn sun with a lens and sets a candle burning and offers a fervent prayer to the God who created and loves the world. By the light of faint lamps, the students listened avidly. But the one on my left—probably exhausted from the day's labors—was stretched out full length, asleep. There were also some who rolled up their sleeves in haste from time to time to catch fleas.[27]

Takeyama wrote about the diligence of his students, too, in "Ichikō in 1944," the first translation in this volume. But almost as remarkable was the diligence of teachers like Takeyama. Witness "The Younger Generation," his address to the school in July 1945, scant weeks before Japan's defeat. Ichikō put Takeyama in touch with the Japanese elite; it put them in touch with a remarkable humanist.

Takeyama's devotion to his Ichikō students, all of them male, all of them best and brightest, did not long outlive the defeat. In 1949 Ichikō became part of Tokyo University, and in 1950 Takeyama took strong exception to the new breed of student activists. Soon thereafter he left teaching permanently.

## Harp of Burma

Outside of Japan Takeyama Michio is most famous for *Harp of Burma*. In Japan, too, it may be his chief claim to fame, in part because the two movies based on it became major hits. Takeyama wrote *Harp of Burma* at the request of the publisher of *Akatombo* [Red Dragonfly], a prestigious journal for children. As he recalled in an essay of 1957, Takeyama spent ten days in the summer of 1946 recuperating from many years of uninterrupted work (no vacations) and from an inflammation of the inner ear. He calls *Harp of Burma* a "product of his imagination," a work that had no models. In 1946 repatriated soldiers were a very common sight; they begged at railroad stations and other busy spots (I remember seeing such men in 1964, my first year in Japan). Hardship was general, and so soon after total defeat there was limited sympathy for these men or respect for their service. Here is Takeyama, writing a decade later, after his own thinking had changed markedly:

> At the time, no sense whatsoever of praying for the souls of the war dead appeared in the press. It wasn't on people's minds. On the contrary, the mood was that "every last one of those who fought were evil men." Speaking ill of the Japanese military was the thing, was righteous. I couldn't accept that, even if people said that wishing for the repose of the souls of all those who did their duty and gave their lives was going back to the old ways. Going back to the old ways was fine. It was something entirely separate from clarifying the causes of the war and assigning blame. The fad for speaking ill of absolutely everything was shockingly insincere. As it proceeded in all areas, I thought the burial of the dead a reason for rejoicing. Indeed, the fact that young men had died in that way was painful beyond words. I think I understand, if dimly, the feelings of General Nogi, who had such deaths on his mind for the rest of his life.

General Nogi Maresuke was the hero of the siege of Port Arthur. On the death of the Meiji Emperor in 1912, he committed ritual suicide with his wife in delayed atonement for the deaths of the men he had ordered into battle. In his recent monograph, Baba Kimihiko argues that "Takeyama Michio's sense of shame [for the war] became the source of his intellectual anguish and worry."[28]

Takeyama writes, "The painful fact of defeat was impressed indelibly on us, and almost daily we saw pitiable repatriated soldiers, so I felt I wanted to portray them inside and out as men who fulfilled their duty and fought that bitter war." At least once, a soldier-beggar whom Takeyama encountered turned out to be one of his Ichikō students. Takeyama had read of a soldier, a young music teacher, who trained his men to sing; in turn, they protected him with their bodies when bullets flew. In contrast to most repatriated units, these men returned in good spirits. Further, a friend back from the Burma front told Takeyama of a soldier who had turned monk. And Takeyama worried about how to rebuild Japan.[29]

He planned at first to set the tale in China, a country to which he had traveled (he remembered seeing a photo during the war of Japanese troops against the backdrop of a walled town in the interior), but for the plot he needed a song that was common to both Japan and a European country. He knew of no songs Japan and China had in common, so he chose "Home, Sweet Home," which meant British soldiers, and that meant Burma. Takeyama had never been to Burma (and in 1946 information about Burma was difficult to obtain), but as a college student he had traveled to Taiwan and had hiked in its near-tropical regions among its aboriginal tribes.

*Harp of Burma* is the heartwarming story of a Japanese military detachment in Burma at the end of the Pacific War. In desperate conditions, the unit maintains its unity and morale, largely through its devotion to choral music. One soldier deserts and becomes a monk (a Japanese Albert Schweitzer?), devoting himself to the burial of the corpses of Japanese soldiers; when the unit returns to Japan, he chooses to stay in Burma. Both as children's tale and as novel of ideas, it is unique among Takeyama's works.[30]

Howard Hibbett's translation, *Harp of Burma*, is masterful.[31] However, the gentleness of the language—the fact that it *is* a children's book—is virtually impossible to convey in translation. Perhaps the English-language reader needs to see the original, in the children's magazine, with lines widely spaced and frequent illustrations. Here is my translation of the prologue:

Most of us have seen, haven't we, our soldier boys demobilized and returning from China and the South Pacific? They all look exhausted, thin, unhealthy, so pitiable. Some of them are sick, carried on stretchers, their faces the color of wax.

Among these soldier boys was one unit that came home very hale and hearty. They were always singing. Moreover, the music was difficult—two parts, three parts, and they sang it well. Those who had gone to greet them when they landed at Yokosuka were astonished. So they asked, "You people are singing so happily—what have you been eating?"

It wasn't that they had been eating anything different, but while this unit was in Burma, they had practiced singing, constantly. Their leader was a young musician just out of music school, and with great earnestness he had taught them choral singing. And thanks to their singing they kept their morale high even during the bad times, and during the boring times they beguiled themselves with music, and they always stayed on good terms with each other, and their cohesion as a unit held. During the long war these things were ever so much their salvation. That's why this unit came back in fine fettle and surprised those who had gone to greet them.

One of the soldiers from this unit told me the tale that follows.

Here (in Hibbett's translation) is the opening of that tale: "We certainly did sing. Whether we were happy or miserable, we sang. Maybe it's because we were always under the threat of battle, of dying, and felt we wanted to do at least this one thing well as long as we were alive. Anyway, we sang with all our hearts. And we preferred serious songs, songs with depth, not the frivolous popular kind. Of course most of us had been only farmers or laborers, but we managed to learn some fine choral music." *Harp of Burma* is uplifting on many counts: happy soldiers, on good terms with their leader, healthy, singing fine music (not popular songs).

The Burma of *Harp of Burma* is a tropical paradise of sorts. One Japanese soldier comments: "We [Japanese] have the tools for civilization, but at heart we're still savages who don't know how to use them. What did we do with these tools but wage a gigantic war, and even come all the way here to invade Burma and cause terrible suffering to its people? Yet they accept it and go on living quietly and peacefully. The Burmese never seem to have committed our stupid blunder of attacking others. You say they're uneducated, but they believe in Buddhism and govern their whole lives by it." Again: "No matter where you go, the Burmese seem happy. They live and die smiling. All the troubles of this world and the next are left to the Buddha, as they pass their days tilling the soil, singing, and dancing, without selfishness or greed." This Burma represents in part the Japanese past: "Still, Japan was probably like that in the old days—it's only during the past eighty years that we've become modern." But Burma represents in part the Japanese future: "Our country has waged a war, lost it, and is now suffering. That is because we were greedy, because we were so arrogant that we forgot human values, because we had only a superficial ideal of civilization. Of course we cannot be as languid as the people of this country, and dream our lives away as they often do. But can we not remain energetic and yet be less avaricious? Is that not essential—for the Japanese and for all humanity?"

It is important to the plot that Corporal Mizushima, the hero, can be taken for Burmese: "The Burmese look very much like us Japanese, except that they have light beards. However, Mizushima was only twenty-one, and had a light beard and large, clear eyes like a Burmese. His skin was deeply tanned. But above all, though he was a man of great courage and daring, he seemed to have the sad, contemplative expression that tropical peoples such as the Burmese often have, perhaps because of their oppressive climate. And when he wrapped the red and yellow patterned *longyi* around himself he looked just like a native." The resemblance is important beyond the plot.

It is also important that his message is as much political as personal. Here Corporal Mizushima tries to talk another Japanese unit into surrendering: "'What good will it do to be wiped out?' I said. 'We've got to live. We've got to live and struggle and work, for the sake of our country.'" Takeyama's true heroes are the silent majority. In this passage, one character speaks with Takeyama's voice: "I cannot help being appalled by what I read in newspapers and magazines nowadays. Many people seem to pride themselves on slandering and blaming others. 'It's all that fellow's fault,' they declare, as arrogantly as if we had won the war. 'That's why the country is in such a mess.' But these are the very people whose attitude during the war was hardly admirable, and who manage to live extravagantly even now. However, men like the old-timer say nothing and simply keep on working. That seems to me to be far better than clamoring for your own selfish interests. No matter how chaotic things are, some people go on working silently and unobtrusively. Aren't they the real patriots? Doesn't the survival of a country depend on them?" In "The End of the War," translated in this volume, Takeyama depicts with scorn a neighbor who is clearly an opportunist.

For Japanese in 1946 and 1947, whether children or adults, this was a heady message. By focusing on 1945 and Burma, it avoided both Japanese prewar imperialism in Korea and Manchuria and the early years of the war in China. By concentrating on British and Japanese casualties (more than half the 300,000 Japanese who fought in Burma died there), it glossed over the tens of thousands of Burmese who died in the war, many of the deaths coming among those forced to construct the Thai-Burmese railroad. By focusing on universals, it avoided the specific cruelties that marked the Burma theater. Mizushima sees British burying Japanese dead: "I could hear a fierce voice whispering deep within me: Foreigners have done this for us—treated our sick and wounded, buried our dead, prayed to console their spirits. . . . *Hanyu no Yado* ["Home, Sweet Home"] is not only a song of yearning for your own home, for your own friends. That harp expresses the longing of every man for the peace of his home."[32] So Japanese and British join in their humanity (although Mizushima doesn't bury British dead), and Japanese and Burmese join in their common search for wholeness. *Harp of Burma* is a parable with particular appeal for Japan just after the lost war.

Takeuchi Yoshimi (1910–1977) was one of the earliest to point out the major flaws in *Harp of Burma* (and also in *Lost Youth*, Takeyama's early volume of essays about German youth). Takeuchi conceded that Takeyama's style was beautiful: *Harp of Burma* was "not only a remarkable piece of children's literature but an outstanding piece of postwar literature." But he "sensed a patrician feeling, an aloofness amid the beauty. I sensed an aura of isolation and decadence, as if the works were looking down from on high, as if they extolled what was dying." Specifically, in *Harp of Burma* the war was "fated, as if controlled by some great unseen hand, and the human beings subject to that fate had to preserve their dignity." Takeuchi concludes, "This is not a solution but the evasion of a solution. The central idea that the author puts into Mizushima's mouth, that peace of mind is all, gives several fatal flaws to a work that at heart should crystallize into a beautiful tale." *Harp of Burma* is unreal (the Japanese army in Burma was not a disciplined body), and its love of humanity is conceptual, not emerging organically from the conflicts in the book. In short, *Harp of Burma* includes "a contempt for humanity and a sort of decadent thinking."[33]

In 1977, many years after Takeuchi's critique, the British scholar Louis Allen commented that *Harp of Burma* "begin[s] as naturalist narrative" and becomes "metaphysics or religion," "a work of fantasy." Allen concludes: "In a sense it is not so much a novel, more a Buddhist tract," with Corporal Mizushima speaking for Takeyama. In a fascinating footnote Allen reports that Hirakawa Sukehiro, Takeyama's son-in-law, challenged Allen on this point of interpretation, then checked with Takeyama and reported that "Mizushima's 'message' was in fact Takeyama's view at the time, though he would not say he was a Buddhist now." For Takeyama, Allen writes, "the war became the subject of a literary exercise."[34]

In his essay, "Japanese Writers and the Greater East Asia War," Donald Keene argues that "contrary to the impression sometimes created by Japanese who are anxious to gloss over the war years, the members of the literary profession were at the outbreak of war almost solidly united behind the militarists. . . . There was no resistance to the militarists save for the negative action of a few authors, mainly older men, who refrained from publishing. . . . Only the writers deeply imbued with European culture had any strong predisposition to oppose the war, though it should be noted that some authors who had lived many years abroad, possibly because of the discrimination they had encountered there, were among the most vociferous of the xenophobes."[35] Keene seems to forget that Japan's ally, Germany, was also European, but measured against this admittedly low standard, Takeyama stands out. In his late thirties, he was not one of the senior figures, but he spoke out against

Germany in 1940 and kept silent thereafter. Though he had spent time in Europe, he was distinctly not among the xenophobes and chauvinists.

A symposium of the late 1990s on "How the war has been told" gives some indication of how significant *Harp of Burma* was at the time and how much the critical evaluation has shifted since, at least among those on the left. How significant? Narita Ryūichi states that *Harp of Burma* (1947) and *24 Eyes* (1952) form the core of how the war was told in the early postwar era. Both works were made into popular films (*24 Eyes* in 1954), and their canonical status is owed in important ways to the film versions. The discussants identify the "early postwar" as the first of three chronological divisions. The characteristics of this early phase: absence of guilt, focus on Japan as victim, a concept of "we Japanese" that claims the postwar nation is a community, and an avoidance of the war itself.

Although the symposium's participants all agree that *Harp of Burma* is canonical, the tone of the discussion is caustic. There is criticism for Takeyama's choice of Burma: had he done the appropriate research, he could not have written this book, but he did none at all. Okuizumi Hikaru, who was reading *Harp of Burma* for the first time, says, "I find it absolutely amazing that this novel received such critical praise." Kawamura Minato comments that *Harp of Burma* epitomized the idea that "the aggression of [Japanese] fathers in Asia was not aggression but liberation." "First, you discard the prewar and wartime experience of Japanese in Asia. Then you gloss over for the kids their fathers' actual war experiences. It's not that the cruelty of war is not written about, but it's the general cruelty of war—Japanese die, Burmese die, English people die—and victims; you shape it from humanism." Not knowing Takeyama's polemic against Germany in 1940, Kawamura goes so far as to link Takeyama with those Japanese specialists in Germany who during the war praised Germany and then after the war—"as alibi"—turned to Hermann Hesse and other German writers of the "universal humanist" stripe. Okuizumi focuses on the relation between Japan and Asia that is implicit in *Harp of Burma*: continental "nature" and Japanese "nature" merge, so "Japan too is Asia." Japan's colonialism in Asia disappears, and Takeyama "presents a vision whereby, with the war over, we [Japanese] return to 'Asian nature'—with a mission. We are 'innocent.'" Adds Narita: the novel "creates a sense of community facing inward, lacking consciousness of the other and denying the historical process." A final comment comes from Kawamura: the recovery of bones takes place outside Japan, but the domestic dead, at Hiroshima and Nagasaki, do not get the same treatment. All in all, it is a stunning indictment.[36]

A recent book by Takada Rieko takes the argument one step further. She emphasizes the humanism of the higher schools—the focus on Hesse and Rilke, Stefan George and Thomas Mann—and the role in particular of teachers of German language. (It is that tradition that Ivan Hall alludes to in his tribute to Takeyama, that Takeyama was "the last living member of one of the great schools of early twentieth-century Japanese literary humanism.") Unlike many of his fellow teachers, Takeyama did not idealize Germany, but he did make Ichikō the model for the Japanese army in Burma; the army becomes "an army modeled on the old-style higher school." In fact, the Japanese army was anything but Ichikō-like in its human relations. It substituted oppression and scorn and fawning for the friendship and fellowship among equals that characterized Ichikō. Takada writes that *Harp of Burma* is "an attempt, conscious or unconscious, to elide the gulf between ideal and real." *Harp of Burma* is the triumph, as it were, of Ichikō over the military: its setting is "a world-wide Ichikō," Ichikō on a universal scale in which the fellowship extends to British troops and even Burmese cannibals, too. It is, Takada comments bitingly, "not a war tale but a school tale, an Ichikō tale"; it is "Ichikō sentimentalism."[37]

In his 2004 book, Baba Kimihiko restates Takeuchi's critique of "the issue of war guilt and how to deal with it. If you skip right over both the awareness of guilt for aggressive war and coming to terms with war crimes, you can't come truly to terms with the war." *Harp of Burma* "isn't war literature. Even more, since it's about what happens after the fighting ends, we simply can't call it a war tale. It is Utopian children's literature that is utterly lacking in battle scenes and weak in historical grounding." Baba argues that "the consciousness of war guilt lurking in *Harp of Burma* fixes its gaze on responsibility to one's own war dead, makes guilt for the suffering inflicted on enemy soldiers a secondary issue, and pivots on the sense of 'shame' for one's own guilt for not having acted, for having been unable to prevent or resist." What is missing? The Burmese (and other Asians). Baba describes Takeyama's goal as "to pray for the happiness in the next world of [Japan's] war dead—this at a time when the Occupation authorities were painting soldiers as evil men." After the war this humanism led in opposite directions: on the left, to the peace movement and neutrality in the Cold War, and on the right, with Takeyama, to opposition to authoritarian communism.[38]

In the present volume the novella "Scars" provides a fascinating second look at Takeyama's early postwar thinking about Japan and Asia. *Harp of Burma* and "Scars" are virtually simultaneous, and "Scars" is set in the China that Takeyama wanted for the setting of *Harp of Burma*. "Scars" includes a minor atrocity by Japanese against Chinese and the retaliation it called forth. The China of "Scars" is at times naïve and simple and at times truly humane (Jiang Kai-shek's pronouncement against vengeance). And although there is explicit admission of Japanese cruelties in China, those cruelties take place offstage, and the focus is less on Japan's invasion and the war than on the psychology of the Japanese, both soldiers and civilians.

## Japan's Culture Wars, the 1950s

Takeyama's postwar ended and his Cold War began in 1950. "Those Who Refuse to Enter the Gate" is Takeyama's white-hot reaction to the student boycott of Tokyo University's entrance examination in 1950.

It is difficult today to imagine the high tension within Japan in the late 1940s and early 1950s. The tension grew out of differing experiences of and reactions to war and Occupation and Cold War, not to mention the personalities of the major players. Japan's culture wars saw Takeyama on one side, sounding the alarm, and on the other most of the Left—from members of the Japan Communist Party to fellow travelers to nonaligned "progressive" intellectuals, some of them Marxist, some not. The American scholar and translator Edward Seidensticker (1921–) witnessed these years, and words he wrote in 2002, nearly fifty years later, still carry the vitriol of the time. In his memoirs, Seidensticker spoke of the intellectuals on the left in the most disparaging terms. They are "the bunch of lunatics known as the *interi* [intelligentsia]," they are "pestilential," they engage in "terrorism," and they are "the enemy." He calls the students of the late 1960s "the most violent student movement in the world." And he sees no problem with clandestine U.S. Central Intelligence Agency financial support of the Congress for Cultural Freedom, in which both he and Takeyama were active: "Not that I myself see that the presence or absence of CIA money makes all that much difference."[39] In their own writings, Seidensticker's "lunatics," including such luminaries as Ienaga Saburō and Maruyama Masao, speak of the student movement of the 1950s as the high point of Japan's postwar democracy.

*Jiyū* was one of many journals around the world supported by the CCF, which in turn received much of its backing from the CIA. These journals included *Encounter* (England) and like-minded journals in Australia, India, West Germany, Italy, Brazil, Lebanon, Nigeria, and other countries. *Jiyū* was created with external support and is the only Japanese magazine linked with clandestine American financial support; the CCF's aim was to offset the influence of such magazines as *Chūō kōron* and *Sekai*, which were too anti-American—whatever that meant—for CCF tastes. At the start the key figure behind the scenes was American anthropologist Herbert Passin (1916–2003), who brought together such important figures as Abe Yoshishige (former minister of education, president of the Peers School), Koizumi Shinyo (educator in charge of tutoring the crown prince [and current emperor]), Tanaka Kōtarō (Supreme Court justice), Takayanagi Kenzō (legal scholar), Hirabayashi Taiko (novelist), Fukuzawa Ichirō (painter), and Takeyama.

But the early issues of *Jiyū* were not tough enough for the CCF; its director John Hunt wrote to Passin in 1960, following the Tokyo riots of June: "Things are in a hell of a mess." *Jiyū* "should have taken up [a] clear-cut stand on behalf of intellectual responsibility and democratic procedure." So Hunt broke with the Japanese publisher and decided to "go on our own with a team composed one hundred percent of our people. Japan is far too tricky ideologically to leave our magazine in the hands of a man who is not tried and true." The new publisher was Takayanagi Kenzō, and the new editorial committee included Takeyama. The ensuing turnabout gratified Hunt, who wrote in April 1961: "*Jiyū* is now generally regarded here as one of the big 4 of Japanese periodical publishing—a remarkable achievement. With more help, they can accomplish very important things." By 1967 the subsidy to *Jiyū*, one of the CCF's largest subsidies, was nearly $50,000 per year, roughly $9 per *Jiyū* purchaser.[40] In 1967 a year's subscription to *Jiyū* cost 1,800 yen—$5 at the exchange rate of the day. So the CCF put in nearly $2 for every $1 subscribers paid. Needless to say, *Jiyū* never apprised its readers of this funding.

The news that the CIA was responsible in part for CCF funding made fewer waves in Japan than elsewhere. In March 1967 John Hunt wrote to the head of Japan Cultural Forum, Ishihara Hōki, a four-page letter that was less than candid: "I am sure that you and your colleagues will appreciate a clarification regarding the Congress' relationships to American Foundations named in recent disclosures in the American press about the use of some Foundations by the CIA for the purpose of providing financial support to a variety of international organizations." Hunt proceeded to describe only the Hoblitzelle Foundation and stated, "At no time did the Hoblitzelle Foundation deal with us in any manner whatsoever except to respond to our request for funds for specific programs originated and developed by us. . . . Any question of influence by the Hoblitzelle Foundation on Congress policies or programs must therefore be definitively ruled out. I hope that the foregoing will be of use to you in clarifying for our friends and colleagues the nature of this Foundation and the way in which the Congress has dealt with it over the years."[41] Hunt did not admit that he himself knew about the CIA support or that Hoblitzelle was not the only foundation laundering CIA money; indeed, Hunt was likely a CIA agent himself. Ishihara responded a month later, in English:

> It has been getting talked about the funds of CIA to some extent in Japan, either. There was a magazine which said that Japan Cultural Forum perhaps

received its funds as it was Japanese branch of Congress for Cultural Freedom, but we did take no account of that. When a weekly magazine called 'Shukan Gendai' brought the question before us, too, I turned upon them saying 'On what authority do you say so?' And then they have never published about it. I am afraid we will meet the problem once in a while in the future, but I believe it will blow over in due course of time so that we don't want to give an impetus of no use. For the present, Japan Cultural Forum has not been publicly injured by the CIA problem.[42]

A year later, citing fiscal hardship, the CCF cut its funding of the Japan Cultural Forum and *Jiyū*. Shepard Stone of the CCF delivered the bad news. As he reported, "For a gay, round-the-world holiday I would not recommend, as a first step, budget cuts involving people who meet you at airports. . . . Our friends Ishihara and Takeyama were in a state of shock over the cut."[43]

One of the most astute American critics of CIA funding was Jason Epstein, founder of the *New York Review of Books*. Writing in that journal in April 1967, Epstein spoke of "a genuine community of interest and conviction between the entrepreneurs of American cold war diplomacy and those intellectuals who, to put it bluntly, were hired to perform tasks which often turned out to be a form of public relations in support of American cold war policies." He continues: "The depressing fact is that the cadre of intellectuals who had been arbitrarily placed in high journalistic and other cultural positions by means of United States funds, were never, as a result of this sponsorship, to be quite free. What limited them was nothing so simple as coercion, though coercion at some levels may have been involved, but something more like the inevitable relations between employer and employee in which the wishes of the former become implicit in the acts of the latter. . . . Organizations ostensibly devoted to cultural freedom and the pursuit of truth were thus based upon lies."[44]

Takeyama's role in *Jiyū* was more important than merely the positions he held. Once Herbert Passin was no longer on the Japanese scene to keep an eye on things, the CCF turned to Edward Seidensticker in the years around 1960 and Ivan Hall in the years around 1970.[45] All of these men—Passin, Seidensticker, Hall—are well-known to Japanese scholars, but Seidensticker is clearly the most prominent. Seidensticker thought very highly of Takeyama. He was "obviously the man"; Takeyama should "take firm control of the magazine."[46] Ishihara Hōki, the chief paid Japanese contact, wrote to "Passin-san" in English: "No matter what is done about the magazine, Takeyama remains the center of the matter. The other day he said to me, 'As long as you are involved in it, I will do it.' So don't worry; it's all right. (Don't mention this to anyone else.)" Seki Yoshihiko wrote to Hunt, also in English, that "the (de facto) chief editor is still Mr. Takeyama."[47]

In 1965 Seidensticker was teaching Japanese literature at Stanford and wrote to Ivan Kats of the CCF, who was thinking about publishing Hibbett's translation of *Harp of Burma*. Seidensticker praised Takeyama even while criticizing *Harp of Burma* (the letter, reproduced here in its entirety, mentions neither the book nor Takeyama by name):

> Dear Mr. Katz [sic],
>
> I did not answer your letter of February 22 because I could think of little to say, and because what I could think of did not seem as pleasant as I would like to have had it. But since you press me, here we go.
>
> I do not much admire the book. It is, as you say, very romantic, and it also seems to me a touch condescending in its attitude toward the Burmese. I was somewhat surprised when Hibbett, a man of very good taste, undertook to translate it, however, and so maybe it is better than I think.
>
> And on the other hand I greatly admire the author. He has been a real friend in need, to me personally and to the Congress, going out to do battle with the pinko intellectuals when almost no one else had the courage to.
>
> So it seems to me that the question comes down to what your motives would be in bringing out the translation. Would you wish strongly enough to help—well, do a favor for—an old friend that you would be willing to overlook certain literary defects? Or would the reverse relationship hold?
>
> Sincerely yours,
> Edward Seidensticker[48]

During Ivan Hall's stint as CCF "consultant" in the late 1960s, the Paris headquarters sought more effective Japan Cultural Forum representation on the board of the International Association for Cultural Freedom. That meant removing Takeyama, whom Paris found "ineffectual" and "not articulate."[49] The solution: invoke the CCF rule of retirement at age sixty-five and move Takeyama to an honorary position, "honorary member of IACF."[50] A tribute to him was placed in the minutes. It included these words: "As a professor of Tokyo University, he has left a deep imprint of his personality as well as of his mind on his pupils. Few great contemporary writers have shown such unswerving attachment to principles of freedom and humanism as Professor Michio Takeyama."[51] Honorary membership had gone to only four others: Ignazio Silone, Michael Polanyi, Hans Oprecht, and Louis Fischer.[52]

A recent book about the CCF's role in Great Britain suggests that "British intellectuals only cooperated . . . when they realized they stood to gain something."[53] We need to ask the same question of the CCF in Japan: Who called the tune? Were Takeyama and the others used by the CIA? Or did they use the CIA? The answer likely lies somewhere in between. On the one hand, the CCF financial stake in *Jiyū* seems to have given it near-absolute authority. On the other, the language barrier and CCF's relative ignorance of the Japanese context seem to have allowed leeway for the local actors; the correspondence between Paris and its men in Japan—Passin, Seidensticker, and Hall—shows how out of touch Paris was, how sorely it needed the guidance of these men in dealing with its Japanese allies. But unless there are Japanese-language archives and correspondence to set against the CCF archives, which are fragmentary at best, we may never know. What was Takeyama's role? In what ways, if any, did his active or passive resistance alter the CCF's goals in supporting the Japan Cultural Forum and *Jiyū*?

In the 1957 postscript to his volume of four essays on Nazi Germany, Takeyama wrote that those essays reflected his strong awareness in the early postwar years of "the relation between the power of contemporary totalitarianism and respect for the individual."[54] In the 1950s Takeyama saw totalitarianism of the Left as the prime threat to the individual and made common cause with the reactionary (but not totalitarian) Japanese state and with the anticommunist Left worldwide.

Takeyama Michio was born in 1903 and died in 1984. His writings ranged widely over the cultural scene—translations, cultural commentary, children's books. The works in this volume span the years 1940 to 1953.

As editor and translator, I hope that these translations shed light on the Japanese home front during the Asia-Pacific War. To be sure, Takeyama was an idiosyncratic and privileged observer. I hope they contribute to current rethinking of the Asia-Pacific War, the major event of Takeyama's lifetime and one of his lifelong concerns. I hope, too, that they lead to further interest in Takeyama. I find myself much in sympathy with him early on and increasingly out of sympathy later, as he moves toward the right. But I respect him for following his conscience, even if doing so took him into unworthy alliance with the Congress for Cultural Freedom. I realize that my sympathies reveal at least as much about me and my times as about Takeyama Michio and his.

## Notes

1. "Professor Michio Takeyama," May 29, 1970 (Congress for Cultural Freedom Archives [University of Chicago], series II, box 177, folder 9). IACF is the International Association for Cultural Freedom, successor organization to the Congress for Cultural Freedom (see below).

2. Baba Kimihiko, *'Biruma no tategoto' o meguru sengoshi* (Tokyo: Hōsei Daigaku Shuppankyaku, 2004).

3. Takeyama's collected works are *Takeyama Michio chosakushū* (8 vols., Tokyo: Fukutake Shoten, 1983), hereafter cited as *Chosakushū*. The best source on Takeya-

ma's life is the chronology in *Chosakushū* 8:323–36; there follows (8:337–92) a bibliography. Both are the work of Hirakawa Sukehiro. Unless otherwise noted, the information here comes from that source.

4. Takeyama Michio, "Saigo no jusha" (November 1953), in *Ransei no naka kara* (Tokyo: Yomiuri, 1974), 111, 121.

5. "Watakushi no bunka henreki," in *Chosakushū*, 2:308–9.

6. Takeyama Michio, *Hikari to ai no senshi* (Tokyo: Shinchōsha, 1942), 2–3, 339, 342, 345–46.

7. Katō Kōmei, Wakatsuki Reijirō, Hamaguchi Sachio, Hirota Kōki, and Hiranuma Kiichirō were the prime ministers before the end of the war; Hatoyama Ichirō and Kishi Nobusuke served in that office after the war. Wakatsuki remembered Ichikō's Inauguration Day ceremonies, for which he had been elected to carry the new flag, as one of "the most moving experiences in his life" (Donald Roden, *Schooldays in Imperial Japan* [Berkeley: University of California Press, 1980], 63).

8. Nishizawa Tadashi, ed., *Aa gyokuhai ni hana ukete* (Tokyo, 1972), 250.

9. Akira Kubota, *Higher Civil Servants in Postwar Japan* (Princeton: Princeton University Press, 1969), 60–62.

10. Miyake Setsurei, Yanagida Kunio, Minobe Tatsukichi, and Watsuji Tetsurō were all prominent intellectuals; writers included Kikuchi Kan, Kurata Hyakuzō, Saitō Mokichi, Ōsaragi Jirō, Tanizaki Junichirō, Masaoka Shiki, and Nobel Laureate Kawabata Yasunari. Kawabata made his debut just five years out of Ichikō with the short story, "The Izu Dancer" (1925). It begins, famously (in Edward Seidensticker's translation [*Izu Dancer*, Tokyo: Hara Shobō, 1964]): "A shower swept toward me from the foot of the mountain, touching the cedar forests white, as the road began to wind up into the pass. I was nineteen and traveling alone through the Izu Peninsula. My clothes were of the sort students wear, dark kimono, high wooden sandals, a school cap, a book sack over my shoulder." Kawabata graduated in 1920, the year Takeyama Michio entered Ichikō. Notable leftists included Fukumoto Kazuo, Hani Gorō, Hirano Yoshitarō, and Morito Tatsuo.

11. "Atogaki," in Takeyama, *Ransei*, 451.

12. Henry D. Smith, *Japan's First Student Radicals* (Cambridge: Harvard University Press, 1972), 3; compare Roden, *Schooldays*, appendixes I and II.

13. Roden, *Schooldays*, 7, 51, 71.

14. Hashida Kunihiko, ed., *Daiichi kōtō gakkō rokujūnenshi* (Tokyo: private, 1939), 597–98.

15. Roden, *Schooldays*, 111, 127–28, 203. *Su-tō-mu* is a phonetic rendering of the English "storm."

16. Hayashi Kentarō, *Utsuriyuku mono no kage* (Tokyo: Bungei Shunjū Shinsha, 1960), 75; quoted in Roden, *Schooldays*, 239.

17. Roden, *Schooldays*, 53–60, 241.

18. Roden, *Schooldays*, 72.

19. The translation is Roden's, *Schooldays*, 137.

20. The Harvard-Yenching Library's copy was once the property of Bruno Petzold (1873–1949), who taught German at Ichikō in the 1930s.

21. Smith, *Japan's First*, 9–10.

22. Roden, *Schooldays*, 98, 227, 260 (appendix III, table 4 note).

23. Roden, *Schooldays*, 245.

24. Ogiya Shozō, ed., *Aa gyokuhai ni hana ukete—waga kyūsei kōkō jidai* (Tokyo: Yuki Shobō, 1967); translated in Smith, *Japan's First*, 10. Much of this discussion relies on Smith, *Japan's First*, 8–11.

25. *Harp of Burma*, trans. Howard Hibbett (Rutland, VT: Charles E. Tuttle Co., 1966), 84–85.

26. *Chosakushū* 1:289.

27. "Akechi," *Chosakushū* 3:215.

28. Baba, *Biruma*, 94.

29. Baba, *Biruma*, 196, 204–5.

30. Nakamura Kōfu, "Commentary," in Takeyama Michio, *Biruma no tategoto* (Tokyo: Shinchō Bunko, 1959), 192–93.

31. There is an earlier English translation, by Ishikawa Kinichi (Tokyo: Chūō Kōronsha, 1950). It includes many of the line drawings of the original (by Inokuma Genichirō) and succeeds in replicating much of its tone: "Boys and girls. I think many of you must have seen ex-soldiers being repatriated from the Asiatic continent and from the Southern regions." It takes liberties: "I deleted some part of the last chapter and changed the order, so that the story would become chronological and clear for the foreign readers," and the soldier/monk becomes Shima, shortened from Mizushima.

32. *Harp of Burma*, 19, 48, 57, 90, 99, 117, 123, 130.

33. Takeuchi, "'Biruma no tategoto' ni tsuite," in *Takeuchi Yoshimi zenshū* (17 vols., Tokyo: Chikuma Shobō, 1981), 7:202–6.

34. Louis Allen, "Japanese Literature of the Second World War," *Proceedings of the British Association for Japanese Studies* 2.1 (1977): 120–23.

35. Donald Keene, "Japanese Writers and the Greater East Asia War," in *Landscapes and Portraits: Appreciations of Japanese Culture* (Tokyo: Kodansha International, 1971), 300, 302.

36. Kawamura Minato, Narita Ryūichi, Ueno Chizuko, Okuizumi Hikaru, Lee Yeonsuk, Inoue Hisashi, and Takahashi Genichirō, *Sensō wa dono yō ni katarete kita ka* (Tokyo: Asahi Shimbunsha, 1999), 57–74.

37. Takada Rieko, *Bungakubu o meguru yamai—kyōyōshugi, Nachizu, kyūsei kōkō* (Tokyo: Shōraisha, 2001), 205–6, 209, 240.

38. Baba, *Biruma*, 7, 10, 136, 158.

39. Edward Seidensticker, *Tokyo Central: A Memoir* (Seattle: University of Washington Press, 2002), 91, 105, 176, 182, 211, 241. A generation younger than Takeyama, Seidensticker learned Japanese in the Navy Language School at Boulder, Colorado (1942–1943), had been at Iwo Jima (February 1945), and arrived in Japan in September 1945, only a month after the surrender. From the navy he joined the

State Department (1946–1950) and then stayed on in Japan, studying at Tokyo University, writing, and translating.

40. Peter Coleman, *The Liberal Conspiracy: The Congress for Cultural Freedom and the Struggle for the Mind of Postwar Europe* (New York: Free Press, 1989), 187–89. Coleman's title is adulatory, not critical. A former CCF employee unaware at the time of the source of CCF funding, he writes (xii–xiii): "I have . . . come to the conviction that cloak-and-dagger questions of who paid whom, how, and for what are in fact far less important than the astonishing story . . . of the idealistic, courageous, and far-sighted men and women of the CCF who fought in this war of ideas—with its attendant suffering and atrocities—against Stalinism and its successors." He identifies the quotations about *Jiyū* as coming from CCF archives at the University of Chicago. See also Frances Stonor Saunders, *The Cultural Cold War: The CIA and the World of Arts and Letters* (New York: New Press, 1999).

41. Hunt to Ishihara, March 16, 1967 (CCF Archives, series II, box 181, folder 1).

42. Ishihara to Hunt, April 5, 1967 (CCF Archives, series II, box 181, folder 1). In a 1983 interview Ishihara told Peter Coleman that his house had been firebombed and he had "sought police protection" (Coleman, *Liberal Conspiracy*, 229). I found no mention of that incident in the CCF Archives.

43. Shepard Stone to Pierre Emmanuel, January 26, 1969 (CCF Archives, series II, box 181, folder 2).

44. Jason Epstein, "The CIA and the Intellectuals," *New York Review of Books*, April 20, 1967, 20–21.

45. Ivan Hall (1932– ) received his BA from Princeton (1954), MA degrees from Fletcher School of Diplomacy (1958) and Harvard (1964), and PhD from Harvard (1969). He had served in the U.S. military in West Germany (1954–1956) and the United States Information Agency in Kabul and Dacca (1958–1960).

46. Seidensticker to Hunt, February 22, 1960 (CCF Archives, series II, box 288, folder 10). Seidensticker to Hunt, April 3, 1959 (CCF Archives, series II, box 177, folder 1). Hunt agreed: "I must ask you in all sincerity to do everything you can to see that Mr. Takeyama will agree to take over sole editorship of the review. If he will not do this, then we must find someone else. Naturally, we would expect to provide a salary to the person who would edit the magazine" (Hunt to Yoshihiko Seki, March 28, 1960; CCF Archives, series II, box 177, folder 2). Hunt had written to Seki earlier: "I should point out . . . that I continue to hold the point of view . . . that the magazine should be run by one man and not by a committee. According to what you yourself told me Michio Takeyama would be the logical person." (Hunt to Seki, February 16, 1960; CCF Archives, series II, box 177, folder 2). In *Tokyo Central* (238) Seidensticker calls Takeyama "a very wise Japanese"—high praise indeed.

47. Ishihara to Passin [letter in romanized Japanese], February 28, 1959 (CCF Archives, series II, box 177, folder 1): "*Magazin wa donna koto ga attemo, Mr. Takeyama ga* Centre *desu.*" Ishihara to Passin, January 26, 1959 (CCF Archives, series II, box 179, folder 2). Seki to Hunt, March 16, 1960 (CCF Archives, series II, box 177, folder 3).

48. Seidensticker to Kats, April 20, 1965 (CCF Archives, series II, box 288, folder 11). Earlier letters provide some context for Seidensticker's epithet "pinko intellectuals." In a letter of 1960 Seidensticker reported to the CCF's John Hunt on events of the day and on his reaction to a Japan Cultural Forum discussion of a paper by Takeyama: "It could not have been predicted that the street mobs would have their way, and, had it not been for the sequence of events beginning with U2, and had the American and Japanese governments shown a little more determination, they need not have. They did, however, and last Saturday all that seemed to stand between us and political chaos was the discipline of the country boys who man the Metropolitan Police. The worst is over, for the moment, provided we can get through the funeral (tomorrow) of the wretched girl the students trampled to death and then accused the police of strangling; but we have had such a demonstration of weakness and ineptitude on the part of the governing party that perhaps complete inaction—letting prosperity and the United States solve all Japan's problems—is the best we can hope for from future governments. . . . (What a ghastly parallel there is, by the way between apologies for the angry young officers twenty-five years ago and the apologies for the students today, from no less a figure than the president of Tokyo University. But try to make any 'intellectual' students see it. There is, naturally, a difference between feudal violence and revolutionary violence; and besides, the police resisted. The brutal police.)" (Seidensticker to Hunt, June 23, 1960; CCF Archives, series II, box 288, folder 10). Of the July issue of *Jiyū*, Seidensticker wrote: "The rioting has been so much on my mind that I have been rather badly collected. The contents are very annoying indeed, and seem to put *Jiyū* right in the middle—or, even worse, somewhat fecklessly on the perimeter—of all the insanity. The lead article . . . is about the Security Treaty, and is full of the usual nonsense—will of the people, tyranny of the majority, dangerous entanglements, blessings of neutrality, and the rest. Or so it would seem. I have had so much of this horseshit these last weeks that I could not bring myself to do any more than look through it. One thing is certain: at a time when *Jiyū* ought to be taking a firm and courageous position, it is weaseling" (Seidensticker to Hunt, July 1, 1960; CCF Archives, series II, box 288, folder 10).

49. Stone to Hall, October 27, 1969 (CCF Archives, series II, box 178, folder 3); Stone to Hall, January 6, 1970 (CCF Archives, series II, box 181, folder 3).

50. The issue was sensitive because—in the words of one CCF memo—Takeyama was "a man with very powerful family connections" ("K. A. [Constantin] Jelenski: First Notes on Tokyo Visit," December 3, 1969; CCF Archives, series II, box 181, folder 2). Jelenski had edited the report of the Berlin Conference (1960) of the CCF, *History and Hope: Progress in Freedom* (London: Routledge & Kegan Paul, 1962); that volume includes a brief intervention (78–79) by Takeyama, which includes these words: "Japan gained its independence and made its ascent in a period of the most barefaced imperialism; whereas nowadays the highly-developed countries are helping the others. Europe and America are ready to help the Asian and African countries. That is noble. I would like them to make sure, as well, that those countries will develop systematically from the spiritual point of view too, looking at the

whole problem not only from the angle of historical ideas, but from the psychological angle as well. Psychology plays a very important part in a country during periods of transition. To take an example, propaganda from the nihilistic-radical side is always up-to-date and psychologically captivating; whereas the propaganda from the side of reason is always outdated and unpsychological." During a visit to Tokyo in 1969, Jelenski had written: "Again to my surprise, I learned that Michio Takeyama, author of 'The Burmese Harp' and member of our General Assembly, whom I knew only as a prestigious novelist, is a member of one of Japan's most influential families. He is first cousin once removed of the young Crown Princess (his father and the Princess's grandfather were brothers) and brother-in-law of a former President of the Japanese Diet, one of Japan's important elder statesmen." Jelenski suggested making him an honorary president; he added: "As a Board member, he would be hopeless. Perhaps the appointment to an honorary presidency of the IACF would be the best solution?" But one important CCF staffer responded: "I told Kot [Jelenski] OK, but I would resign!" (Jelenski to Stone, April 30, 1970; CCF Archives, series II, box 178, folder 3). The handwritten reaction is apparently that of D. Goldstein.

51. "Professor Michio Takeyama," undated, CCF Archives, series II, box 15, folder 5. This tribute is based on the biographical statement by Ivan Hall that we have already quoted at length. Hall wrote to Stone (May 20, 1970; CCF Archives, series II, box 178, folder 3): "I am delighted and immensely relieved that there is a legitimate way out of our quandary with respect to Prof. Takeyama. . . . I'm sure that the honorary membership for Takeyama will mean even more [to] him than an appointment to your board—and it is precisely the sort of honor that the Japanese are accustomed to bestow on their senior leaders."

52. Stone to Hall, May 5, 1970 (CCF Archives, series II, box 178, folder 3).

53. Hugh Wilford, *The CIA, the British Left and the Cold War: Calling the Tune?* (London: Frank Cass, 2003), 299–300.

54. Takeyama Michio, *Ushinawareta seishun* (Tokyo: Shinchōsha, 1957), 210.

*Part I*

# THE WAR

# Ichikō in 1944

*"Ichikō in 1944" details Takeyama's experiences as faculty member and dormitory overseer, both on the Komaba campus and at one of several work sites. It tells of friction between two student cohorts, between the school and its neighbors, and also between the school and the military. It describes students without shoes, students getting called up into the military, students studying despite everything.*

*"Ichikō in 1944" appeared in the December 31, 1946, issue of the Ichikō bulletin.*

1944 was a most difficult year for our school. My memories are vivid, and the year was eventful. Were I to write about it in detail, I'd go on forever, so I'll simply note here some things I experienced, material for a page of the school's history.

Since the spring of 1944, second-year students had been working at a factory in Hitachi.[1] To write about the months at Hitachi in detail would make a fascinating tale. Young people being young people, even in hard times they fashioned their own lives. But doing so in those times was completely unacceptable. In particular, in that militarized factory town, Ichikō student life itself was defiant and provocative. Sometimes it was taken as insulting.

The Ichikō students borrowed a vocational school dorm; the teachers there had often said to their pupils, "The Ichikō students will arrive soon. Model

---

1. Hitachi, a city seventy-five miles northeast of Tokyo, on the eastern coast of Honshu (see map 1). It was bombed heavily in the last months of the war.

yourselves on them." But soon after the Ichikō students arrived, the teachers stopped staying that. Instead, they warned: "Don't ever imitate them!"

At night, under complete blackout, the entire city turned dark. Only the Ichikō dorm on the hill above the ocean had lights on, unshaded. Seeing this, the townspeople worried. At the time American submarines were already a constant presence fifty miles offshore.

At the factory the students worked hard and earned trust, and they studied hard for the few hours in the day after they returned to the dorm. But to outsiders, the idiosyncrasies of students raised in the Magic Mountain that was Ichikō were incomprehensible.[2] Ichikō students walked in big groups, singing as they went. That was what drunks or crazy people did. Walking in the rain, they covered themselves from head to toe with their capes. Encountering these weird figures, girls grew frightened and ran away. (During the war, these capes had a symbolic meaning and became the butt of criticism. How many teachers' meetings the capes occasioned!)

Hitachi being the sort of town it was, it had its brothel. Go there, and you could buy a meal.[3] The hungry Ichikō students would form a line and, singing the school song,[4] parade to the brothel in broad daylight to eat. This shocked the townspeople: "*These* are the vaunted Ichikō students?"[5]

What the people of the town had expected, of course, was that Ichikō students above all others would show the way in their "absolute faith in victory." To reassure people that this was not false, an illusion, the students would have learned to follow to the letter the behavior the times called for: clothes, rules, salutes, and the like. They of all people would always sing out, "Draw the sword that slays evil"[6] and carry on unchanged the tradition of resistance to the "siren call of the West."

But Ichikō students maintained neither this illusion nor this behavior. Nor was that all: by a strange irony of the changing times, the very spirit that in the old days opposed liberalism had now become a defender of liberalism. Here for better or worse was an ingrained idealism, and it whispered, "Don't follow fashion blindly." The esprit d'corps that always develops when one sort of people of the same age gather in one place, and their age—twenty or thereabouts—produced here a special spirit. It was a pure idealism, seeing everything conceptually, and a related lack of concern with reality.

---

2. The allusion is to Thomas Mann's *Magic Mountain*.

3. Legitimate restaurants, controlled more closely by the authorities, had little food to sell, but brothels had illicit access to food. The "meal" was *oden*, a concoction of potatoes and *kon'yaku* in broth.

4. *Aa, gyokuhai*.

5. Roden, *Schooldays*, 139, 146, 152, gives numerous examples of misogynistic attitudes and practices in the higher schools.

6. A line from a school song.

Leaving their own world behind, these young people came here to work in a weapons arsenal. And this is what they saw.

For example, when, at the ringing of a handbell, they enter the cafeteria, they find several hundred vocational school pupils sitting there. Up front is one aluminum bowl, and each waits with his own lunch box for lunch to be given him. The pupils range widely in age, some of them already adult in appearance, some still childish. Their expressions are uniformly empty and horribly docile. Ask them the sum of three plus four, and some of them would count on the fingers of both hands, so every stage of the meal, too, takes place on command.

There is a large Shinto altar high in front and here, on a step below it, epaulettes on their shoulders, the supervisors are lined up. All through the meal, supervisors walk about, keeping watch.

On command, the entire hall stands, bows to the altar, and observes a moment of silence. On command, they sit back down, and the several hundred recite in unison. Ancient words of ritual blessing, they express gratitude for the meal and for the good fortune of prosperity under the emperor's reign; the Ichikō students call it an incantation.

When this is over, again on command, one squad leader per table stands up. In sequence, the pupils raise their lunch boxes high and incline their heads. The squad leader then takes these boxes and dishes up the food. Thus begins the meager meal.

The Ichikō tables were in a long line under the windows. If the Ichikō students did not arrive on time, they neither bowed nor recited the incantation. For the vocational school, control via regimentation was a practical necessity, so the cafeteria observances became a fractious issue. But days passed without any solution being arrived at, and finally a cold, tough atmosphere of callousness between them and us became the solution.

As I ate on the high step, I often thought I had seen it before, as a prison scene in a movie.

This cavalier attitude on the part of Ichikō students was a cause of worry for the teachers who had accompanied them. We made excuses and apologized to the townspeople; we scolded and pleaded with the students. A thing of no consequence as far as intent was concerned gave rise to fearsome misunderstanding; it was looked at askance, as an outrageous lack of common sense or as evidence that in essence Ichikō students didn't support national policy.

This last point was particularly tricky. Insist on pursuing it, and there were things for which we had no response. During the war, we lived a strange contradiction.

Our shaky position was as follows. That the country lose the war and fall to ruins was of course not something we desired. Yet we couldn't bring ourselves to hope that those now ruling us should win. But as of now they *were* the country. There was no way to change that. To separate leaders from country and topple them ourselves was inconceivable. Modern organization and weapons[7]—they were destiny, pure and simple.

The emissary this destiny sent to Ichikō was a man with three stars on his shoulder, a short moustache, and a simple heart. He tried to insert into official documents the words, "School is a branch of the military," but he encountered the opposition of the head teacher and, after heated words, backed off for a time. Further, he asserted that the proper way to salute was not to remove one's hat but to touch one's hat, and again he encountered opposition. Whether one saluted by touching one's hat became an index of whether Ichikō itself intended to obey the military.[8]

True to his profession, this man was deeply troubled because at Ichikō military training wasn't enough of an everyday thing. "Routinization of training as daily affair" was the legal expression. Military training in the schools was under the supervision of the military. It had to be a daily affair. Student activities as a whole were termed "internal affairs," and they were to be guided by military principles; the military had a serious interest in the success or otherwise of "internal affairs." Thus, via this one opening, "routinization of training as daily affair," the military came to exercise control over the entire school. Finding himself unable to fulfill his duty on this point, this man presented a memorandum to the military authorities in the spring and asked to be reassigned from his post at Ichikō.

The organization immediately had the chief of the Military Affairs Bureau of the Utsunomiya Division, I believe it was, appear one day unannounced at the dorm on Hatogaoka in Hitachi and, without asking to be shown, inspect the dorm and listen to the appraisals of the locals.

He reported the results to the regiment: "The disorder defies description."

Had it not been Ichikō, the school would have been done for. But we were given a temporary reprieve—a last chance, and a second officer was assigned to the school. Moreover, the division chief, a prince, would redo the inspection. This time he would inspect the extent to which military training had become a daily affair. The deadline was announced—the end of August.

Ichikō faced its darkest hour.

---

7. See "The Trial of Mr. Hyde" (translated in this volume) for Takeyama's emphasis on organization and weapons.

8. Through middle school, students performed a military salute; higher school students celebrated their status by instead removing their hats and bowing.

The summer was hot, dry, long, awful. The sun burned on, unblocked; glittering clouds towered, threatening. Suffocating winds blew through town, and ash-like dust piled up on rooftops. Even around Shibuya whole rows of shops were closed and roads dug up,[9] and few people were to be seen, except that here and there, in front of food stores, there were long lines.

Everyone was listless and bored. In the South Pacific, islands were wrested from us, one after the other, but even such dire developments didn't stir us. The argument to be heard was that contrary to what one might expect, these developments had their advantages. From this point on the lives of city residents became more chaotic still; every last person focused his wits on getting food, and human beings of a new type emerged, champions at making do.

Headmaster Abe grew thin. He became a different person from the ruddy-cheeked person he was when he took that job. His jaw narrowed; his neck shrank, pathetically. With unruly white hair, eyes glittering beneath baggy eyelids, gradually wrinkling skin, he often looked like an old carved mask. Clearly, it was not merely the flukeworms that infested his liver.

One day high school headmasters were summoned to army headquarters and given training in saluting and the like.

This time the head teacher went in his stead, and Abe was angry at the disrespect: "To make elderly headmasters ride horseback . . . " Why the Japanese military—its core, no less—should have degenerated to this sort of foolishness was beyond explaining.

Head teacher Hidaka helped the headmaster and, being the kind of person he was, took on himself all the unthinking criticism. In a bind no matter what the situation and not being permitted to explain, he made the best of things, bore up under things, and without holding a grudge took criticism even from people he himself was defending. Thomas Mann said, "Those capable now of defending liberalism are not normal liberals. They are fighting liberals," and Hidaka was one of the few who lived up to those words. In order to set our own house in order, he had to put us under tight discipline.

One time he said, "Unless we operate from the premise of accepting their sensible demands voluntarily, we'll lose the whole thing. Accepting them will enable us also to put forward our own case. For us to offer nit-picking resistance is like being in a besieged castle and signaling the enemy—'Here's a weak point!' 'Aim here!'" With this intent he worked himself to the bone, but he couldn't even explain his approach publicly.

Had such men not existed, Ichikō would have been beyond rescue. And even had it been rescued, it would probably have become merely safe and

---

9. For roadside air-raid trenches.

mediocre. Ichikō was unquestionably fortunate in 1944 to have this head-master and this head teacher.

X has absolute coercive power but, without showing his hand, uses Y to control Z. Y loves Z, so he has to take on this distasteful role. If he says no, someone worse than he will make a worse job of it. Y keeps X's demands to a minimum, and he has to speak to Z as if the intent of X, who doesn't show his hand, is really his own, Y's. Among the three, unreasonable logic will appear. It will also likely be necessary that compulsion accompany responsibility. Moreover, some among Z truckle to X; some believe sincerely that even if they don't truckle to X, they won't be able to save the situation unless they make common cause with X; some criticize Y to Z to gain popularity; and there are various other permutations. That's the situation a sacrificial goat like Y faces—this I learned for the first time during the war.

I also learned this: the person in charge has no leisure time and enjoys no freedom of speech or action. By contrast, those not in charge get a good bit of leisure and can say what they want to say, and they can keep their own hands clean, at least by not doing what they don't want to do. There are other complications in the contrast between the two, but no matter what, those not in charge are in a safe zone and pass judgment on the ones in charge, who aren't free to defend themselves. At times responsibility treats people quite pitilessly, callously.

It was a summer with no summer vacation.

After all the difficulties, dorm reform took place, student self-government was abolished, and a "manager system" introduced. I was appointed manager of Middle Dorm and on August 6 moved to the third floor of Middle Dorm.

Dorm life had a deep impact on me. Looking back, I think that it even changed me somewhat as a person. It was tough, but I'm thankful I did it.

Mornings at 5:20, as manager of Middle Dorm, I made the rounds ringing the wake-up bell. Then we gathered on the roof, took the roll, reported the count, observed morning ceremony, and did physical training. Then after an hour of class, the juniors went to their new place of work, a factory in Kawasaki,[10] to return after dark. Taking their deportment on the way there and back as an index of their training, the military officer assigned to the school exercised strict control, mornings in particular. As winter approached, morning meeting took place in total darkness. In the dark on the roof of North Dorm, Kimura Kenkō materialized, shoulders hunched against the cold, ringing the bell. Dawn broke while we were doing physical training,

---

10. Kawasaki is a major industrial city ten miles south of Tokyo (see map 2).

and the snowcapped mountains appeared beyond the reddish plain to the west, beautiful.

In early autumn the days continued bright and clear, and as far as concerned me, life in the cleaned-up dorm was surprisingly pleasant. But in October came the long rains and then the cold, befitting the problems at the front, and a grim oppression was added to daily life.

The Ichikō students wore their capes against snow and cold. But out on the streets and in the factory, the capes raised eyebrows. Angry letters of protest arrived, calling it "ivory tower Gatsby-like romanticism."[11]

But although it might have been okay to take his cape away from Gatsby, we couldn't now take these useful capes away from Ichikō students who didn't have money for clothing. After much thought, we finally solved the difficulty provisionally: wearing the capes was OK, but whenever the students set foot outside the school gate, they wrapped on gaiters, donned air-raid gear, and an announcement was made, "Prepare for air raids!"

The shortages were severe.

One afternoon a student returned from the Kawasaki factory ahead of time. Ichikō students had a poor attendance record, and this was a cause of real worry for the school, so on that score the teacher assigned to the factory had a tough job. Leaving the factory early was also controlled strictly. I asked this student why he had left early, and his answer caught me off guard: "Because I don't have shoes." He had walked home in his bare feet. "When it gets late, the streetcars are crowded, and people are always stepping on my toes. So I left early." Having said this, he entered the dorm, nonchalantly singing the dorm song in a loud voice.

Many students had minor injuries that became infected and didn't respond to treatment. It was because of malnutrition. A student named Ueno on the third floor of Middle Dorm had his instep swell to twice normal size, and the skin became soft and transparent; underneath the dirty bandage you could see the wound. Still, whenever you inquired, he simply smiled gently and didn't take it seriously. It astonished me that about such issues young people are all in fact calm, indifferent, nonchalant, stoic.

When ordinary people got together, they'd talk always about food; but despite their meager diet, these young people didn't talk about food.

Thinking to add some elegance to dorm life, the school planned to put together a magazine and asked for submissions. I too wrote a piece about the dorm day. Manuscripts piled up, and after much effort things got to the proofreading stage. But among the finished pieces there wasn't a single militarist

---

11. Literally, "of the *Konjiki yasha* variety." *Konjiki yasha* (1897–1902) was a tragic novel of Ichikō life by Ōzaki Kōyō (1867–1903).

line, and that fact surprised and angered the people at the printer's. What is more, when we got finally to the printing stage, military police in plain clothes were coming and going, searching our wastebaskets, so we gave up the idea of publishing it.

This journal that in the end never appeared we named "Oak Leaves." We wanted to name it "The Lamp of Self-Government," but that name we had to avoid.[12]

Against the winter we tilled the playing field assiduously. But nothing much grew.

Alerts sounded constantly. At all hours, Yanagida's sharp commanding voice from atop the tower could be heard as far away as Shibuya.[13] Every last thing became a rush. Dread winter approached. Along with it, the liveliness of the dorm died, and one no longer heard voices singing dorm songs. Some students grew reckless and didn't even go out for labor duty; they stayed in bed during the day and went out at night. Their nutrition was bad, their spirits sank, and they looked miserable. Many anguished over tough questions: What point is there in this labor-brigade life? No matter how you look at it, can you see any raison d'être in living this way? To resolve them, some people read recondite philosophy of history, and some, unable to reach any resolution, agonized. For young people, intellectual problems turn into virtual bodily pain. Agonizing for different reasons, several of the adults deteriorated visibly.

Call-up notices came daily. Faces we had grown used to seeing were suddenly gone. At this late date there were no more send-off parties; some people stood and chatted for a bit at the shoe rack in the entryway before departing with an "I'm off now." Everyone realized his own day would come. Voices singing the sad "Skies over the Capital" rang endlessly atop the tower, in front of the buildings, and in our ears even after we returned to our own homes.[14]

Washio joined a special attack [kamikaze] unit and, wearing a new military uniform, came to school to say goodbye; he died soon thereafter, as I learned a bit later. I confess: speaking with him on that occasion was tough, unendurable. Perhaps sensing my coolness, he hesitated briefly on the stairs, then went resolutely on down and left the building alone.

Morning ceremonies, roll call, cleanup, and the rest—until the air raids grew fierce, we carried out this new regimen to the letter. Ichikō had

---

12. Self-government was a cherished higher school tradition; Ichikō students pinned oak-leaf medallions to the front of their caps.

13. Yanagida was a veteran instructor of athletics; there was a loudspeaker atop the tower. Shibuya was a mile or more east of Komaba (see map 2).

14. "Skies over the Capital" was an Ichikō school song and hence sung as students left for the military.

achieved the desired attitude: of the demands made on it from outside, it had put into practice off its own bat those that made sense. Still, it did so at the cost of much internal distress. . . .

Mid-autumn came, and the second-year students who had gone to Hitachi came back, leaving one group there. Seeing the state of the dorm, they were extremely angry. They said, "What's this? What happened to our traditions? Our glory? Our pride?" Many of the students had grown to maturity in the dorm. For them, it was the only world, and this atmosphere their only home. As, finally, they graduated and came to know that other lives existed, their ardor cooled, but while they were in the dorms, many of them liked to think that the dorm was an extraterritorial zone where the laws of the state didn't apply. There were other motives behind the conservatism of these young people, but no matter what, seeing the sea change the dorms had undergone while they were away, the second-year students who came back to the dorm were extremely unhappy.

The school made strenuous efforts. The pretense had been that in reforming the dorms, the school hadn't been bowing to outside pressure, so to some extent the difficulty was logical as well. This attack was a real setback for the new, post-reform mood. Those students who had lived through the reform answered back, but their position had the handicap of conceding, "I'm a dorm student, but . . . "

I gazed awestruck at the organization, execution, and rhetoric of the Ichikō students who became leaders, regardless of their stance. Even if they only slept in class, lacked spirit, or were passive, when they got back to the dorm they were spectacularly active. I hope someone writes a detailed account of the good fight these students put up in those difficult days.

I'd like to note that even at such a time, some students really studied hard. They came back from the factory, hauled chairs to the only corridor with a light on all night, and set books on the chairs; squatting on the floor, wrapping their capes about them, they read with a will. This was against regulations, and it caused concern for their health, but I couldn't bring myself to put a stop to it. Walking past them late at night, I worried about them . . .

Scheduled for the end of August, the inspection by the prince who was divisional commander was called off because he happened to be reassigned just before then; instead, Major General Y, director of the Military Affairs Bureau, came to inspect us—it was at the beginning of December, if I'm not mistaken.

Few of the students understood just how critical for school and dorms this inspection was.

In preparation for the fateful day, we had to put the whole school in such order that even the military couldn't find fault.

To this end we needed first to persuade the students, get them in the mood.

There were many purists: "Why dissemble by prettying up the surfaces of things for just the one day? Why not let them see us the way we are?"

In the dorm, meetings were held, and debate took place. The discussion took one of two familiar paths: people either used subjective words difficult to grasp, sometimes tracing the issue back to human fundamentals, or they piled abstraction on abstraction until finally they themselves didn't understand what they were saying to each other. In South Dorm, after strenuous efforts by the dorm manager, they finally reached this conclusion: "OK. We'll do it. But it's not to show the brass. It's to prove to ourselves that if we decide to do so, even Ichikō students can clean all this up."

On the day before inspection, I went into the toilets on each floor, braving the stench, and erased the graffiti on the walls. They were a real danger. Reluctantly, I erased an eloquent one: "We thought it was the beginning, but in fact it was the beginning of the end. Fate is laughing cynically."

In one room I erased a profusion of ink graffiti. For a long time this room had had graffiti all the way up to the ceiling, but at the time of the dorm reform, at a cost of 3,000 yen, all the dorm walls had been whitewashed. These graffiti were on top of the whitewash, so where they had scraped off the new graffiti, the old showed through. Their solution was to paste paper over the old graffiti and then write on it. The words appealed to me, but I've forgotten them.

In another room the whole wall was covered with GEBA[15] in huge letters. That was ominous.

The rooms I had absolutely no hope of cleaning up I locked up and decided to say they belonged to second-year students still in Ibaraki.[16]

One cold day we cleaned up outside the dorms. We didn't have tools of any kind, so we picked everything up by hand. Dorm rain[17] froze, green and bubbly, and embedded in it were pieces of broken glass. These we grabbed with our fingers and pulled out. I wondered how to kill the penetrating ammonia smell from the triangular depressions beneath the windows of the dorm rooms, but there was no way.

The students' way of cleaning up was to set fire to everything. At the end thickets and grass were burning fiercely. As the fires burned, the students

---

15. *Ge-ba* are the first two syllables of *ge-ba-ru-to*, the phonetic Japanese for the German *Gewalt* (power); the graffito calls for violent revolution.

16. Ibaraki Prefecture, in which the city of Hitachi is located (see map 1).

17. "Dorm rain" is a euphemism for urine. Pissing out dorm windows was a cherished practice, part of the grunge style—"higher school barbarism"—that characterized Ichikō, apparently throughout its existence. See Roden, *Schooldays*, 111, 219.

searched the ground carefully where the flames were. I wondered what they were doing; it turned out that the chestnuts that had fallen in the grass were now roasted, and they were picking them up to eat.

Most students disappeared midway, but a dozen worked with a will and cleaned up the area around the dorms completely. At the end I walked around and put out the last traces of fire. Because it was already dark and embers were visible from the air.

Inspection day arrived at last. Their leather boots clattering, the director of the Military Affairs Bureau and a group of ten officers went through the dorms.

Major General Y was an older man, slight and thin and grizzled. Fidgety and short-tempered, he engaged in loud, one-way communication. He was a haughty and proud man accustomed to command and control. Entering without ceremony, he looked around, gimlet-eyed. But on this day there wasn't a single chink in Ichikō's armor. The general seemed displeased, almost as if he didn't like it.

There was an air raid that day. It was the third or fourth time that B-29s had appeared in the skies over Tokyo. In the clear early winter air, they floated calmly, violet and sparkling. Shining like a firework, a Japanese plane approached like a shooting star and rammed a B-29. Then, spinning and giving off black smoke, it fell to earth. Drawing long white frosty lines, the B-29s faded slowly into the crystalline distance.

We had dug an air-raid shelter in the schoolyard. Our flawless enterprise, command, communication, and report surprised the officers.

On the second floor of Middle Dorm, General Y questioned one of the students lined up in the corridor outside their rooms and saluting: "How did you feel when you saw that plane ram the B-29?" The student answered, "I was sorry 'Japanese science isn't up to the task.'" This was a popular phrase at the time. The general nodded. Then he asked, again in a loud voice, "So what do you think we should do now?" The student froze and, face red, couldn't come up with an answer. Pointing at the chest of the student, the general said, "You students—that's your responsibility. Right?" and walked on.

The inspection ended without incident. The general said nothing to the school, but on departing, he supposedly commented to the officer assigned to the school, "Satisfactory."

Watching him leave, I commented: "If the director of the Military Affairs Bureau has time now to come inspect us, the war must be going fine." The man standing next to me responded, "No. He's got time because things *aren't* going well."

Thus, the danger passed for the present, and the school regained the standing it had enjoyed before.

The winter that followed was a truly bitter one. Air raids continued one after the other. Any number of times the fuel and food necessary for the large household of a thousand people seemed on the point of running out. During this time military police in civilian clothes came and went at the school, and in the new year Professor Kimura and dorm students were arrested by the military police and held for some two weeks; that was the second time the school faced danger. Because of a fire that started in Middle Dorm, room 26, at dawn on February 10, I was dismissed as dorm manager. About that time the graduation of the second-year students was decided on, and solely because of poor performance of labor duty, several of them were deemed ineligible. The dorm was in an uproar, that sanction being unacceptable, and for several nights, late into the night and with snow falling, there was a constant coming and going of students complaining to Headmaster Abe, who slept at the school. After many twists and turns, the upshot was that these people did graduate. There was also the dilemma of how to evacuate the school itself out of Tokyo. The pupils scattered to several places—from Yamagata Prefecture in the north to Shizuoka Prefecture in the south, lived in dispersed lodgings, and did labor service. Some became firemen and, when air raids came, raced to their assigned posts in the dead of night. In May a third of the school went up in flames. But in July, when Tokyo was already largely destroyed, the school celebrated an all-dorm dinner assembly and a culture day, listened to the orchestra, and presented research reports.[18]

Should the opportunity arise, I'm thinking of setting down very brief notes about all these things. With ten times the space I've used for this essay, I could write down what I remember.

---

18. It was at this banquet that Takeyama delivered the speech, "The Younger Generation" (translated in this volume).

# The End of the War

*"The End of the War" begins in May 1945. The key dates in late summer 1945 are the Potsdam Conference (July 17–August 2) and Declaration (July 26), the atomic bombing of Hiroshima (August 6), the atomic bombing of Nagasaki (August 9), the Soviet attack on Japan in Manchuria (August 9), Japan's surrender (August 15), and the surrender ceremony (September 2).*

*This essay appeared first in the September 1953 issue of the national magazine Shinchō.*

On May 25 I was staying the night in Kanazawa Hakkei,[1] at the site of the school's labor assignment, so from the beach there I watched at a distance the bombing of Tokyo across the water.

In the humid, late-spring sky there were many clouds, and the fire in the city reflected off them; bit by bit the layers of cloud came clearly into view, even those off in the distance. The radio reported continually: "Large enemy squadrons attacking from the direction of Bōsō and from Shizuoka";[2] to the east and to the west, searchlight beams rose up, a forest of them. At the prescribed separation, pairs of beams intersected, and at the points of in-

---

1. Kanazawa Hakkei is a small stretch of waterfront on the southern edge of Yokohama (see map 2).
2. The Bōsō peninsula, south and east of Tokyo, forms the eastern shore of Tokyo Bay. Shizuoka is the prefecture of Fuji, the distinctive mountain American pilots and navigators used to orient themselves (see map 1).

tersection floated enemy planes, violet-colored. These pillars of light moved slowly from left and right toward the center, keeping the enemy planes on their pedestals, as if silently transporting them. The beams were pale, like a hallucination but ordered, and the sky was tense with a strange sense of oppression. From the dark behind the clouds, plane after plane appeared, astonishing in their numbers. They seemed virtually beyond counting.

Transported one after the other on the pillars of light, the enemy bombers soon enter the area in the center that is burning with dazzling brightness. There it's a red lotus of fire. In it, lights glitter prism-like and flow, a veritable symphony of colors.

Lights like red snakes race horizontally high in the sky, and some are falling, still horizontal. Green and orange balls of light also rise from the earth, slowly. Antiaircraft shells open out just like fireworks, and some hang like mercury lamps. All of this is artificial light to which we're not accustomed, but it bears no resemblance to streetlights; it flows together, flashes in complicated ways. As I think back now, I don't hear even the slightest explosions in my head; could I really not have heard any?

Sometimes a plane breaks up in midair. First flames flare out, suddenly, then always die out for a bit. But then, quickly, they flare up again. The plane turns gradually into a ball of fire and continues to gyrate. Twisting and spiraling, falling almost to the ground, then climbing once more, it's just like a creature in agony. Then, finally, just when you think the flames have been brought under control and died out, they flare up suddenly again, and the plane breaks into pieces and falls.

I myself counted seventeen planes that fell. At the time, I took them all to be enemy planes, but they probably included a good many friendlies, too.

It was truly an eerie spectacle. And it was filled with strange new sensations. In those days of air raids, each new day, we thought, was "the end of the world," and it was a surprise that the end of the world was so beautiful, like the hallucinations of a madman. It was exactly like one of Baudelaire's sketches.[3] Weird arcs and rich colors. A terrifying sense of disintegration. Eerie realities. In a corner of the painting, a self-portrait of the silk-hatted Baudelaire, looking on skeptically with an unsettling nihilistic sidelong glance—the sketch seemed horribly lifelike.

It wasn't clear to me that it was indeed Tokyo that was being demolished; I simply couldn't guess the amount of damage such an air raid would inflict. In those days we had no way of knowing what the larger picture was or how we ourselves fit into it. What would happen tomorrow? We had no way to

---

3. Charles Baudelaire (1821–1867), French symbolist poet and critic.

judge. Driven day by day, struggling physically, we merely observed what took place before our eyes. We could grasp neither significance nor substance. When I read accounts of the end of the war now, they are written as if the authors acted on the basis of clear judgments of the situation, but those must be after-the-fact feelings.

Utterly exhausted in body and soul, I had little strength left over to react freshly. The "postwar lethargy of the people"—hadn't it really set in around 1944? Except for the few who managed to live in comfort, most of us were exhausted long since. From the sense of powerlessness I'd had for some time, I'd lost all will of my own and merely reacted to the changes taking place before me. The end of the war meant the whip impelling those changes forward was gone—that was all. In the novel *Oblomov*,[4] the main character passes day after day watching with empty eyes as the house across the way sparkles in the evening rays of the sun, and it was in precisely that manner that I observed Tokyo going up in flames on May 25.

But enemy planes came twice to the very spot where we were standing on the beach and watching. Appearing suddenly from behind the hills at our back, they came on in the blink of an eye, low, right over our heads. From the silent black hills and woods all around us, antiaircraft fire went up, a surprising volume of it. It went up also from the island in front of us. Echoes resounded all around. Wrapped in dense smoke, the planes disappeared from sight. I saw my first tracer shells; they sounded different from ordinary shells, as if someone were pumping water. Many balls of flame, linked like sausages, flew slowly through the air. The speed of the bullets was something we could see with astonishing clarity. These sausages of flame seemed about to reach the planes but never did, turning and falling and dying out. The planes emerged from the smoke undamaged and flew on.

When the enemy planes appeared suddenly, we forgot everything we'd been taught. We didn't take refuge—there wasn't anywhere to go, nor did we hit the dirt. Looking up in astonishment, we simply watched. The modern feel of vessels passing overhead, purple light shining on fuselages covered with duralumin skin, was entirely novel. It had no connection with terror for our lives. What occupied our minds was mere curiosity—"What will happen next?" It was like witnessing a traffic accident: the tension—"What's happening?"—and then the body, as if paralyzed, unable to move.

We had gotten out of bed and gone to the beach—another teacher, of mathematics, A., assigned to this work site, and I. Exhausted from the day's work and with empty stomachs, the students slept on, even through the sirens. This lodging on the waterfront in Kanazawa Hakkei was on the edge

---

4. *Oblomov* (1858), by Russian novelist Ivan Goncharov (1812–1891).

of the breakwater, and if you dug in the sand, you hit water immediately, so we couldn't dig air-raid shelters and in case of emergency were supposed to run to a cave in a hill a half mile off; but that was in fact impossible to do. Indeed, the people who had been working here had left this spot to us, and they themselves had moved to a safer spot.

Meanwhile, there were sharp reports in the air, and shrapnel fell around us. The sound came from the sand and from the clumps of reeds. Roof tiles on huts nearby shattered. Shrapnel falling into the ocean sounded quite like a red-hot sword plunged into water. We stood there amid the steadily increasing shrapnel falling on all sides. Unable to do anything—as I think back now, it seems completely stupid of us, we simply grinned.

Once July came, I accompanied the first-year students to a new labor site, the Tachikawa aircraft factory, and slept in the dorm there.[5] This factory had already been nearly destroyed by the bombs, and great iron beams were askew, broken glass all over the place, and concrete broken; on many consecutive nights that March and April the radio had said, "Enemy planes over Tachikawa," so this post was a bit unsettling.

About a year earlier, in a room with blackout curtains drawn, I had spread out a map of Japan and searched for somewhere to evacuate to. Of course, the map itself couldn't tell me anything, but luckily there was a family in Nagatoro in Chichibu[6] willing to take us in, and I rented the loft of a silkworm breeding building and in the spring of 1945 moved my family there.

Relatives who had been burned out of Tokyo moved into our own home in Kamakura, and I myself went to Tachikawa, and we waited to see how things would turn out. By chance, things turned out fine for the whole family. The Tachikawa factory was building an underground factory in the mountains of Chichibu, and when that was completed, it was expected that the whole factory would move there. In that case I too would go to that underground factory and be close to my family in Nagatoro. I'd be able on occasion to spend the night on the wooden floor of the silkworm loft. And I'd be able to see my children, then four and two. Besides, there was the difficult problem of the school itself: one day it would go up in flames, so what to do about evacuating it? The students were on labor details at scattered sites, from Yamagata Prefecture in the north to Shizuoka Prefecture in the south, and we needed to prepare a base of operations against the day we lost the main campus. As for that base, I went as emissary and got approval for the school to move to a primary school in Chichibu, close to the underground factory. Thus, with

5. Tachikawa is twenty-five miles due west of Tokyo (see map 2).
6. Chichibu is forty-five miles west-northwest of Tokyo; Nagatoro is a village fifteen miles due north of Chichibu (see map 1).

my move to Tachikawa and my family's to Nagatoro, we would achieve in the end the goal of a family rendezvous in the Chichibu basin.

The Kanto plain might become a battlefield. But even then, the fires of war probably wouldn't reach the Chichibu basin. All this was the very best we could plan, forecast, and pull off at the time (but when I went as emissary to Chichibu, I was surprised to learn that the townspeople there had already begun to evacuate to places still farther out).

Even accomplishing just this was indescribably difficult. However, I didn't lose my home, and I cut corners in my official duties; but some people discharged their official duties scrupulously even though they had been burned out and were fighting economic distress. Most people had all they could do to save their own skins, and morale crumbled, but thanks to a small number of people with real mettle, the whole held. Those people kept silent even after the war and continued their unsung labors. Thanks to these people, the whole barely held through the long crisis. By contrast, those in the limelight after the war were for the most part people who had been in the limelight during the war. And they disparaged the others.

Finally the day came to leave for Tachikawa, and I squatted among the luggage that we couldn't take with us and turned on the phonograph. The record was a Bach chaconne played by Busch.[7] I thought, "This is the last time I'll hear it." Listening to this piece that brought with it so many memories, I wept a tear or two.

. . . Depending on events, off in the mountains of Chichibu we may have to live in caves like the residents of Chongqing.[8] Even should the war end, we'll probably have to live for a decade with a standard of living like that of the aborigines of the South Pacific. This is indeed the end of what we call civilization . . .

A relative who had moved in with us, an old man, frequently intoned the slogan about 100 million Japanese dying together. But his was not the usual logic. He said, "You think on the whole the war Japan waged was essentially right? Having done what we did and lost—you think if we simply put our hands up they'll let us live?"

At the Tachikawa labor site, I spent my mornings teaching German and afternoons weeding the potato patch, consoling homesick students, and making charts and compiling statistics. The fine weather continued day after day, and sometimes I lay in the sweet-smelling grass and watched the air war. At night when the sirens sounded, I jumped out of bed, wrapped on my puttees

---

7. Adolf Busch (1891–1952).
8. Chongqing (Chungking) was the Chinese nationalist wartime capital, inland on the Yangtze River. Heavy Japanese aerial bombardment drove the residents underground.

and clapped on my helmet, and ran to Tanashi,[9] and sometimes when the Tanashi airfield just ahead was bombed, there'd be a huge explosion, so I'd return to the house and hide under the covers. But the bombing of Tachikawa was over and done with, so to my surprise Tachikawa was safe. Enemy squadrons were always passing overhead, and soon in the distance the usual smoke would billow up, like ash-colored brains. Tachikawa was just like an outlying island in the Pacific after the enemy forces had bypassed it.

The factory had sent foodstuffs to the construction site of the underground factory in Chichibu, so we here were really desperate for food. We often said, "The chopsticks fall right over,"[10] and if we stood the chopsticks upright in the bean stew, they did fall right over. We too suffered constant hunger pangs, but for the young students it was really bad.

One morning, taking a look in the washroom mirror, I gave a start. My own face had aged so much I didn't recognize it, and a sort of shadow of death appeared. To be sure, in those days malnutrition caused changes in appearance, and lots of people looked ghastly . . .

One day a telegram came for me. The family that had gone to Nagatoro had taken sick and returned to Kamakura. Please come immediately.

Obtaining permission, I came back to Kamakura. The two children and my sister-in-law having played outside and come down with diphtheria, the whole family returned home in a great rush, and they had been admitted to the hospital (fortunately, things went well, and they were soon discharged). Because they had left Chichibu in a hurry, they hadn't gone to town hall to stop the rations they'd been getting. So they couldn't get food here in Kamakura, and there was nothing to eat. My family moved in with the relatives who were in our house, and by the time I arrived, dog-tired, the complications of communal living had already set in.

The complications that began now were absolutely extraordinary: just like fighting cocks with cockscombs shaking, the women were hateful to each other, snarled at each other, clamored fiercely, seemed virtually to have gone mad; it made a very deep impression on me, but because it concerns private matters and the parties are still living, I'm not going to write about it. Everything was a mess. Particularly at that time when I was utterly incapable of supporting my family, I wanted desperately to wash my hands of the duties of head of the house. But if we were put out, we had nowhere to go, so I swallowed my bile. These were all people who had been living in comparatively easy circumstances; had the war continued another three months, my family would surely have disintegrated completely.

9. Tanashi is a dozen miles northwest of Tokyo (see map 2).
10. In other words, the food was meager.

Sirens, lack of sleep, shortage of food, pressure of business, rations, drills—with all this, the hall was muddy, and the bedroom a mess. When I listened to the radio at night, I often heard enemy propaganda broadcasts. But those I listened to were in clumsy Japanese and missed the mark—not effective psychological warfare.

At the time of the early-spring air raids, a mysterious fellow moved into the house next door.

This Mr. —— was thirty-two or -three, dark-skinned, with compact body, and a fierce and sly look. On the name card he gave me were printed several titles: Attached to the Secretariat of Minister ——; Seconded to —— Main Office. He was living with his mistress, and the wealth of material goods of this house was something to be envied. They seemed to lack for absolutely nothing. The difficulties and exhaustion of wartime life appeared not to touch them at all. Their shelves were always weighed down with Chinese cigarettes—*Ha-tamon*; since my mother-in-law was landlady of the house he rented, he appeared occasionally with gifts. He wore a brand-new civilian uniform with shining leather puttees and cut a dashing figure. Evidently he belonged to that special class of people that appeared in those days, a member presumably of a Pan-Asianist organization.

I had seen his name on handbills plastered on Tokyo streets. They were handbills for a session of anti-Jewish propaganda, with Lieutenant General S. presiding and Mr. —— as one of the speakers. From this fact and from his style of living, one could surmise that he belonged to the extreme right wing and had ties to the continent, but the rest was unclear. Rumor had it that he had graduated from university in the Dutch East Indies or somewhere and traveled in Europe and Africa, scouted New Guinea and made the first map of it, but who knew how much of this was true?

Although I couldn't guess what he was up to, he was without doubt a bigwig of the day, living an adventurous life ably and expeditiously. He was on a scale and dimension beyond my comprehension. Likely he belonged to some powerful organization in society's shadows: that must have been how he gained his privileges.

Magnanimous in spirit and somewhat haughty, he seemed charitably inclined to the little people who came for favors. When my aged mother became ill in the country, I couldn't lay my hands on a train ticket, that being the way things were then. Timidly, I asked his help. And Mr. —— lent me casually his own nationwide second-class pass.

Other than that we had no contact, but in the meantime came Hiroshima, Nagasaki, and the Soviet Union's entry into the war, and it seemed the catastrophe was finally at hand. As before, we had no way of knowing how things really stood; we knew only what we saw and heard within our own narrow radius. In fear amid the chaos, we could only conjecture and surmise from the rumors, yet we could tell from the newspapers that something was afoot. I too was beside myself with worry for the future of the country, and on August 10—probably that was the day—I mustered my courage, went to the big man next door, and asked him to tell me what was happening.

Mr. —— said: "They've just delivered this. It's about the meeting at dawn this morning in the emperor's presence." With no compunctions he reached up and took a mimeographed sheet from the mantelpiece and read it off to me.

On hearing it, I was thunderstruck.

Foreign Minister Tōgō reported to the effect that there was no alternative but to accept the Potsdam Declaration unconditionally, and in response Army Minister Anami said that Japan should land a major blow at the time of the invasion of the main islands, but that if an end to the war became possible based on the conditions our side had proposed, he would give his assent; Navy Minister Yonai. . . . The Prime Minister stated that although the discussion had already gone on for several hours, they hadn't reached a conclusion, but the situation did not permit a moment's delay; so with deep respect he would receive the emperor's decision as the decision of the meeting. In response, the emperor made his decision. . . . To endure the unendurable, for the sake of generations to come, he wants to clear the way for peace. It was not necessary to worry about his own fate or that of the Imperial House. . . . Hearing these words, the whole room wept.

Mr. —— read this off in the completely matter-of-fact tone well-suited to an energetic man of affairs, twisting his oily lips. He seemed utterly untroubled. On reflection, I thought that various plans for the future must already have been percolating in Mr. ——'s head at the time; as for the defeat, it was just as if he were speaking of a horse race. I was dumbfounded.

So it had come to this! Still, what sort of person was he, this man who got same-day reports of the nation's most important news, news we were utterly unable to divine? Moreover, though a right-winger, he seemed completely unmoved by the defeat, seemed to treat it as if it was someone else's business, not his. Did he have emotions? No? Was he a great man? A fool?

I sank into gloomy thoughts. I didn't register Mr. ——'s commonplaces thereafter, and I couldn't really respond. All I remember is hearing him say quite cheerfully and with some self-consciousness: "I'm not going to Tokyo today. If I went, I'd have to join the revolution."

As I made my departure, left the entryway, and walked along beneath the windows of Mr. ——'s room, I heard him say to his mistress: "Hmm—dealing with someone like him makes me tired." It was probably his first encounter with someone as exhausted as I was then.

Right after the war Mr. —— moved away and soon was publishing a photo magazine, *Democracy*. Even in Kamakura I caught sight of him wearing a sharp suit and riding about in a car with Americans. But because we moved in completely different worlds, I took no note and forgot him.

But quite recently his name has become prominent in the press. After the war he "made his fortune riding the wave of textiles and metals," "bustling about the political and financial worlds, he elbowed his way into the front ranks of the business world"; now he's applying his talents as an executive of a great armaments factory.

I heard the emperor's broadcast in Tachikawa. For another week or so Japanese military planes still flew. In the late-autumn sky, the roar of their engines sounded imprudent, almost reckless.

From the city authorities in Kamakura came a notice that the U.S. Army was landing, so evacuate women and children to a safe place. At our house the dispute was raging, I thought the danger might be real, and I was worried in particular about food in the coming winter, so thinking it would be until there was some prospect of things settling down, I sent the family off again to Chichibu.

~

# White Pine and Rose

*"White Pine and Rose" takes its title from a poem by the German Eduard Friedrich Mörike (1804–1875), the pine and rose that will be planted on Mörike's grave. The essay is Takeyama's reflection on his own mortality, on his experiences in wartime and in the early postwar era of the U.S. Occupation, and on man's powerlessness before fate. Takeyama's comment that "three years was plenty of time for a country to fall to ruins" will resonate with many Americans in the twenty-first century.*

*The essay appeared first in the April 1947 issue of the national magazine* Shinchō.

~

## On Destiny

Dear T. K.,

Thank you for your letter from the Heights.[1] It'll be hard for you to come back to Tokyo. And there's no hurry, is there? In your letter you write about days and months of eating thistles and getting lifts to town on the milk wagon at dawn as the stars fade about the slopes of Mount Asama—I'm jealous. I hope that you're making progress meanwhile on great work, such as the complete writings of Romain Rolland.

---

1. Katayama Toshihiko (1898–1961), a senior colleague at Ichikō, translated the complete works of Romain Rolland. Mount Asama lies in Nagano Prefecture in central Honshu, north and west of Tokyo (see map 1).

As for me, I commute to work through a burned-out city. Every last thing is complicated and difficult. This must be what life's like in a defeated country. The monster that is daily life has devoured our psyches completely. We pass the days one after the other, busy and driven.

Still, things have calmed down some. On occasion, I even have a bit of free time to sit by myself, quietly. It's been a very long time since I was able to do that. And I look about my shabby room as if for the first time.

At such times, a sensation I hadn't known before bubbles up inside. I forget it when I'm at work during the day, but when night falls, it raises its head. Chased into the depths of my heart, turned there into an idée fixe, it affects all my current thoughts and feelings.

After ten years of horrible experiences, life has come floating up, bringing new prospects. For me the war experience was not simply war experience. It was life experience. Life used the opportunity of the war to lay bare its hidden aspects.

I want to write about these prospects and my own emotional state living amid them.

Still, I needed an occasion to put my thoughts on paper. You wrote, "At last the time has come when human dignity is restored," and those words spoke directly to my thoughts; so I've decided to address that issue here.

## 2.

The experiences of the last ten years gave me an uncanny awareness. I came to feel something I'd not felt before. Here are examples.

With high-speed photography and its opposite and with other techniques, movies show us things the naked eye can't see. For example, in three minutes on the movie screen we can see frogs' eggs turning into tadpoles and then frogs.

Before, I had thought that countries fell to ruin by gradual disintegration, over a century or more; but countries in Europe were toppled one after the other, and at a time when our country, too, created enemies on all sides, I realized that three years was plenty of time for a country to fall to ruins. I saw that happen as if on the screen.

Again, on the screen, changes we're normally utterly unable to see can be filmed, enlarged, and shown us in full view. One time I saw how skin sloughed off and grew back. Recently I've watched close-up how people in our society little by little straggle, fall, get weeded out, and disappear from sight, and with my own eyes I've seen people of a different sort appear and re-form society's crust.

I also became aware for the first time of my own perception of my surroundings. I was surprised by what a strange thing it is, simultaneously sensitive and insensitive. On the one hand, people are extremely sensitive at any moment to their surroundings and absorb those surroundings, whatever they are. They accept that the surroundings, whatever they are, are as they should be. When all others accept these surroundings, it's difficult for the person who thinks differently to hold out. At one time we ate without thinking twice about food that, were we to eat it now, would surely shock us. Still, I'm the sort of person who clings to an awareness different from everyone else's. It surprised me during the war to see a friend who has a reputation as an intellectual bow at a small roadside shrine.

At the same time, humans are quite insensitive to conditions that don't affect them directly. Future danger to society and the like: it's hopeless no matter how much you admonish them. And they immediately forget past emotions. We forget the past in the same way that in the moment of waking we forget the nightmare we've just had. For most people, the everyday life of the war is already becoming stale, meaningless. If one still thinks of that great occurrence as a fact of his own psyche, he'll be ridiculed, thought silly. It's true: "Mankind learns only one thing from history—that he learns nothing from history."[2]

As for that different awareness, there were, for example, the delayed-action bombs. When we were taught to be wary of them, we were deeply impressed. They may explode; they may not explode. If they explode, there's absolutely no way to know when—now? an hour from now? a day from now? And their point is to threaten the nerves. That is, they exemplify perfectly the fearsomeness of chance, of destiny. In the old times destiny was ascribed to the gods, and men could only prostrate themselves in fear before it. Now human artifice has caught up with divine artifice—truly frightening, don't you think?

In olden times, poets plucked their lyres and sang to make people aware of this unfathomable force. Mörike[3] put us on notice with that elegant poem "O Soul, Think of It!"

> In the woods—who knows where?—
> Grows a pine tree;
> In some garden—who says which?—

---

2. Georg Friedrich Hegel, *Vorlesungen uber die Philosophie der Weltgeschichte* (Hamburg: Felix Meiner Verlag, 1996), 12:10: "Die Geschichte und die Erfahrung lehren, dass Völker überhaupt nicht aus der Geschichte gelernt haben."

3. Eduard Friedrich Mörike, *Mozart auf der Reise nach Prag* (Dusseldorf, 1913); Mozart on the Way to Prague, trans. W. Alison Phillips and Catherine Alison Phillips (Oxford, 1934).

Blooms a rose.
They've already been chosen—
O soul, think of it!—
To take root on your grave
And grow there.

Two black ponies graze
On the meadow,
. . . . . . . . . . . .
They will go step by step
Pulling your corpse;
Perhaps, perhaps even before
They lose the iron
That I see gleaming
From their hooves.[4]

In Mörike's novel, Mozart set this poem to music while imagining that the hour of his own death was approaching. Shouldering that fate, this incomparable genius who would die young burned with sublime creativity.

It's truly a riddle that at that young age, while creating that rich, bright music, Mozart thought constantly of death. The famous letter addressed to his father was written when he was thirty-one:

Since Death (to name it precisely) is the true and ultimate purpose of our life, I have over the last several years come to know so well this true and best friend of humankind that his image not only holds nothing terrifying for me anymore but instead much that is soothing and consoling. And I thank my God that he has blessed me with the opportunity . . . to perceive death as the key to our ultimate happiness. I never go to bed without thinking that perhaps, as young as I am, I will not live to see another day.[5]

Mozart's letters are all cheery, happy, filled with details of everyday talk, and this letter too is filled with happy innocence. There's absolutely no darkness. Still, we can glimpse here the boundless void beneath that bright ethereal genius.

Four years after writing this letter, Mozart was buried in an unmarked grave in Vienna.

---

4. Mörike, *Mozart's Journey to Prague*, *Selected Poems*, trans. David Luke (London: Libris, 1997), 71. I have altered the translation considerably to accord with Takeyama's translation. Cf. Mörike, *Mozart auf der Reise nach Prag* (Editions Montaigne, 1931), 73.

5. Letter from Wolfgang to Leopold, April 4, 1787, in *Mozart's Letters, Mozart's Life: Selected Letters*, ed. and trans. Robert Spaethling (New York: W. W. Norton, 2000), 389. I have altered the translation (cf. *Wolfgang Amadeus Mozarts Leben*, ed. Albert Leitzmann [Leipzig: Insel-Verlag, 1931], 414–15).

Treating a single day late in the life of this genius, Mörike depicts a figure who, while shouldering the destiny that has not yet made itself apparent, creates, is sociable, plays, and makes happy small blunders. And he composes "O Soul, Think of It!," a song in the form of a simple Bohemian folksong.

People of old were warned by philosophy and sermons and poems about the unknowable that is hiding somewhere and will attack sometime. We were made aware of it in more violent, naked form.

## 3.

Thus ten years' experience brought me into contact day and night with something I'd previously had no contact with, and I gained an impression of this strange thing. I mean fate.

I'd never had any concept of fate. I'd thought of it just vaguely—something that doesn't exist, merely a word devised by mankind to help explain, something that in fact represents nothing. I thought it was just like the meaningless stains on old walls that lead kids to guess, "That's a giant," "This is a sailboat."

But today fate has become the very frame of my psyche. It's an external force that exists independent of our will; it may constrain us or appear as chance. Against it we're utterly powerless. This memory is something I can't erase. And it floats above our future. How we come to terms with it, I've come to think, is a precondition for the restoration of human dignity.

At the dawn of history, mankind constantly cowered in awe before the forces of nature. When this external force interfered in life, people called it fate and imagined behind it someone pulling the strings. The ancient tragedians depicted man as controlled by it. The chorus of the old men of Colonus sang:

> I am not one to say, 'This is in vain,'
> Of anything allotted to mankind.
> Though some must fall, or fall to rise again,
> Time watches all things steadily—[6]

Like children deciphering stains on the old wall, the ancients divined this inscrutable someone by means of the cracks in the burned shell of a tortoise or the state of an animal's entrails. Thus, when some doom befell them, they consoled themselves with an explanation: this must be revenge for something, so look for a human crime that needs to be atoned.

---

6. Sophocles, *Oedipus at Colonus* (Robert Fitzgerald translation), in *The Oedipus Cycle*, trans. Dudley Fitts and Robert Fitzgerald (New York: Harcourt, Brace, Jovanovich, 1939), 155.

But finally mankind ascended from that status as servant to the status of master.

In the sixteenth century Hutten is said to have cried, "Psyche woke up. It's a joy to be alive!"[7] From that time on, man became aware of his own unblockable strength and believed firmly that all external forces could be overcome. Turning the old view upside down, he thought he himself could control all external force, that sometime his knowledge and will would be able to eliminate all chance. Man's awareness of fate disappeared gradually. Fate became simply a lie told by a fool.

The ancients divided fate into three parts—*moira* was fate, *tyche* chance, and *daimon* character, and modern man recognized at most only the last of these. In his arrogance, even the man who is the authority on knowing the fearsomeness of this world spoke of the "love of fate," asserted that fate would be won over to his side, and taught that man should become superman.[8]

This push to expand the realm of the human would go on forever—so it was thought. People called it progress, and in fact it did go on. But as it went on, this progress began to undergo a strange transformation. In the end, though created by humans, it came to have its own rules and dynamic and to confront mankind, paradoxically as force from without. In our time, it went back to filling the same role as the natural forces of the ancients.

The delayed-action bombs I mentioned earlier are a very small example.

During the last ten years, like humans at the dawn of history, we were at the mercy of external force. Sometimes it was absolutely unbending, sometimes utterly quirky. Human beings were wholly powerless before it. Fate appeared before us once more in concrete form. Coming into contact with it, some people sought for a crime that could be laid to someone or other and reproached these persons with great clamor. That must be human nature. And some people consciously or unconsciously made bold to challenge it, remake it with their own strength.

Once you're sure what the shape on the wall is, you can't see it as anything else. When I'd deciphered it as fate, I tried to identify its lines and smudges.

## 4.

What emerged first of all and oh, so clearly, was politics.

In ancient times, no matter how he tried, Oedipus Rex couldn't outrun the fate decreed for him. Now it's politics that has us in its grasp and won't let go, no matter what we do. With modern organization and weapons, rulers have

---

7. Ulrich von Hutten (1488–1523), German humanist.
8. This paragraph is an allusion to Nietzsche.

godlike power. Try though they may, the ruled can't resist the rulers. Even the most stalwart person can only endure. This was the reality we faced.

Nearly 150 years ago, Napoleon said, "How would we compose a drama of fate today? In this modern age, politics is fate." During the past several years I was reminded of these words any number of times.

The army's power to coerce was absolute. It had organization and power; nothing happened except as it decreed. Military people said, "I want this. You can't deviate from it. If you don't obey, such and such fearsome results will ensue. Those results are solely the responsibility of those who don't obey." With this formula, the military pressed at home and abroad and got its way. To be sure, it wasn't only the military that used this formula; it may be the formula for the application of every modern political power.

To resist, to borrow the expression somebody once used, was truly like "using chopsticks to stir ferroconcrete."

Military spokesmen used this expression. All the people supported the formation of an Ugaki cabinet, yet the military opposed it.[9] That's how they described efforts to oppose the army. Ultimately, these efforts were in vain, and an external power that transcended the political parties came to rule the people. Our fate was sealed.

Thereafter, thick ferroconcrete walls were erected, encircling us. No matter what we did, our lives could no longer venture outside them.

Inside those walls, astonishing things began to happen.

Once people understood that they couldn't venture outside, they flip-flopped and came to want to think that these walls were a good thing, that the walls were what they themselves wanted, that the walls were the realization of their own desires. Philosophers sought to prove it. They deployed jargon and logic to that end. They repeated over and over that reason obeyed will, and this assertion was self-fulfilling—less by conclusion than by process.

Not only that. Still more hair-raising things happened.

Within the walls, the rulers set out to change the psychology of the ruled. It wasn't a matter of controlling the masses by force alone; rather, they made the masses follow them voluntarily, enthusiastically, actively. Finally, they succeeded in becoming just like the hypnotist who implants his will in his subject and makes the subject act as if of his own volition. The ability to do this is, I think, a great difference between ancient despotisms and today's despotism.

To this end, they used every last fruit of modern man's efforts. Man had created these things to conquer external fate, but now an external fate was

---

9. General Ugaki Kazushige (1868–1956) had been the chief advocate of the 1920s disarmament; his attempt to organize a cabinet failed in January 1937.

using them. It mobilized not only cultural tools like communications and propaganda, but also scholarship—all the natural sciences, political science, sociology, even philosophy and psychology. Using the methods these disciplines taught, organization and weapons became more effective and demonstrated astonishing efficacy. In the span of two or three years, the people within the walls had been transformed to the depths of their psyches, believed the worldview given them, and finally, thinking that nihilism was how one "lived in eternal righteousness," didn't even hesitate before jettisoning their own human dignity.[10]

Nietzsche says something to this effect: to control people, make them enthusiastic about an idea. This is a fearsome insight. Our politics implemented this insight. As the rulers wished, people were made to embrace fierce emotions about an idea. When I think back now, it's like a dream, but many young men did not hesitate to let themselves be made into human bullets to be shot out by cannons[11]—that's how far things went.

People in great numbers seem to be like the elephant. Its body is big, its strength is great, and once enraged, it's uncontrollable; but a clever elephant trainer can make it do exactly what he wants. Today, aren't ideas the slim whip of the elephant trainer? Thus, politics meddles with and controls people's minds. In ancient times the chorus in *Antigone* sang of the power of *moira* to decide and enforce. It said:

> No power in wealth or war
> Or tough sea-blackened ships
> Can prevail against untiring Destiny!

Still, emphasizing human greatness, the chorus sang this, too:

> Words also, and thought as rapid as air
> He fashions to his good use; statecraft is his.[12]

But the modern politics that is our fate not only robbed us of the sea-blackened ships on which to flee the walls, but even saw to it that whenever we talked, we'd use given words, that the thought as rapid as air had a given content.

We came face-to-face with this external force.

I repeat: against it, even the most stalwart person was powerless. Some people resisted in their hearts. But that didn't move fate in the slightest. Even

---

10. "To live in eternal righteousness" was a wartime slogan rationalizing the sacrifice of life.
11. This is an allusion to the suicidal tactics of the *kamikaze*.
12. Sophocles, *Antigone*, in *The Oedipus Cycle*, 223, 199.

if they were thinking reeds, they were still only single reeds, flattened along with all the other reeds by the storm.[13] A few didn't knuckle under even though in prison chains for eighteen long years.[14] They were like Prometheus bound. They vindicated faith in human nature. But like Prometheus, these people were utterly powerless so long as their fate held. For the duration they were noble, but not great. What I mean here by great has to do with human power and its potential against external force.

In the end, so long as modern organization and force are used for control, if one wants to guarantee the dignity of one's own person today, there's no alternative but to involve oneself in politics and be the victor. There's no alternative but to join hands with organization. That's the road one has to take even if one's goal is to ensure that organization and weapons can't be used this way. Those who don't take that road can't know when their entire external and internal existence will come to be controlled by external force. One must take part in politics; one must become part of the group and fight and win, making its will his own—for someone like me, at least, that's a dreadful fate. To take part in today's practical politics is to reduce oneself as an individual to the very minimum, to subordinate one's own judgment to the judgment of the party, to jettison all but one's political self. To the extent that I cling to my own independent existence, this too is external fate forcing me to obey.

## 5.

Politics was decisive fate pressing in from outside. It was our *moira*.

To be sure, we also experienced fate as *tyche*. Our lives were ephemeral, bubbles that piled up, faded, bumped, flowed at the mercy of chance. The weather was unseasonable, so foodstuffs ran out. Packages we had taken pains to pack and finally found the means to send off to supposedly safer places went up in flames there. As if possessed by demons, things flew up, vanished, laughed. Chance, about which we could do nothing but shrug, toyed with us. The delayed-action bombs I wrote about earlier were this kind of thing. But I didn't encounter any of them myself.

Of countless experiences, the air raids made me feel most immediately that I was a plaything of fate.

They happened entirely without regularity. You couldn't predict them. No matter where you were, you might encounter one. In ancient times, oracles gave warnings about fate; for us sirens gave warnings twenty or thirty minutes ahead.

---

13. The reference is to Blaise Pascal's *roseau pensant* (thinking reeds).
14. Several members of the Communist Party spent the years 1927–1945 in prison.

In ancient times in Athens, there were statues of the Fates embracing the bewitching Sirens who lured men with their beautiful voices. These Sirens, it goes without saying, are the source of the word "siren." In our case, the Fates embraced the sirens that gave off that awful sound.

This is a bit of a digression, but in ancient Greece, oracles protected men against fate; what protected us at the end, too, was an oracle. But the modern oracle was not the whispers of oak leaves or wind echoing in crevices; it was broadcast on August 15, on radio waves through antennas.[15] The guardian spirits issuing the ancient oracles had possessed a natural authority among the people ever since ancestral times; that's the way it was in our case, too. This is something entirely different from God, who creates and judges. Its misuse by usurpers to lend themselves authority was very similar, too.

The sirens sounded one day in every three, one day in every five. Soon brilliant violet shining cross shapes came floating from among the clouds, in regular patterns, beautiful. In the winter, with their tails of frozen vapor, they looked like slender jellyfish trailing transparent white tentacles. They appeared, completed their great destruction, and disappeared quietly over the horizon.

At night, part of the sky turned red, and we heard cities crumbling. We lived with the thought that we'd survived yesterday, that today too had passed.

As I think back now, it was all utterly unreal. For ten months we lived in unbearable suspense. Moreover, at the time, it was suspense without limit of time. We could only be absolutely passive. As the burned-out area gradually spread, the odds worsened for those living in areas that still hadn't burned. Some philosopher should study life lived with an awareness of such odds.

As the odds worsened, chance turned imperceptibly into certainty. "If they come this way, we may go up in flames" became "We're sure to go up in flames." *Tyche* became *moira*. Every last person came to have the wisdom of Heraclitus: "One way or another, we're doomed." As more and more places burned, people became breezy and said things like "I'm fine." But this liveliness was only a passing thing . . .

Amid the suspense, we weren't all that uneasy. It makes people uneasy not to know what's just ahead, but when the crisis finally hits, mankind seems to say either "I can't know, so there's no point in worrying" or "It's certain doom, so don't think about it." The sense that I myself will be OK is deep-rooted, and above all, suffering isn't real so long as it's other people doing the suffering.

---

15. On August 15, 1945, the emperor broadcast his statement of surrender; he called on the Japanese people to "bear the unbearable and endure the unendurable."

Clear awareness of the uncertainty of life, it seems, can exist only when life is secure to an extent. One may sense it the most when the degree of security stops increasing and awareness of insecurity starts to grow. The time we felt most acutely uneasy was before the war. Once the war started, a lot of people felt relieved: "Well, that's settled." Kierkegaard lived in a peaceful age in Denmark and was so secure that he could make it all the way through life without ever finding a job, but he suffered from melancholy and worry. Read him, and you'll find surprising things becoming the source of deep anguish: for example, "My lover kneels before me, but the responsibility is too much for me to bear," or "A man visits a prostitute once in his life, and walking there and back, shudders every time he sees children playing. He may be the cause of any one of these lives. Should one of these children curse the father's existence." This may be the true uncertainty of life. If so, it's only natural that we had no philosophical uncertainty.

We were, if anything, lively. It was an animal liveliness, focusing on the barest essentials of life . . .

And we were fit. Carrying things, hoeing the fields, standing and waiting for hours, working in the factory—we were constantly busy, doing practical and physical things. There were no gaps through which psychic collapse could slip in. The fact that in all countries suicides decrease in wartime and increase after the war likely relates to these factors.

What I mean is that the capacity to be uneasy about life is one proof of human dignity. As a precondition for dignity, in order to be fully human, man needs a positive and fulfilled world of his own. Then he has a stable ego and the ability to interact actively with others and make choices. We didn't have those things. What we had once had, had been taken from us; we had only what was given us. We didn't really exist. Since we didn't really exist, we weren't uneasy, either.

In this perpetual suspense, people were lively and fit, but at odd moments in the busyness that kept them on the double, they were forever painting illusions. I can't forget the strangely optimistic illusions that arose back then.

Beginning long before, people had used fictions to keep up a bold front. A whole range of schemes became frameworks that offered public support for people's psyches: changing organizations; changing titles; wearing prescribed clothing; rousing people at dawn, making them undergo ritual cleansing and shout their beliefs and shouting at them and making them listen.

When the air raids finally became frequent, illusions sprang up. There was "The enemy has fallen into our trap." And "If Japan withdraws its troops from the continent, America will have lost its war aim. After that, if we turn all of Japan into a fortress like Rabaul, the war will go on forever, so the enemy will grow tired and quit." And "You lose because you surrender. But we won't surrender, so we can't lose. If each of us kills one of them, our numbers will prevail."[16] All these ridiculous illusions—even relatively sophisticated people voiced them. Thanks to those concrete walls, there was absolutely no way to prove whether these were illusion or reality, and these castles in the air actually became a force that stirred the people.

But even as people were embracing such optimistic views, in reality chance was running amok. About all we could do was calculate the odds.

Take this experience of mine.

One night I returned home late. From Tokyo Station to Kamakura took about an hour by train, and two-thirds of that distance was a dense industrial belt. At the time, it had been burned out on all sides; it seemed strange somehow when houses were still there, unburned. Yet from the windows of the train we could still see diapers hanging out to dry in houses crowded together and children playing in the streets.

There was an iron bridge, and everyone figured that it was the prime target. So if the raid came before we crossed the bridge—for me that became a matter of life and death.

On this line where the fatal odds were great, I commuted with one eye on the clock, and that night, because I had things to do, the hour grew inauspicious.

Air raids normally began twenty minutes after the alert. So if the alert sounded after we'd crossed the bridge, in twenty minutes we'd be at Hodogaya, and after that was farmland, not dangerous. That's how I calculated it. And each time I got past the bridge, I'd suddenly cheer up.

But soon after we left Shinagawa Station that night—it was just after ten, the woman conductor entered the car and called out: "Here's the report. A large squadron of enemy planes is now proceeding northeast in the skies over the Izu islands; the target is likely the Tokyo-Yokohama area."

It was pitch dark in the car. Fastening the strap of the large cap under her chin and lighting her footsteps with her pocket flashlight, the woman conductor made her way to the next car. That light revealed that there were very few passengers, and all had on metal helmets and thick hoods and were bent against the night wind that blew in through broken windows; silent, no one asking questions, they sat there unmoving.

Head down, too, I did the mental calculation: in twenty minutes we'll reach Yokohama. The odds are still great, but since we'll have crossed that

---

16. "Fallen into our trap" is literally "the enemy has entered our belly," a comment attributed to General Yamashita Tomoyuki at the time of the American landing on Luzon in the Philippines. Rabaul is a port on the island of New Britain, just east of New Guinea.

horrible bridge, even if this is the area of the raid, my chances of disaster are 20 percent, no, 15 percent.

But my reasoning was mistaken. The train didn't keep running until the enemy planes appeared. It stopped partway, and the passengers were all ordered to get off and take cover.

Silently, we all jumped down onto ties and gravel. Over our heads, the sky, suddenly the object of everyone's attention, spread out into the distance, the color of polished steel.

Straight ahead we could see the gleaming surface of the river. The train had stopped just short of the bridge.

I had to stay here—on the most dangerous point on the line, at the most dangerous hour. So under these conditions, all I could do was search for the safest possible spot.

The other passengers all seemed to have the same thought. Naturally moving as a group down onto the broad riverbank, we tried to put as much distance as we could between ourselves and the bridge. Each person suspicious of the next—isn't he outwitting me and finding a safe refuge?—and seeking for ourselves a good spot, we looked around in the dark. But the riverbank held no cover.

Then a bunch of people came walking from the direction of the town, hurrying in the direction we had just come from.

As our paths crossed, one of us asked, "Isn't there an air raid shelter here?" One of them answered, "No." And added, "Go to the bridge. They seem to be leaving attacks on transportation to the last, so the bridge is safer than the town. It blocks shrapnel, too." Hearing these conclusive words, we too turned back and followed these people. At the base of a small bluff, in the shadow of the bridge, twenty or thirty dark figures were already squatting.

The people who lived in this most dangerous area had made this calculation of the odds.

At length, the sky in the distance turned red, bright, billowing clouds gradually became visible off in the distance, and explosions sounded. Tonight, they said, it seems to be the Tachikawa area.

## 6.

That is how I experienced fate. I became acutely aware that man is powerless in the face of fate. My trust in human dignity collapsed.

"Man is wretched, and at the same time great. Because he knows his own wretchedness"—the classical words offer some consolation in that although one is utterly powerless against fate, he knows it; but I don't feel that can be called greatness. Moreover, I had witnessed how once fate is decreed, man can come to think his own wretchedness great. I had witnessed how he can boast that his own folly is wisdom. That is, I had passed the point where a thinker who "knows his own wretchedness" could exist. And I had seen the state of affairs when ideology and fantasy take its place. Had it not been possible for that fate to be overthrown from without,[17] the very few people remaining who had not gone down that path would all have been arrested.

Still, I'm not particularly depressed now. For one thing, I'm busy; for another overstimulation has left me dull and insensitive; and for still another, in these ten years I've been steeled somewhat, so in daily life I'm healthy, calm, even somewhat more practical than before.

My life is unsettled, hand-to-mouth. In particular, I've come with some difficulty to accept as part of life the hours I spend each day on the train. Occasionally I've even been transported on trains with iron lattices over the windows, trains once used for luggage and livestock.

But this doesn't cause me any great inner anguish. Thanks to this external resistance, I'm becoming simpler, straighter, harder—in short, pragmatic. I haven't faced psychic dissociation, fatigue, emptiness. For me now, individual tragedy, hypersensitivity, romantic dreams, interior awareness, and, even more, that logic of "gratuitous action"[18]—they feel as if they belong to long ago and far away. Why read Proust now? We have no time to savor such things as the dissolution of the ego. To the contrary, threading its way through the external forces pressing in on it, my ego is congealing in the most primitive form possible.

As humans, we are much smaller than the norm. Our possibilities are strictly limited. If only for that reason, we have a certain fitness. Our insecurity is an insecurity of the sort man had at the dawn of history, toward external forces that threaten our lives. We can't have the insecurity human beings had when they were just past their golden age, the grand insecurity characteristic of human dignity.

But the war is over. I'm busy, but I do have free moments. At such times, I sit by myself, quietly, and sometimes I experience a strange shudder. These may be the times my human potential has expanded a bit. From nooks and corners of my heart, after-images of the war return. Moreover, sensing that in what now lies ahead I'll be abandoned once more to external forces and chance, the person I am today wants to reread the Greek tragedies.

What's particularly frightening is when I wake up in the middle of the night. Recently that's happened a lot. Waking suddenly after a horrible

---

17. Takeyama's reference here is to the defeat of the Japanese empire by the Allied forces.
18. This is a reference to French literary critic Charles DuBos (1882–1939).

dream, I don't know which way I'm facing, as if I'm floating in space, or I think I've become a firework tossed into the void. At such times, I'm overcome with the fear of death. As if my heart has suddenly failed, my retinas see white glittering in the dark. I go rigid and wait for the terror to pass.

This double life—working normally during the day, feeling these paroxysms at night—has gone on for some time.

One night I felt the terror. The bed under my back seemed a scorching-hot anvil. Carried away by agony, my hand reached out involuntarily. It touched the small hand of the infant sleeping beside me. I grasped that hand that always smells so sweet.

Then my fingers felt an inexpressibly miraculous thing. In the baby's wrist, a pulse was beating—faint, soft, but sure. In the great lonely darkness, the pulse in that small wrist beat steadily on.

Feeling this small pulse in my palm, I was struck by a strange thought. What a joyful song in that sound, in the only thing echoing in the dark, the sound of my child's pulse! I am touching something absolutely solid, and it murmurs something utterly different from fear and despair. Something like Mozart's music—that's what I sensed. It came to me from somewhere warm, soft, far away; it contained an ultimately irrepressible and rising energy. It was alive.

I heaved a sigh of relief. Like barbarians, to escape the fearsomeness of being alive we humans may have no alternative but in some sense to seek life in the tribe.

It wasn't as if I'd reached any logical solution, but I calmed down. In touch with that pulse, I felt the terror retreat like a tide ebbing. Peace of mind came to me, as it had at times when in my own searching I'd done my very best. The cold sweat on my forehead evaporated, and in its place a smile creased my cheeks. And I thought, "This is the hand that will plant white pine and rose on my grave. Until that time . . . "

What followed "Until that time . . . " was "I'll profit as much as I can from Mozart's example."

From that time on, my reading of the shapes on the wall has taken on new meaning. Fate is an external force we simply can't fathom; I don't know when or in what form it will appear again. It's certain I can do nothing to affect it. That I'm terrified by it is inescapable. But the new meaning is this: until what comes comes, live fully!

This is truly a banal lesson. It's trite. But in my case deciphering it took the war experience. As I said before, for me the war experience was a life experience. I realized for the first time that because we are alive, our backs are against the wall in the face of unpredictable fate.

Now I think: we don't know when the forces that constrain us will appear again in the form of chance. To exaggerate, in human life the delayed-action bombs are always falling. We can forget this fact, but we can't deny it. We have to recognize this fact and submit. And we have to live in its cracks and crannies. For us, human dignity cannot transcend this limit. But strangely and contrary to what one might expect, when we're conscious of this absolute limit, the desire arises to live a better life.

We can't make long-term plans and schedules. We can't have absolute peace of mind. We can't rejoice in that possibility. When air raids came several times a day, I left the shelter in the intervals, hoed the fields, sowed seeds. Then, when the siren sounded, I retreated once more, and with my heart in my throat, heard things down from out of the clouds exploding on earth. That was wartime life; it is in fact life itself. That's my realization today.

While sensing his own death ahead of time, Mozart devoted himself to exquisite creation; I want to listen with new ears to Mozart's music.

# 7.

As I've said, I began writing this letter basically to report to you about the strange feelings of my recent double life. But the prologue has become so long I can't get to the body. And even the prologue isn't at an end.

I've no choice now but to write, in very abbreviated form, a conclusion to this prologue.

What I've learned from past experience I see once again as I look ahead into the future. I mean *moira* and *tyche*.

First, we don't know when we'll encounter again that awful starvation. The weather and the like will determine that. Next, we don't know when our livelihood will be changed from the roots up. Our everyday life too is filled with difficulty and unforeseen events. We can't establish a routine. A day-to-day, hand-to-mouth existence has to be the fundamental style of life.

I can depend on only one thing. The rays of a lens. Here's what I mean. I roll cigarettes with rationed tobacco and pages torn from an old dictionary. I've got no matches. Even if I had some, they'd only break. So I take out a lens and focus the rays of the sun on the tip of the cigarette. After two or three minutes, thin smoke always rises. In my life this is the only certainty I have. Albeit only when the sun's shining . . .

Moreover, the workings of society defy comprehension. If goods aren't in somewhat short supply, they're sorely lacking, and things at black market prices are the rule, with virtually nothing at the official price; if by chance there's something at the official price, the only people who can lay their hands on it are the wily black marketeers—these and countless other things are like a riddle, something out of the *Arabian Nights*.

Moreover, many people I know have already fallen by the wayside, and some have died. In society today a great weeding out is taking place. Looking about me, I'm startled at how the faces have changed. Many people have dropped from sight because they aren't adept at accommodating themselves to this strange new life. Many old people worry lest they fall ill; many couples fear they'll have children and not be able to feed them. We ourselves can't know when we'll join the unfortunate ranks of the fallen.

Most startling of all, some people are now saying there'll be another war, some that there won't be. In the broad world into which we're not permitted to peek, there seems to be tremendous movement. In the January *Reader's Digest*, a famous American critic spoke of war strategy in Europe . . . [19]

On our path ahead such things lie in wait everywhere. We don't know when they'll explode. Even the odds are unclear. We have no alternative but simply to live well until we encounter them, and when we encounter them, to submit to fate.

These beautiful words come from one of the tragedies of Euripides:[20]

> We all must suffer.
> It's men who bear their ordained fate nobly
> Who are the sages.

I can't become a shaper of fate, so I'm not about to take the path to greatness. I hope to advance, if I can, toward nobility.

---

19. That issue contains an article by prominent Protestant theologian Reinhold Niebuhr (1892–1971), "The Struggle for Germany."
20. This passage is not, in fact, from a tragedy; it is fragment 37.

~

# Scars

Unlike the other essays in this volume, "Scars" is fiction, at least in part. Takeyama had been in North China in 1931 and then again in 1938, but the North China part of this short story cannot have been Takeyama's own experience, involving as it does events that took place after Japan's surrender. Moreover, the justice of the tale—seven fingers for seven fingers—is surely too poetic to be true. But the central part of this short story—the Japan part—is Takeyama's own experience. He lived in Kamakura, and his children were about the ages of these two children.

When "Scars" first appeared in print in 1949, Takeyama noted the date on which he finished this short story: September 2, 1947, the second anniversary of the surrender ceremony on the battleship Missouri in Tokyo Bay. He didn't always note dates of composition, so September 2 had particular meaning. Moreover, this was the period in which he was writing his other fictional account relating to the war, Harp of Burma. Harp of Burma appeared in serial form between March 1946 and February 1948. Takeyama had never been to Burma and wanted to set Harp of Burma in China, but he needed British troops to recognize the song the Japanese troops sing, and there were no British troops in China. The attitude toward non-Japanese Asia and Asians that permeates "Scars" is similar to that in Harp of Burma, as are the fact that major Japanese atrocities happen offstage ("They say very horrible things happened elsewhere") and the focus on the Japanese soldiers. There is also a seeming disdain, in the absence of elite figures, for ordinary soldiers, the noncommissioned officer and the men, who can survive in the postwar world without fingers—as porters, perhaps; the paragons of virtue who are the two main characters in Harp of Burma have no counterpart. The comparison of war front and home front is new here.

In the second section of "Scars," Takeyama refers to "the Mereon Island tragedy." Mereon (or Mereyon) is the Japanese rendering of the name of one of the specks of

71

*land in Woleai Atoll in the Western Carolines, hundreds of miles east of Yap. The Japanese used that name, not Woleai, to refer to the whole atoll. During the war some 7,000 Japanese troops guarded an airstrip and seaplane landing there, and 5,000 of them died. The United States bypassed Woleai, so there was no ground fighting; almost all the deaths came from malnutrition and disease.[1] The February 1946 issue of the national magazine Sekai carried an article, "Mereyon Island Tragedy," and the officers' mistreatment of the men under their command became a major issue. I use Woleai Atoll, not Mereon Island.*

*"Scars" appeared in the March 1949 issue of the national magazine Kokoro.*

Two friends, one older and one younger, came to visit. No matter who's talking, the topic doesn't change, and these men, too, spoke of their wartime experiences. The younger one was a demobilized soldier, so he spoke in particular of his experience overseas.

## 1.

I was stationed in the mountains of North China, and it was a most boring place. All the way through the war, to the very end, there was no war worthy of the name.

It was a basin smack in the middle of the boundless yellow-soil belt; on all four sides there were steep cliffs. When you looked up at the precipices, they seemed just like stale sponge cake, ready at any moment to crumble. And probably because of floods every few hundred years and incessant weathering, the ground had split open everywhere, and here and there in the depths gaped the mouths of caves. Those places looked just like candle stands when the candles have melted all the way down; there were no trees, and grass didn't grow. Of course, people didn't live there. Like ribs of the earth's crust, these places connected meanderingly, one to the next. Call it bleak, call it desolate; when we looked at the scene, for instance in the evenings, it gave us the shivers.

On all sides: soil, soil, soil. Nothing but crumbly, soft yellow soil. . . . And there were weird things. For example, there was no particular spot in the houses to dispose of wastewater, so you simply threw it on the dirt floor. The water was swallowed up, silently, by the soil. It couldn't run horizontally on the floor. It penetrated straight into the sponge-like soil and finally, tens of miles, hundreds of miles later, flowed into the distant Yellow River.

---

1. See Mark R. Peattie, *Nan'yō: The Rise and Fall of the Japanese in Micronesia, 1885–1945* (Honolulu: University of Hawaii Press, 1988), 303–9.

On a hill in this belt, we made an old temple our barracks. Below the hill was the river that ran through this basin, and on its edge was a cluster of houses. They were all constructed of earth, in irregular shapes, but their roofs were interesting. Each house was decorated strangely. Like prehistoric hieroglyphs, like fetish signs, their simple lines stood out and, since each house was different, the simplicity packed extraordinary power. Together, these houses clung to the sponge-cake cliffs—an impressive sight.

When we climbed down the cliffs and went to the village, the houses were all one-room or two-room dwellings, with neither floors nor furniture. At night there weren't even lamplights. If you went up close to the mud walls and listened carefully, people inside were talking in the dark, but once the sun went down, they soon went to sleep. People were born here, multiplied here, and died here, so this small world was a strange place. It was poor and peaceful, rough and wild; it was what you thought life must have been like in antiquity.

The inhabitants were well behaved and didn't put up any resistance. And for our part, too, we didn't do anything bad. Still, the houses in the village all closed their doors during the day. We saw only the men, scattered in the fields, at work farming; the women absolutely never showed themselves.

One woman, and she alone, was the exception. When she appeared in the small square at the center of the village, we cheered from atop the hill.

I mean, she wasn't a very womanly woman. She was a large ugly farm woman—stout, slow, always angry-looking, probably past forty, though that wasn't the issue. She always wore a short tunic that left her chest bare, and, suckling a baby at her great, cow-like breasts, she walked with back and neck tall, like a giant. It was as if she was showing her pride: I'm a mother, not a woman. She strutted on her bound feet as if to prove they could support her heavy body. Those feet were like small triangular yachts about to sink under the weight of an enormous mast. It was quite a sight: willows drooped over the river beside her, and domestic ducks bathed, and ducks on the shore wobbled their fat behinds from side to side as they followed her.

That was our only amusement. We were utterly bored and homesick.

The boredom was just indescribable. One mountain range back, there were guerrillas, but they didn't move about much. Sometimes there were shots, and they'd echo among the hills—*boing!* just like a spring—and make the quiet air quiver; but tranquility soon returned. Our nerves went taut for a bit, then sagged once more, and we forgot even to speak, and every night we drank, and when we talked, we talked nonsense; as I think back now, our whole unit must have been suffering from nervous exhaustion.

Day after day was the same. The sun rose; the sun set. In between donkeys brayed; mountain doves cooed. Time and space both stretched out absurdly; we had no aim and knew no meaning, and we dawdled and dawdled. In the end it was as if our blood had become sluggish and impure, had stopped circulating; it was very tough. The voices of donkeys and doves were enough to make our heads hurt, and sometimes we almost hated them.

That's how our life was, so in our unit we had no unspeakable atrocities such as they say happened on battlefields elsewhere.

The single atrocity-like act at this post happened as follows.

To haul our water we hired a boy. He was the son of that village giant with the big breasts. Already seventeen or eighteen, he was good-looking, like many Chinese and unlike his mother. Taciturn, obedient, he was popular throughout the unit. He too liked us, knew a few words of Japanese, and called each of us "So-and-so-san." Though thin and slender, he was used to labor, so he was strong; it gave us pleasure to see this boy come climbing up the steep path from village to barracks—transporting water on donkey back and putting buckets on either end of a slender pole, hoisting it to his own shoulder, bending forward so that his hands nearly touched the ground, swaying rhythmically.

We all gave this boy things, so sometimes his mother on her bound feet climbed up the hill road to thank us. Before each of us, this stout woman, whose flesh hung off her, whose eyes looked like slits in her chubby cheeks, repeated the same words, hands clasped in front of her. She was so tall we looked up at her, so we were all surprised and, with embarrassed smiles, nodded our heads.

But for some reason this obedient and unselfish boy pilfered things from us. Moreover, he stole one after the other items of military issue you had to account for, shirts and helmets and the like. It was probably simple curiosity . . .

As you know, lose something in the army, and you have to replace it even if that means stealing from others. So the damage fanned out, ever wider, and the damage was great: some men got punished, and some, suspecting each other, got into fistfights.

No matter how we searched the unit, we didn't find the thief, so suspicion fell on this boy, and when we investigated, evidence turned up, and the boy was dragged to the trunk of the pagoda tree in the courtyard of the temple that served as our barracks.

The boy cried out, almost beat his head on the ground again and again, and apologized.

Much to our surprise, this boy we'd made a pet of was the guilty party, so everyone was angry.

There was the brouhaha about the robberies, and periodically a mood sharp as shards of glass permeated the unit, and men beat each other up. The fact that something novel had happened even pleased everyone. The story was told in exaggerated form, and, churning with anger and curiosity, the men gathered round.

The men standing around the pagoda tree looked down at the boy, and soon one of the men came forward, hit him on the head, and shouted, "Because of you people, we've had to come to this spot and face hardship!" He kicked him. The boy toppled over for a moment, but then, holding his side, sat up again.

On hearing what the first man said, voices rose, suddenly, in agreement: "Right! Right!" the men cried in unison. "Because of you people, we've had to . . . "

And the beating began.

"Show them some kindness, and this is what you get! Beat them all up!"

"They marched me off first for three years, and just when I thought I was bound for home, they marched me off again!"

Blood rushed to the men's heads, their faces turned red, and they applied brute force. Some among them were mortified almost to tears. In the boy, these men discovered someone on whom to vent their unhappiness at their own fate. The atmosphere moved past the point of stopping, and the boy became an unexpected scapegoat. The angry eyes of the men gave off a mad gleam as they beat him one after another, and the boy stayed crouched there, arms about his head. He was a mere lump of flesh wrapped in rough cotton cloth, no more. By this time there was no sense that he was a human being. However, a strange contradictory feeling ruled the men, that precisely because he *was* human, it made sense to vent their anger on him.

What in the world was it with young men, something stored up so that it couldn't be pacified short of exploding? Something unfocused and itchy, that could not be resolved short of blowing out in the most cynical and crude form. Destructiveness that bubbled up virtually against our own will and interest. Vague resentment against everything. Unfocused lust for revenge . . . That evil power pulling the men along—what was it? In our unit military discipline had kept it in check, but I think I understand how, once discipline collapses, and toward something that discipline doesn't cover, unbelievable cruelty can be carried out, in particular by an army running amok.

Our CO was a man past forty, jaded and lazy; wearing a faded officer's uniform, standing with legs spread, stroking his thin mustache, and smoking a cigarette, he had watched the scene develop. Finally, he raised his hand to stop them: "Enough. He's gotten what was coming to him. You've beaten him enough; now let him go."

But the men didn't obey: "Sir, I got punished because of him." "Please give us a bit more time."

Some men were still panting, and it didn't look as if things could be kept in check.

Seeming not to want to bother resolving the situation himself, the CO said, "OK, go ahead and punish him a bit more. Those with light fingers need shaping up."

He started to leave. But when he'd gone a half-dozen steps, he stopped, turned, and said, "But don't kill him. Got that?" He seemed to sense the danger in the air.

After he left, three or four men stood right in front of the boy, arms folded on their chests, as if discussing what to do with this scapegoat.

Holding absolute power, they looked down on the defenseless boy crouching before them, and the mood seethed up inside, of itself: if we're going to do something, let's have some fun.

One of them made as if to raise his hand against the boy again, but an NCO checked him. And he ordered a raw recruit at his side: "Hey! There's a straw cutter we use for provisions for the horses. Go get it. On the double!" He smiled meaningfully. He was an archetypical NCO: a tall man, sunken cheeks sunburned, chin pointed, brimming with confidence in the power of education through duress.

NCOs played a large role in the daily experience of every unit. We really found them unbearable.

This NCO was a curious character. As an individual he was a good man, yet under such circumstances he sometimes did inhuman things. Starting in primary school, humans torment those weaker than they for no reason at all. Women become mothers-in-law and give brides a hard time. In the case of NCOs, it's as if the army institutionalizes that trait. Moreover, their every whim has absolute authority, and there's absolutely nothing to hold them in check—the system's truly screwed up.

The recruit ran and soon came back carrying the straw cutter, which had a sharp blade on one side of its square iron base. You piled bundles of barley on it and then—*snick!*—dropped the blade.

No one grasped what the NCO had in mind. We all looked on with curiosity and anticipation, wondering what was about to happen.

"A bit farther forward. Yes. Raise the right side some, make it level . . . fine." He gave directions, setting up the cutter in the shade of the pagoda tree. The thin steel curved flexibly, a gleaming blue. Raising one foot onto the iron platform to steady it, the NCO surveyed the unit and said, "We're gonna correct the kid's light fingers."

Then he called to me: "Hey, bring the kid over here!"

I was shocked. I had started to have an idea what was coming. It happens all the time—for example, you see someone on the street about to get run over by a car, and yet you look on, absorbed in wondering, "will he?" "won't he?" and the idea of rescuing him doesn't come instantaneously. We don't know what the future holds or even what lies three seconds ahead. All the more so when someone's ordering you. In this strange confusion, I grabbed the boy, who was lying on the ground.

The sun was shining brightly, and far off in the cool, clear mountain air donkeys were braying, and in the branches of the pagoda tree overhead mountain doves were cooing. The boy was limp, his skin soaked with sweat; my hand slipped off his shoulder.

The NCO said, "C'mon. Get a firm grasp!"

With a start of comprehension, I braced both feet and heaved the boy to his feet. It's a curious thing, but just then the leather belt of my trousers broke. It was old and ragged.

Grinning wryly, I pulled my trousers back up, and as I was doing so, a man named Tanaka, ordered to take my place, grabbed the boy.

Supported from behind, the boy had both his hands lined up on the plate of the cutter. And at a signal the blade fell, and without a sound seven fingers fell to the ground.

Everyone had watched in silence, but now the boy screamed. It was a long, eerie scream. Then he bent over, hands in armpits, and ran off. Watching, we saw him grow gradually smaller on the road down the yellow-dirt cliff, screams continuing, until finally he entered the village.

Watching him go, the NCO jutted his jaw and smiled, but the smile turned then into a forced grin. Chilled, we scattered.

The cutter was put back, and where it had stood fingers lay scattered like pebbles. One man trampled on them as he left, burying them in the dirt.

That night, when we drank at the canteen, we were all strangely excited. No one approached the NCO, so he sat alone, staring fixedly, drinking glass after glass. He was dangerous when he got that way, so we were all nervous.

That was the only atrocity that took place in our unit.

They say very horrible things happened elsewhere. The men were tired of a long and aimless war, and their caliber was sinking; everyone's mood broke down, and they became slipshod: where that happened, the sordid ran rampant, utterly inhuman. You know, thinking back now, I feel keenly what an empty life I had to live and for how many years I had to do absolutely crazy things.

Try that kind of life. You see things differently. When I talk with comrades who were overseas, in this war we experienced in fact horrors you won't find written in any harrowing tale, ancient or modern. Then, after coming home and getting back to normal, we felt we were in some completely different country among a different people.

We were seeing things differently. We hadn't lost arms or legs and returned in the same body, but in our hearts we'd become different human beings.

## 2.

On hearing this tale, the older friend said:

You know, I don't really understand it, but young men who've been repatriated are always saying, "We see things differently now." And "In our lives the war lingers."

But ask them, "Well, differently in what sense? How does it linger?" and you can't get a precise answer. They simply repeat, "There's a difference. It's as if we're seeing things through someone else's glasses," and they can't explain. It makes me think, "It seems just like fiction!" "We see things differently now"—it's a striking, beautiful phrase. These men look for conclusions about war, want to believe such things exist, and set out from that point and arrive at a point that confirms their illusion. Or so I've thought.

Young men simply aren't in contact with reality. Thinking and feeling young men are all schizophrenic. They *imagine* life. Whether or not there's a war, there's always a gap between their perceptions and reality. It's not that the war brought any hard-and-fast change in their perceptions. Rather, the "vague resentment" in the story we've just heard is at work here, too: they may want to defend themselves against their critics by saying, "We're a damaged generation." In their schizophrenic world, this assertion of theirs is hanging out a sign—"We see things differently now." That's my take.

The schizophrenic tendencies of young men calm down with the years, and they gain balance. Reality enters their consciousness, and they all become healthy, run-of-the-mill realists. But the gap that today's young men claim, that "We see things differently now"—there'll be exceptions, of course, but won't its scars too disappear with the years? Won't they get their own glasses back? Those who've lost arms or legs are different, of course, but wounds to the soul will surely close up. They're young.

Young men's wounds are one thing, but in this war, it seems to me, every last person in Japan received wounds to the soul. At least, all those of us in the middle class who didn't go off to fight are bleeding in invisible places.

What I'm getting at is this: for a time it was all we could do simply to survive. In all sorts of cases close friends betrayed each other; relatives antagonized each other. In those grim days we all bared unattractive sides of our character, and these unattractive sides all had to do with a sort of cunning. We all have memories we'd prefer to leave undisturbed today of how callous—cruel—to others we were able to be. The closer the tie, the truer this was. People who normally loved each other and helped each other became disagreeable in ways they would never have done except for the war. Distrust and enmity were rampant. There are lots of people even today who barely get by using an egotism like that of the old man in *The Arabian Nights* who climbed onto someone else's shoulders, clung tight, and couldn't be shaken off. It'll be a good bit before we know whether time will heal these real, ugly scars.

First and foremost in our lives, there was the shortage of food.

This problem was a constant, so most households each had their small version of the Woleai Atoll tragedy. On isolated islands where food was wholly inadequate, fierce antagonism arose between well-fed officers and starving men—from our experience that was only natural. Men who were on other islands said, "What the officers in that account said in their own defense—that's a lie! There may be differences in degree, but that's what happens." I'm sure that's so.

We spent years in the household, that small atoll that lacked adequate food. We haven't been demobilized yet; we're still there. Food has gradually become easier, but the wounds are still open. Here, clearly, the war lingers on in our lives.

I'll let you in on the Woleai Atoll tragedy that happened in our household. The story's about food, so please forgive me if that's all it's about.

Almost all Japanese have made light of the laws—"Keeping to the letter of the law costs you," "Wait a bit, and the law will lapse," "How do we work around the rules?"—and even housewives came to think this way. I think this was one of the largest national wounds. As you know, my wife's normal, not savvy at all, so at first she listened to what the government said. She read it fearfully, the circular that came round the neighborhood—"Hoarding and stockpiling are treasonous acts." So already by 1941 our household was in a bind for food.

But soon it became clear we couldn't survive that way. We came to understand for the first time that we couldn't live without evading the law and fighting for our lives. We came to understand, too, that the black market was the normal state of things and that the black market had its own "official" prices. This hidden system—until then we hadn't dreamed it existed—became the system on which our lives depended. So we began to buy on the black market and, taking it for granted, felt not the slightest pangs of conscience; indeed, we celebrated our successes.

Yet my wife's black market dealings were quite minor things. They amounted merely to pleading with those who knew their way around and possessed a kind of Aladdin's lamp, following their lead, and setting out to search for each day's food.

This was a strange business, simultaneously criminal and not criminal, and the women formed groups, made up battalions, struck up connections, sought out information, posted lookouts, even developed signals—in short, they did as all organized criminals do; they donned strange clothing and loitered around the farms outside the city.

Truly, back then the world changed in fearsome ways! Our life and thinking entered a truly new epoch, more so than after the defeat.

And in our home, too, after life got difficult, discord arose, little by little. The two women—my wife and her mother—sometimes quarreled.

"I tell you the truth!" my sixty-year-old mother-in-law grumbled. "I won't live with anyone as assertive as you."

"Yeah, yeah. I'm assertive. If I weren't, we'd be in trouble. Grandma too should be a bit more assertive, go out looking for food," my wife would say, furious, on her high horse.

"You say, 'Go search for food,' 'Go search for food,' but I'm the one who tends the garden."

"Oh, you think so? Yesterday I did the weeding."

"Those weeds? I told you long since they had to go."

"Weed them when they've grown big, and they pull up much more easily!"

Thus were repeated arguments unique to women: when you hear them, they have logic of a sort, but think back afterward, and they make absolutely no sense.

Finally, by 1944 we had virtually nothing to eat. Hodgepodge, soybean drainings . . . sorting the weeds to pick out the wild spinach and mix that in—bitter pitch-black lumps followed each other onto the dining table. When on occasion there was a ration of fish, it was some strange small fish—"Ethiopian," "Korean"—we'd never heard of. Wherever you went, the talk was of food, only food. People talked of food with the only passion they showed, as if possessed. Today it's considered vulgar to talk of food—that's how differently we see things now; but back then if the topic of some fine treat arose, people looked up with sunken, haggard eyes, and their faces showed insuppressible lust and agony . . .

In this way, totally, slowly, certainly, hunger came to us. It's a bitter thing to be aware constantly of an empty stomach. Somewhere under your chest there's always something strange and twisted, and it cries out for sweets and fats . . . That new word "malnutrition" echoed horribly in our ears. One time, as I sat on a small hill looking down at town, it was as if all the people in all the houses I could see and all the cells in all their bodies were famished, shriveled, crying out for nourishment—Creation was truly evil.

I'm utterly impractical, so I was completely unable to do as the other husbands and find a way to get stuff. My wife's mother—my mother-in-law—was diffident in the traditional style; even when she was in the house, one never knew where she was, and quite like a cat, she never made a sound. Once she had lived in luxury and with her pale skin must have been a beauty, and her two hobbies were puppet play chants and clothes; even in the midst of busy days during the war, she often sat for long periods before her mirror. Mother tired easily, so after noon she was exhausted and fell asleep. Going out in search of food was the thing she detested most of all, and it was truly painful for her, a curious figure carrying a shopping bag, to go to the farm fields, bow her head, and ask that they sell to her. So the procurement of food for our house: my wife did that alone.

One evening the same topic of conversation arose again at table. My wife pestered me angrily: "Mrs. Miyajima was picked up at the train station, had her bags confiscated, and was scolded. They took her to the police station. They say buying stuff is bad even when there are no rations, but what can you do?"

"You're asking me?"

"Day after day—I've had it! Really, it's because people like the Miyajimas buy on the black market that there's not enough food in the ration system. They *should* have scolded her at the police station. Serves her right!"

"Recently," Mother put in a word, "many of the farm fields in the neighborhood have been raided by thieves. They pull up a *daikon* and in its place, I hear, leave fifty *sen*."

"Wow! Fifty *sen* for one *daikon?*"

"But that kind of theft—it's hardly something to get angry about," I say. "Because people truly in need pay more than a fair price. Farmers really ought to be more considerate."

"True! True!" says my wife. "Grandma, this time you go out in search of food. The authorities won't suspect you, and the farmers will be more considerate."

The next evening, Mother takes a one-*yen* note out of her *obi*, places it on the table, and after a bit she says, crestfallen: "I stood twenty minutes in this spot, twenty minutes in that spot. I just couldn't bring myself to do it."

Because going in search of food terrified Mother, she had gone out to steal from the neighborhood farms. But that terrified her, too. The rows of fresh green *daikon* in the rich dirt of the fields belonging to some lucky person stood there, to no purpose. She complained weakly, "I did *think* of leaving one *yen* and taking one."

At table were my wife and I, Mother, and the two small children. Usually one helping of a fixed amount of food was set on each person's plate. The food the children spilled we picked up, washed, threw together, and reheated; the adults ate it.

There was always the same amount on the children's plates as on the adults'. This was because we wanted the five-year-old and the three-year-old to have enough to eat. So the children pretty much didn't go hungry. Apart from the times we were really short, there were even occasions when the children, spoiled, left the awful food uneaten.

"Makoto, clean off your plate now, won't you?" said my wife, looking into the child's eyes. "If you don't eat, you won't grow."

Pouting, the child eyed the table with its spilled liquid and scattered bits of food. "If I eat it, do I get something?"

"Something? What do you mean?"

"Something good."

"What do you mean, good?"

Stretching out his legs and poking with his chopsticks at his hateful plate, the child leaned his head to one side, thinking how to answer. My wife, angry, slapped him. He burst into tears.

"Well, OK, don't eat it." Saying this, my wife, put the plate that still held food under the fly netting.

And what was left on the plate—afterwards, late at night, my wife ate it.

"They may leave food uneaten; they may not. In any case, we always give the children adult portions. Who knows if they'll eat it?"—Both Mother and I understood my wife's sly wisdom, but we didn't say a thing. Silently, beneath the shaded lamp, we ate what was set before us.

Everyone in Japan grew thin. I grew thin, too. Once, going to the bath for the first time in a while, I was shocked that my thighs had shriveled and become like an old man's. And when I pinched the flesh of my stomach, it was paper-thin, and my thumb and forefinger met.

During the war, the males all grew thin, but not the females. They say females are able to grow fat even on little nourishment. They can turn starch into fat. Their digestive apparatus is superior—that's the idea that was current, and I think it's probably true. But we can't deny that the NCO of the kitchen has special privileges.

In my case, the NCO of the kitchen at our house said I was of course the man of the house and that if I didn't work, we'd be in trouble, and she favored me whenever she could; in her mother's case, she seems not to have been so charitable—"You're really not all that active." And Mother could suffer in silence. But little by little, even I heard the disputes. I really don't understand what goes on even in one small house. From my room to the kitchen was less than fifteen feet, but I was quite aloof and lazy—"I want absolutely nothing to do with it!"—and by the time I tuned in, the situation was already very bad.

One day, at the time the air raids had begun, I came home in the evening from work. Back then, when the train arrived in the station, you know, everybody rushed off. Puttees around shins, helmets on shoulders, people ran down the stairs, rushed through the stile, and raced off to their homes, as if pursued. It seemed our house alone had insulated itself from all fear.

As I stepped into the entryway, I heard the two women arguing as they prepared supper.

By now I was used to this sort of conversation, with its edge and its bated breath. It was a petty, absurd, determined battle, of the sort that makes you think women just love to argue. My breast froze listening to it—I loved peace and quiet; I thought I'd rather be ordered into battle amid shot and shell than wade into assertions woven of such complicated, twisted, and strange logic. When they make determined assertions, women can convince themselves on the spot that those assertions are completely factual. Moreover, their way of mounting the final assault is weird. For a comparison, it's like the battle between hedgehogs I once saw in a nature film. Both animals raise the spines that cover their bodies, stand there stock-still, apart. Then there's the slightest of contact, and one side is already injured; its spines droop, and it turns, dejected, and departs. Into the bargain, the strange thing was that by the next morning this household's hedgehogs usually had already holstered their weapons and carried on normal conversation.

I tiptoed to my room.

My wife's voice: "I'm completely exhausted, too. What can you be thinking? Making others do all the work . . . No. When Father gets home tonight, I'll ask him to say which of us is right. That man always, always pretends to be above it all . . . "

The origin of the argument was butter someone had sent us.

Some three months earlier, I had chanced to meet on the train an old man, a distant relative. An entrepreneur, he had wormed his way into the privileged class of the day. At the time there had arisen a class that made one think, "So this is what the old samurai class was like!" They were able to use freely the trains for which ordinary people couldn't buy tickets even if they stood in line two nights running, they knew everything, and they were never hard up for material goods. Walking in the streets, you could spot them at a glance. This man established connections with military men on the financial and accounting side of things and by about 1943 had already seen what was coming, got access to transportation and so on, and moved to the country and there managed an estate and became self-sustaining; then he got a second-class rail pass, came up to Tokyo, and began to deal. Hearing my grumbling and sympathizing with me, he was kind enough to say, "Well, let me send you some butter from my farm."

Those were tumultuous times, so I had no way of telling whether his good-will would bear fruit. But when I'd almost forgotten it, two packages of butter arrived, entrusted to someone to deliver.

When we opened the packages and saw the soft mounds of fat the color of golden honey, our joy knew no bounds. We put small bits on our tongues, and the softness spread to fill our mouths, slid down our throats. And luxuriously, our entire bodies seemed to recover; for years they'd had nothing fatty to eat, and flesh and bones, as it were, had turned dry, tiny holes opening up all over. Another lick, and the extraordinary itchiness that permeated our bodies would be soothed, the mental balance we had lost would be restored: that's how it felt.

Then, when we first tasted food cooked with the butter, we all licked our plates clean. And when we poured hot water on the plates, we delighted at the pearl-like drops that congealed on the surface. We let the children have one extra spoonful each.

When the smell of butter frying wafted my way, it suddenly evoked for me the smell of art paper. That good old smooth, thick paper—it had been ages since I last touched any. Then the smell of the hair of a girl I had scented long ago. Breakfast toast, a breeze, music, the Heights in summer, sweet repletion . . . it was the smell of past peace.

But butter sowed the seeds of discord.

In the letter accompanying the butter, the old man said: "It's only a small amount, but given the current shortage . . . one package for the lady of the house, one for the children, a little present I earnestly hope will suit their palates . . . "

This was a letter suited to a time of peace and plenty. It held, too, the incomprehension of a country person for the lives of townspeople assailed by empty stomachs. This benefactor had sent one package of butter for Mother, one for the children! That was an old-style presentation. It certainly showed that "things looked very differently now."

Mother rejoiced. An unenergetic and weak person, she was already completely beaten down, so, dimples floating on a white face that had once been plump, she said, "Butter really is nutritious, isn't it. Please thank him kindly. Before, I hated even the smell of butter . . . " and she put her package in a jar for her own use.

On the dining table stood two jars with lids, each holding a package of butter wrapped in greasy wax paper. At each meal, Mother and the children each ate a spoonful from their jars.

After three or four days, my wife suddenly raised her voice during a meal: "Uh oh!" Shock and worry mingled in her voice. Finally, sniffing the smell from the jars and staring fixedly, she said: "If we leave the butter here, it'll go bad. Look, it's already turning color."

Mother too sniffed, stared fixedly, and said: "Really? I don't see any change."

"So? No, the color *is* changing. Grandma's eyes are weak. Butter's good for you. But when butter gets old, you know, its vitamins die, and its nourishment disappears. We can't leave both out like this. We'll use one at a time. I'll put this one in the well."

Mother said nothing and kept on eating, but her breathing quickened.

Then my wife got up and cleared off the table, happily, singing a song. It was a tune from a girls' musical popular in her childhood . . .

My wife put the children's butter in the well. And from then on we fed the children too from Grandma's jar. Gradually, that butter came to be used for cooking, too. In this way, Mother's monopoly on that butter was broken.

Other issues that had been dormant were involved, too, and this event became a wretched wrangle.

"But it's better this way, isn't it? When we use up the one jar, we'll start in on the other. It doesn't make sense to distinguish between first and last."

"I didn't mean that. If we lump it together and we all use it, it'll all be gone just like that."

"Terrible! Maybe we should let both jars spoil."

"The way I use it it won't spoil."

"The way *I* use it it won't spoil!"

"Sure. You're famous for not letting things spoil! Ha!"

Up till now my wife had sometimes let things spoil. So this irony was an unexpected counterattack from my timid mother-in-law. It told us how upset she was.

The two women fell silent. They faced each other, and you could hear them taking deep breaths.

Then her voice muffled, my wife said something, short and incomprehensible. Suddenly, weakly, in a voice choked with tears: "Really, Grandma, I'm not *that* bad!"

So the evening's argument ended without resolution. And afterwards as before, the children's butter was put in the well.

Thus the final summer arrived. We lived busily, feverishly, as if driven, and sleeplessness from night after night of air raids continued. Already everything in the house was muddy and dusty. Luggage left behind when the family evacuated to the countryside was piled up everywhere, in a jumble, and *futon*, too, were left out. And during that time we got strafed by machine guns, and onto our roof, too, fell shrapnel, setting off a loud, harsh sound on the tiles.

It was a morning during that period. I was still in bed, and outside the storm shutter I heard the sound of conversation between Mother and my daughter, who was about to turn five. Mother had tended a tomato plant that had finally borne fruit that turned red. That whole year these were our only tomatoes.

During this conversation, my daughter cried out in a loud voice, "Uh-oh! Mama! Grandma's picking the tomatoes!"

I raised my head off the *futon*. Simultaneously there came a scream—it was Mother. Then the sound of tools being thrown down and of someone quickly wiping dirt off hands and feet, and she pitter-patted off to her own room. The words came as she ran, "You don't let me eat a thing!" and I could almost see her extreme agitation.

I thought, "Something has to be done. I hadn't realized things were this bad." But as always I lacked the courage to address this complex tangle. If, for once, I addressed it, I'd be drawn into a maze from which male logic could find no way out and in the end be criticized for my lack of savvy, and undoubtedly things would return in the end to the status quo: all that I understood well.

Finally, the war ended. That saved me. Things had piled up that were much more trying than this incident, and I think our house would not have survived three more months. The women were half-mad, and the house was on the point of collapse. Families in the same condition as ours, weren't they the rule everywhere? I think so.

Suddenly all was quiet, and I heaved a sigh of relief. But we had been buffeted for so long by flashes of light, the sound of planes, angry voices; thrown suddenly into an infinite void, we found this new time at first passing strange. And step by step, as we grew accustomed to it, a disturbing emptiness—we had lost our inner balance—began to open up . . .

One such day I was given ten delicious bean-jam buns.

The company where I had done labor service had built an underground factory in the hills, and since the need for that factory had evaporated, they used everything they had in stock for a going-out-of-business party. The buns had been made for the occasion, and the leftover ones were divided up. It was so huge a luxury—unimaginable at the time. I carried them home, a treasure.

When I got home late that night and showed what I had, my wife was overjoyed: "Oh, the children will be delighted!"

The next day was Sunday. It was a bracing, clear, early-autumn day. Though it still held an aura of threat, the sky was beautiful. Beautiful. It was typical of a few days of early autumn, filled with a sort of white wine jelly, bubbling. Out of the sky a breeze came blowing, fluttering the pages of the book out on the shelf, and lifting the blackout curtains we still hadn't taken down. I heaved a deep sigh.

"Well, today let's all go somewhere with Father, shall we? It's been a while," said my wife.

Asking Mother to stay and watch the house, my wife and I took the children and left.

This neighborhood had escaped being burned, but all the roads were dug up. The shops were all awry, their dust-covered glass display cases all empty. In the city, we often heard, you could see the bodies of people who had starved to death, but in this neighborhood there were none. Still, we occasionally met people walking slowly, heads swathed, leaning on someone. The white heads were unsettling, only the eyes and mouth peeking through, as if smiling. On the curb at one corner, silently, a woman, apparently a housewife, had opened out her *furoshiki* and on it had set out her wares—three slices of roasted potato, one bar of soap, and when she had sold them, she left.

Radios were on in the houses along the street, so as we walked we got the general meaning; it was an announcement from the Occupation army.

After walking only ten minutes, we came to the edge of the pond in the park in the vicinity of Kichijōji, a noted beauty spot.

Here too there was extreme devastation. Many of the tall trees had been cut down. I looked again at the sky.

Clouds floated in the sky. Once I had peered through a microscope at amoebas, and under the lens half-transparent fuzzy blobs expanded and contracted irregularly; it was hard to tell if they moved according to their own will or in response to some stimulus, and they swallowed and digested bits of food. The low clouds were exactly the same. Their edges were like gold threads in a brocade, and small U.S. planes flew in and out. The sound was like the humming of bees, and listening, I stretched my legs out and shut my eyes.

I felt all the more keenly a dizziness, as if I had just got off a ship tossed on the high seas and stood for the first time on solid ground. I relaxed, and yet I had nothing to lean on, and my insides were still trembling, as if I had lost all my senses; the ground under my feet seemed to tilt, and I didn't know where to look for balance.

The children were playing happily. There was no one else around, but now and then figures passed, all in the same bedraggled state.

My wife said, excitedly, "Come here. I've something good for you."

Her voice was so proud and happy that I looked up through half-closed eyes.

She pulled a package from her shopping bag and opened it. It was the ten bean-jam buns I'd brought home last night.

"It's a gift Father brought home. Delicious buns! Tell him thank you!" Speaking to them so very politely, she gave the children buns. And she and I ate, too.

They were delicious, indeed. Crushing the hardened sugar between my teeth, I felt a strange sadness. It might have been because my sense of taste, long forgotten, asleep, suddenly reawakened, and I had a vivid sense of how things had been long ago.

The children were eating happily, their legs jiggling as they sat, and then my daughter said, "Look! It's Grandma!"

Clad in wartime work pants, an old woman was walking in the shade of the trees to one side; reflected in the surface of the pond, her figure trembled. The work pants had been sewn with care and were of good quality, but her figure, once captivating, had completely fallen apart, and she walked pigeon-toed, as if lurching.

Mother came toward us, cheeks dimpling characteristically beneath the stray locks, but then, looking our way, she stopped.

And then, still staring our way, she smiled again, and—I can't forget that look even now—her frozen white smile, which was like crumpled paper, dissolved almost into tears.

"Uh, I'm going for a moment to the Miyajimas' . . . " she said and seemed to nod slightly in my direction; her figure reflected once more in the pond, she went off.

Strange—why had Mother come here? I didn't know if it was by chance or on purpose. She'd left the house completely unattended, so she apparently came to check on us; still, how did she know where? Perhaps instinctive suspicion led her here.

The last piece of bun in her hand, silent, my wife hung her head. On my stone seat, I stretched my legs out and closed my eyes . . .

From the next day on, Mother separated herself entirely from us. Since there had been incidents before this, she had probably intended doing so; but on that day, the fact that she alone had been excluded probably drove her to the final decision. Thereafter she withdrew into her own room and made her own meals. Food rations she divided precisely. She put cooking utensils on the veranda and cooked with them. Even today she continues to do so and simply will not change.

She separated out her finances. How she's surviving this inflation is incomprehensible, but she's on her own. Sometimes the used-clothes dealer and the stockbroker go and come to her back room, so it appears she's selling off her belongings and her stocks. For the rest, there's no particular change, and usually when we meet and talk, it's as it was before; but there's no doubt that in her old woman's soul there's been a major revolution. I can rely only on myself: that's what she undoubtedly felt in her heart. It's a fundamental life change. And for that matter, the life of our house has been upset, with many unfortunate disagreements.

Mother is the archetype of those Japanese who didn't lose arms or legs yet became different persons inside. In her case the change is surely greater than in the case of the young men who came back from the battlefield.

During the war I was invited to the home of one Westerner. There I saw a strange thing. In this house an old person (quite a famous scholar) was a lodger, and they ate at the same table, but his food alone was entirely different. This old man prepared his own food himself and got along with only that. It really was crude, poor, and miserable. The others ate much better. They didn't share butter—that goes without saying. Yet no one doubted that this was as it should be, and the whole company chatted and smiled.

While being served the better food, I thought, "Aha! This is modern life in the West, based on the individual." Watching the old scholar right there before me, I was troubled that his lot was bad, and I felt ill at ease.

But on this point Mother had modernized totally. At one go she purged her entire being of feudalism. You see, the war awakened her to herself. Commentators today are forever urging Japanese to become more modern, but although she neither wrote nor argued about it, Mother's feelings had changed to the modern, and not just theoretically.

Compared with such real scars, young men's scars have a heavy element of the imagination, don't you think? They'll soon heal, won't they? The day will come when they'll forget. Whether they plunge into nihilism and dissipation or devote themselves to changing society—in either case it's not the wound itself but something comparable to the workings of white corpuscles against infection from an injury—it will heal sometime, and the person will become normal, with sound senses. Their wounds will heal. If life is ultimately imagination, then scars too are of the imagination . . .

# 3.

On hearing this story, I thought: Yes, indeed—during that hungry time, something like that happened in every last household. My own family got by without anything so terrible, but I had the same doubt—whether, had the war lasted three more months, my household would survive. I don't ever want to be in that situation again.

The younger friend thought a bit and then said:

Hmm. Young people don't have real wounds? While young, they're invulnerable? We may *feel* that way, but . . .

Actually, I've never known anyone who went off to war and experienced all the idiocies and miseries and then fell apart on that account and became a different person. That's a fact. And I don't think the war awakened anyone to his true self. That feeling came more from the magazines than from the war. And those people who fell apart after coming home—all of them collapsed because they'd been sucked into the atmosphere of social collapse.

But there's something there. Something—there's something more than a figment of the imagination, as you'd have it.

The sense that I've been wounded in my heart is vague, even to me, hard for me to grasp, hard to speak of clearly.

The finger-chopping story I told you has an epilogue.

After the war ended our unit stayed on another ten days in those yellow-dirt mountains. News of Japan's surrender apparently was transmitted even to that backwater, and in the village below us, several blue-and-white flags were raised. Those blue flags dyed with sun and flame fluttered over the earthen roofs, as if they bore an incantation.

There was no change in the villagers' attitude toward us. There'd been virtually no contact between us, and they were like simple people of the ancient past, so they didn't treat us with contempt. On the contrary, when we met in the village, some even stepped aside and bowed their heads respectfully, just as they used to.

That large woman, too: as was her way, she bared her huge breasts to suckle her baby and walked about on her bound feet in the square with long strides, face hard-grained. Her son never came to the barracks, but we often saw him at work shouldering loads on his carrying pole. Sometimes, when we went down into the valley to wash our clothes at the riverside on the edge of the village, he would come to get water, and he would raise a hand that had only a finger or two and throw us a smile. Sometimes he came with his mother, but then she'd stop him in a spot off a bit, sending baleful glances our way.

On the second or third day after the war ended, when we were relaxing at the river, she came with her son and stared at us from the shade of a tree. We knew we'd done something truly awful to the boy, so before we left we wanted to have a leisurely talk with him, the kind we'd had before, and thought to give him any number of the helmets and such he craved, so we beckoned to him. He appeared to want to come, but his mother wouldn't let go of him.

Waving a shirt at the mother, one comrade shouted, "Hey, how about doing our laundry?" but she didn't move. Then, smiling, we all got back to our laundry in the river.

This river was an elegant one. This river!—it "passes on, not ceasing day or night." Flowing down out of the ranks of mountains of the yellow-soil backcountry, it streamed past day and night. Eating away at the soil carried here over the millennia from distant deserts, it rippled its way past the earthen houses of the village. Remarkably, it had yellow days and blue days, depending on the weather. No, it even changed color on the same day. Look at it from one angle, and the pure-yellow water suddenly turned deep blue. Crouch over it, and it looked just like a rusted sheet of iron; stand up, and it ran cold and clear. Because it reflected the sky. It was just such a river as Confucius sighed over.

Finally, it came time to take our departure from the river, too, and leave. They had reorganized the unit—I was put in the advance guard, and leaving about half the unit behind, we marched off to the county seat in the center of this yellow-soil basin.

This county seat was just visible from the mountains. On the far side of the sponge-cake cliffs one side of the basin opened out, and especially on bright mornings, we could see clearly the square town walls, the crenellations, the dragons rearing back on the towers, the pennants on the towers. In the evening, in reflected light, it appeared a dim gold. In this semiarid backcountry where no matter how many days you walked, you met not a soul, this city reared up, and crowds of people gathered and bought and sold, so it was also important strategically.

The area around the city was poppy-growing country. When we first moved in, the whole area was covered with poppies in bloom. This ancient city seemed to float on a sea of poppy blossoms. The May heat shimmered. And far off on a red hill, like a trail of ants, wound a line of refugees. We entered the city without a fight, and fires were still burning in the hearths of the deserted houses.

Now, several years later, we entered the county seat again, and this time the season of poppy blossoms was already past. Instead, there were millions of ripe poppies, oval-shaped and green. By the time we'd got to the city walls, it was already night, and the light of the moon poured down on the opium fields; it might have been because of the air, but the gentle wind blowing our way seemed somehow intoxicating, and it was as if we had gone completely flat. We trudged through the endless fields, our shadows the black shadows of surrender.

When we emerged from the tunnel through the wall into the city, it was pitch-black, and no one was to be seen. This dark postwar city—devastated, unfamiliar, with no sign of life—really gave off a bitter feeling. All the more so because we were the defeated side. Not knowing what awaited us or when, we were scared. Even the sound of our leather boots, echoing off the ceiling of the tunnel, was chilling.

After we'd gone a bit, we came to a large intersection. For the most part county seats are built the same way, so we guessed this was the city center.

Here there were bright lanterns, and they illuminated the walls of the houses along the sides. On these walls a long announcement in large letters was posted. It was new, only just put up. As if to make it possible to read it even in the dead of night when no one was around, here and only here were bright lamps lit.

We stopped and read it. I translated the gist into Japanese, and it was the pronouncement of Chairman Jiang that became well known later. I made it out to say, "Don't repay violence with violence."

That night, when I first read it, I got only the meaning of the words; I didn't understand their significance. Still, I breathed a sigh of relief. I thought, now I may make it home alive.

That pronouncement was really huge. Without it, we would have been utterly helpless. The statement was truly commendable, and when I think of it now, I can't say how much it means to me for my life now—even subconsciously—that those in authority should have shown such humanity. Except for it, both our spirits and our lives would have been in total disarray.

I mean, the Chinese were extremely angry at us, and not without reason. That pronouncement kept that anger from exploding. It caught the moment and demanded self-restraint on the part of the Chinese. It may have nipped in the bud the catastrophe that would otherwise have taken place. Things did happen in places that pronouncement didn't get to.

Even in that distant village in the hills of yellow-soil country, there was a minor incident.

On the second day after we got to this country seat, the rest of the unit arrived.

This time it was during the day. They entered as dust danced and oxcarts and herds of sheep came and went. They were all bent over, carrying mountainous loads on their backs, and they'd become a crowd without discipline or order; the unit was shabby in the extreme. Watching as they streamed out of the mouth of the gate in the wall, I thought, "We too, did we look that bad?"

At the rear came three men, alone in having tiny packs tied onto their backs. They trudged along, faces pale, looking exactly as if they were ill. One of them was the NCO, and on this day that guy who always looked fierce and terrified the smaller recruits seemed utterly despondent, floored. These three all had both hands in slings, wrapped in thick, clean bandages.

We were shocked and gathered round them, took their packs from them, and asked, "Your hands—what happened?" "You're so pale!"

But none of the three answered. The other men with them also kept silent.

Then, probably because we persisted with our questions, the NCO, edgy, spat out only the single word, "Wounded."

So we too held our peace.

Here's what other men told us later: on the previous evening as these three had been doing their laundry at the river, they were taken captive by the villagers, wounded, and all three came back with their hands tight under their arms. The three were the NCO, Tanaka, who'd held the boy's wrists, and the man who on order had dropped the cutter's blade.

They'd each had seven fingers cut off, and according to those who'd seen them getting treatment after they returned, the hands they stuck out in the light of the oil lamp were swollen and looked just like raw red ginger. On the front of red stumps small fingers remained, trembling forlornly. Otherwise they were uninjured.

The three made it a point to call these war wounds and wore the slings for a while, but when we got back to Japan, they did without. No one asked them how they had gotten their wounds, and they wouldn't talk about it, either; but their fingers had been chopped off with a straw cutter, so I took it that that giant mother had been the one who dropped the blade.

When we chopped off that boy's fingers, at the order of the NCO I had grabbed him briefly. Then my belt broke, so Tanaka took my place. Except for that happenstance, these fingers of mine would have been cut off, gone. That saved me. Of course, I kept silent and said nothing to Tanaka or anyone else.

Afterwards, I managed to get hold of a new leather belt, but I wanted to keep the one that broke as a souvenir of sorts.

From that county seat we rattled for days on end on a train and came to Tianjin, passing along the way any number of county seats. Everywhere we went that pronouncement was posted. It was our sole support, and we read it, again and again, with tangled emotions. And as time passed and we came little by little to know the situation, we were alternately terrified and relieved. Had that hatred not been kept in check and the whole country exploded—when I think of that, even now I go cold.

One dawn along the way I woke up, and the train was running through thick mist. Right outside the window were walking a dozen or so camels, loaded down, with skin like ragged blankets, dripping tassels, slender joints moving feet that seemed about to fall off. When I came awake, there before my eyes, in the haze, was an astonishingly high city wall that stretched on and on, like a lizard. Looking up, I saw, high above, the outlines of a multi-storied tower. This was . . . Beijing. Here, too, the pronouncement was posted. When I saw it, I thought, "The fires of war—over at last?" and felt for the first time like weeping.

Back in Japan, we got on a train, for the first time in ages a Japanese passenger train with seats. The train ran along the Inland Sea, and we were relaxed and chatting. Staring at my belt, Tanaka said suddenly, "That's a nice belt you've got there. Back there, if your belt hadn't broken, you'd be sitting here with no fingers, and I'd still have mine."

Saying this, he touched my belt with his fingerless hand. So Tanaka *was* aware of the situation. After a bit, he said, "How about giving it to me for a souvenir?"

I pulled the belt off and tied it to his duffel.

At that moment the duty officer came by distributing two cigarettes to each man. Above our heads, as we were talking, he suddenly said, "Cigarettes!" and the three automatically stuck out their hands. The man on duty placed the cigarettes in their hands. With the fingers he had left, the NCO caught his adroitly, but the other two let theirs fall clumsily to the floor. They scrabbled at the cigarettes with their stubby hands, and the cigarettes wound up rolling under the seats.

At this, strangely, we burst out laughing. And the three, stooping to scoop up the cigarettes with both hands, as if rescuing them, put them to their lips, lit up, and puffing away, laughed and laughed and laughed.

"Ha!" The NCO smiled at his small triumph. "I caught them with my thumb, but you two couldn't catch a thing."

"Whee! They slide off this hand, and there's no point in hurrying to stick the other one out, either!" Grasping the cigarettes with the hands that still had two fingers, they had a fine time.

Tanaka pointed his tongue and blew a neat small smoke ring.

That was it as far as my contact with them went, and I never met them again; no doubt they're feeling the inconvenience now. They weren't artists or musicians, so they may still get by; maybe they've become porters.

It's not really that I feel my own fingers are borrowed, but still somehow, somewhere I'm wounded. The war lives on even in my current life. You see, "I see things differently now."

I can't quite express it, but in our case what was warped wasn't life itself, but what we imagined life to be. That which will shape our lives from here on: it's run into a block. Even when our imaginations want to soar, some invisible evil clips their wings . . . That's the wound to the soul the war dealt us young men.

—September 2, 1947

*Part II*

# CRISIS AND CHALLENGE

~

# Germany: A New Middle Ages?

*This essay is the eleventh of twelve essays on "The Future of European Culture" making up the April 1940 issue of Shisō, influential national journal of ideas. The lead pieces were by famous philosophers and had titles like "The Ideal of World History" and "Japan and the Future of European Civilization." Takeyama's title then was simply "Germany."*

*In a note appended to this essay in his Collected Works, Takeyama mentions deletions from the manuscript. There are only a few such deletions, and they are minor. Takeyama's trenchant conclusion—"If Germany wins, [freedom of thought] will be wrested from us, fundamentally and instantly"—remains untouched, so it's unlikely that the deletions were for reasons of political correctness. Encountering this essay in the twenty-first century, readers will react negatively to the facile attribution of characteristics to "the Germans" and "the Japanese." But this mode of thinking was common in many countries at the time; witness the vogue in the United States at mid-century of "national character" studies of "the Japanese" and other national groups.*

*Takeyama was outspokenly hostile to Nazi Germany at a time when the Japanese government was aligned with Germany. The Anti-Comintern Pact was signed in late 1936, and the Tripartite Pact (Axis Alliance) was signed in September 1940, less than six months after this essay appeared. In his commentary to volume 1 of the Collected Works, Hayashi Kentarō describes Takeyama's conclusion as "truly brave."*

*This essay does not make easy reading today. But it is valuable not only for Takeyama's thinking before the Pacific War but also for the expectations of readers of national magazines like Shisō: the sentences in German, in parentheses, are in German, in parentheses, in the original. The lengthy quotations (here from Goebbels and Hitler) attest to the role men like Takeyama played as interpreters of Europe to Japan.*

*At Tokyo Imperial University Takeyama specialized in German language and literature, and that was what he taught at Ichikō for twenty-five years beginning in 1926. One wonders what it meant in the late 1920s for Takeyama, then in his mid-twenties, to discover in Europe that he responded less to Germany and more to France. In his chronology in Takeyama's Collected Works (7:327), Hirakawa Sukehiro states, "Each time he crossed the border [into France], his spirits rose." Takeyama's disappointment with Weimar Germany colors this analysis of Nazi Germany.*

*There are strong echoes of this essay in Takeyama's postwar essay on the Tokyo trial ("The Trial of Mr. Hyde," translated in this volume). However, there he puts Japan in the same "late developer" category as Germany; here he does not.*

## On the Seventh Anniversary of the Nazi Accession to Power

For the last seven years, May 1 has been a national day of celebration for Nazi Germany. Last year this day began at the Berlin Stadium with the *Führer's* address to youth. At the German Opera House, the National Academy's culture prizes were awarded, and *Reichskulturminister* Goebbels spoke on the guiding principles of Nazi culture. Then, at the Lustgarten, Hitler addressed the people as a whole, his speech broadcast nationally over all the radio stations, the grand parade took place, and the ceremony ended.

The speech of the *Reichskulturminister* on that day was most interesting. The logic he's given to was repeated and emphasized, the Nazi view of culture was expressed frankly, and many hints about its future characteristics were offered.

According to the newspaper, the order of events was as follows: when to the acclaim of the crowds lining the way Hitler entered the German Opera House in Charlottenburg, the opera house orchestra under the baton of Music Director Rother began playing. The piece was the Festival Overture of Richard Strauss. Then royal singer Rudolf Bockelman sang Goethe's "Prometheus," set to music by Hugo Wolf. Anton Bruckner's Seventh Symphony was performed, and a somber mood filled the hall for the hearing of a grand pronouncement on German culture. (The photographs show the hundred-plus members of the orchestra lined up onstage and the front of the stage buried in bouquets. The backdrop was gold, and on it hung the huge silver festival medallion. The medallion featured a goddess carrying flowers and an eagle bearing the swastika.) The assembly included the *Führer*, cabinet ministers, party leaders, representatives of the military and the diplomatic corps, and leading lights from among writers, artists, and actors.

The cultural prizes awarded at this ceremony were the Book Prize, to Bruno Brehm, and the Film Prize, to Carl Froelich, and also a citation for film production, to Professor Karl Ritter.

At the end, the *Reichskulturminister* arose, and his speech was interrupted repeatedly by applause. The *Reichskulturminister* spoke first of the fact that Germany had reached such glory through the party's strength and, after praising the party's achievements, he spoke as follows:[1]

### Strength, Peace, Culture

The adage says, *inter arma silent musae*: "When weapons speak, the muses are silent." But that is only partly true. For it cannot be doubted that eras of political and military achievement bring with them eras of cultural achievement. Power is not merely a mechanical expression of the strength and glory of a people. The culture of a people is expressed also in power. For power is the precondition for true and enduring peace. Peace gives the people the firm confidence that maintains and creates culture.

For this reason, in National Socialist Germany building up the military and building up culture go hand in hand . . . (Here Goebbels emphasizes that beginning with their seizure of power in 1933, the Nazis provided for cultural construction by spending national funds on it even in difficult financial times.)

### Democratic "Critics"

New racial construction must think of the people as a whole, in all areas of life. That is, politics, culture, military construction, economics—all must be in step. Statesmen have an important duty to give full play to all these.

Thus it stands to reason that the Nazi state subordinates all issues of public life to the people's welfare and to the demands of the national community. So it also stands to reason that to this end limits are set and that politics takes priority over other functions of our national life.

It is precisely on this point that criticism is offered by the democratic states, in particular our neighbors to the west. They howl that it is their duty to protect what they contend is their traditional civilization from the German danger. But when you consider this one thing, their arrogance is laughable and foolish. That is, the authoritarian form of state has made its appearance in precisely those countries whose cultural life flourished in the past, and by contrast, democracy still rules in those countries that live in the cultural shadow of these states or that avail themselves of the spillover from these states.

---

1. In fact, Goebbels's introductory words don't mention the party. What follows is an extended quotation from Goebbels's speech, in Takeyama's translation—accurate if somewhat loose.

For example, take America. American publicists assert that German culture must be defended against the Nazis, but this is the greatest insolence imaginable. To this day, American culture is extremely limited in scope. In music, literature, and art, that country has still contributed to the Western cultural treasury nothing that can be expected to last for centuries. Its culture is for the most part only the result of centuries of work by European countries. If America insists that European culture must be saved from Germany and Italy, we may well ask: Wouldn't it be better if America first created a culture of its own? Wouldn't it be better to exert itself in the creation of its own culture, which it might then defend as its own national duty, national right? Until that time, we have no reason to listen to such empty exaggeration.

Intellectualism clouds the national intellect.[2] The democracies say that in authoritarian states freedom of spirit is repressed, but this assertion, too, cuts no water in Nazi Germany. To be sure, in cases in which it is incompatible with the national interest, authoritarian nations limit freedom of spirit. In the democracies, freedom of spirit may not be restricted on this point, but when it doesn't suit the interests of the capitalists, it is restricted. So the question arises: which is more pleasant and glorious for those who labor at works of the spirit—to subordinate their spiritual labor to the national welfare of the entire nation, or to subordinate their labor to the capitalist welfare of a small number of unseen plutocrats?

Whatever the case, we maintain forcefully that never before has the German spirit shown such broad possibilities for development as in the Nazi age. All our cultural workers, all our artists know this. Only a few of the intelligentsia deny this, and they confuse false intellectual complexity with true spirituality and enslave the strong and moving forces of the heart to cold, calculating reason.

It is necessary to make this difference clear. For we must never equate intellectualism and national intellect. In the last few years our national intellect has accomplished veritable miracles in all fields of public life. The few liberal-democratic intellectuals remaining in our country have only carped. And they've simply looked for their models in the Western European democracies that have long since exhausted themselves not merely politically, but also spiritually, artistically, and culturally. Culture has no connection at all with cold reason. *(Kultur hat ihrem Wesen nach nichts mit Wissen und vor allem nichts mit kalter Intellektualität zu tun.)* Culture is the deepest and purest expression of the life of a people. Culture gains its true significance only when joined to the people's national power.[3]

---

2. In the original, this sentence is a subtitle; for Takeyama, it becomes part of the text.
3. This sentence doesn't appear in Goebbels's speech.

## The Status of Journalists

The work of the press is a particular problem. In Nazi Germany, because journalists serve the interests of the state and the people, they should be considered the professional equals of soldiers and officials; theirs is an honorable calling. In the democratic states, journalists are mere note takers for anonymous capitalists, so there can be no talk of honorable profession. Such journalists must write what they are told to write. And they can't even know what is desired. [Goebbels's original says, "They can't even know who is doing the desiring."] Under democracy, freedom of the press exists only on paper. Freedom of the spirit in liberal states is merely a fiction; it serves the sole purpose of convincing the intellectual rabble that a situation exists that in fact does not exist.

But why all the talk? It's not our job to argue principle with the democracies. What proves the rightness of a course is its achievements. And insofar as concerns our achievements to date, in cultural accomplishments, too, we need not yield to the democracies; we have achieved a superiority they can no longer overtake. The German stage is blossoming. German film is taking bold steps. Great publications that contribute to the national good, radio that reaches the entire people, original music in the tradition of the great works of the past already returning to the basic concept of musicality—melody. Literature that is rich and proceeding ever upward. Film that serves beauty and harmony, art that is young and imaginative; in particular, architecture already astonishing the people with monumental structures, plans, designs—all these are clear evidence of cultural construction unique in the twentieth-century world.

The Nazis have also accomplished the following miracles. We succeeded in giving spirit once again to modern industry that was on the point of completely enslaving modern man, to fill the factory not merely with a sense of purpose but with artistic beauty. Our magnificent roads and the harmony of our bridges demonstrate the changes in the relation of people and industry beyond the shadow of a doubt.

## The German Achievement

How can our democratic critics counter these facts? And we emphasize that what has been accomplished thus far in the cultural sphere is no more than a beginning. While the democracies are merely yakking, our theater is performing. With magnificent performances it has delighted the masses, consoled them, exalted them. Our film has continued its production. The world acclaim of German film cannot be denied. And we have written poetry, composed, painted, built. We ask ourselves: What will remain a century from now of the chatter of democratic journalists? And which of our cultural creations will last more than a century? Which of the two ennobles itself and can look down on the other with clear contempt—we can decide with no room for debate.

Even though we say this, we're not in the least throwing our weight around. We know our own faults better than anyone else. With the profoundest internal vigor and the greatest responsibility, we are working to achieve the people's new life-sense and culture-sense. We wish to set a truly meaningful brand on the twentieth century, which has yet to achieve a unified style overall. In contrast, the democracies are still stuck in the nineteenth century. Democracy is the last remnant of the modern age. Both in spirit and in soul, it has been conquered long since by the fortunate races.

Democracy claims with impudent arrogance to be modern, but in fact it gives off the foul stench of rot. To modern ears its loud slogans sound shallow and give off a sense of exhaustion. The culture of democracy mixes the stench of poverty with the perfume of prostitutes. Together, the two reach the stomach and induce vomiting. For all its riches, in its cultural expressions democracy is sterile; it has lost the power of fantasy. Against our modern European states, it maintains itself by persistence and a certain dogmatism, but these elements have already lost the vigor to show signs of new life. . . . Its false morality is a gaudy thick makeup that it uses to cover up the countless cracks and wrinkles in a face marred by death.

The *Reichskulturminister* praises the German people's strong youthfulness and then speaks of the recipients of the prizes. I translate only the part concerning the Book Prize.

### Brehm's *Austrian Trilogy*

The 1939 People's Book Prize is awarded to the writer Bruno Brehm. His *Austrian Trilogy* is one of the most noteworthy achievements of modern German literature. Its national-political significance lies in its sharp criticism of the monarchy of the Danube (Austria); for pre-*Anschluss* German readers, it deepened their understanding of the general problem of the southeastern territories, and it contributed importantly to the preparation for a Greater German solution to this problem.

And we should point out in particular the stylistic and artistic achievement of this work; it gives real life and striking weight to his storytelling. Beyond his literary achievement, Bruno Brehm is himself one of the most soldierly figures in the German literary world. He was born in Laibach, became a captain in the former Austro-Hungarian army, and then went to the university and earned a doctorate. Because until last year he was still a citizen of Czechoslovakia, he was ineligible for the national prize; that he receives the prize this year has all the more significance. That is, he is a Sudeten German, an eastern German who in the recent months of danger has finally returned to the Reich.

The *Reichskulturminister's* speech goes on to explain the film prizes and ends with thanks to the *Führer*. The above is according to the *Deutsche Allgemeine Zeitung* for May 2, 1939; I have translated about two-thirds of it. What I haven't translated isn't crucial to the Nazis' view of culture. This speech is a statement by a leading light of the government on a most public occasion; under strong dictatorship, modern German culture is controlled and guided by this ideology.

Skimming German newspapers occasionally over the last few years, I have been stunned by the sudden changes in the country. That this would happen to Germany, recognized by all as the font of modern Europe's humanism, to Germans, who preach the freedom of the person and amass wisdom, has sometimes left me in open-mouthed amazement. For example, in the Ministry of Culture, committees to regulate scholarship are convened, and they assemble teachers at the higher school and vocational school levels and examine them on successive days in various subjects. On such occasions the instructions from the bureaucrats are truly remarkable. For example, in physics, the theory of relativity is sophistry that relativizes everything and rejects authority, so it isn't German. Again, at one time the names Jews are permitted to have were listed, some thirty each for males and females. Among them were some very strange names. And again, all merchants had to post their names on their storefronts, and there were photographs showing that in order to camouflage the place of their shop's name, Jewish merchants cover up the area with placards; the caption reads, "Jews are cunning and base and use every means to destroy the national economy of Germans." In the newspaper countless times I've read things utterly inexplicable in terms of what we once knew, but if we take the assertions of the *Reichskulturminister's* speech to be the tone of Germany's new cultural life, these too carry weight.

Of course, even inside Germany there seem to be some who even now can't be persuaded to this way of thinking. Hints appear here and there even in the speeches at celebrations. For example, the following passage appeared in Hitler's speech that day. (This speech is of interest in various senses, but I can't go into it here.) The dictator places his hopes on the next generation and wishes to educate them according to the new worldview that he embraces, so

If some old fuddy-duddy sometimes brings me to despair, I have only to look at his son. When I do, I immediately have hope. (Applause again.)

That which can no longer be fixed in such dotards is already long since overcome in their sons—thank God. They are a new generation coming to maturity, such as we hope for in the future.

We are doing everything possible to make this education effective. At this time it is natural that we eliminate "freedom of the individual." I can foresee that some will say, or would like to say but can't, "I don't see why my son has to do labor service. He was born to do better things. Why should he go around carrying a shovel? Wouldn't something intellectual be better? Some work of the mind?"

But my dear friend, what you think of as mind! (*Was Du, mein lieber Freund, schon unter Geist verstehst!*) (Again, a storm of laughter from the hundreds of thousands.) Now your son working in the western territory for Germany is accomplishing in fact more for Germany than you've accomplished with your mind in your whole life. (The masses spur the *Führer* on with loud applause.) And your son is working to do away with the worst confusion—internal divisions among the people. Don't expect me to say, "If he doesn't want to work, he doesn't need to."

As can be seen from the above speech, the Nazi leaders aim normally at young people. With absolute power, they are gradually educating them. And the above points of Goebbels are the morals the Nazis usually repeat; to the extent the situation doesn't change, they are the guiding principles of German culture in the future. To summarize, they proclaim state supremacy, the primacy of politics, the rejection of the individual, the rejection of intellect, restraints on freedom, the collapse of modern democratic society, and the dawn of a new age in history.

## 2.

Already ten years ago in Europe, I often heard the phrase "a new Middle Ages."

Each year, in the name of Franco-German cultural rapprochement, leading lights of the intellectual communities in the two countries get together. In a speech at the Trocadero in Paris, Heinrich Mann began by quoting the words of Anatole France: "Our status is similar to that of the men of letters in the last days of ancient Rome. The Middle Ages approach, and there will be no one to read what we write." Again, Leopold Ziegler spoke in Berlin on the topic "the European spirit," and one section of his talk had the title, "A New Middle Ages?" His general argument was as follows: In its current stage, the European spirit has been seized by excessive scientism, it has diverged from basic human psychology, and it has estranged itself from world consciousness.

In today's Europe, human beings have broken entirely with the past; they are changing psychologically. To save the situation, Europe must be reecclesiasticized; Augustine's "City of God" must be built. Such medievalism goes back as far as the Romantic movement, with Comte de Maistre in France and Novalis in Germany. The latter's meditation, *Christianity or Europe,* written in 1799, is its great prophecy.[4]

But I didn't really understand this phrase, "a new Middle Ages." The era, of course, had picked up where the fad of Spengler and Keyserling left off,[5] and although I sensed acutely the abnormal atmosphere throughout society as a whole, the moral crisis, and the weakening and deterioration of ideas, I couldn't fathom why so wholly individualistic a society could speak of a return of the Middle Ages. From time to time here and there I saw and heard voices calling, "Dictator, arise!" but in general people indulged in wholly unrestrained liberty. Authority was rejected, criticized, derided, caricatured. Rationalism gave free rein to the play of logic. Living in Berlin in contact with people around me, I sensed that no limits were placed on their desires. They seemed insatiable in enjoying all the freedoms, from very overt materialistic desires to self-indulgent pleasures.

Then, beginning in 1933, Germany emerged before our eyes in new and unexpected guise. Germany truly is the country that thought up the dialectic. Germany swerves from one extreme to the other. In contact with its people, I came to understand, if vaguely, that in a given quality there lurks already an opposite quality, the element that will destroy it. In the people of this country, even in their daily affairs, there is something excessive, off balance. Germany since 1933 has been seized by some elemental force and is rushing in a completely opposite direction than before. And even if we can't conclude right off that it is the Middle Ages, the end of the modern world has been proclaimed at least insofar as that country is concerned, as in the Goebbels speech I quoted earlier.

The modern starts from the proposition, "The truth still hasn't been discovered"; the Middle Ages stand atop the statement, "The truth has already been determined." And in the medieval world, there is an established authority that guarantees this absolute truth. It is sacred and inviolate, beyond reach. In the face of this authority, the premise that "for human beings, human beings are sacred" no longer applies. Rational thought and reason are restricted. Individuals are members of nation, group, tribe; individuals as individuals have no standing.

---

4. Heinrich Mann (1871–1950); Anatole France (1844–1924); Leopold Ziegler (1881–1958); Joseph de Maistre (1754?–1821); Novalis (Friedrich von Hardenberg, 1772–1801).

5. Oswald Spengler (1880–1936; *The Decline of the West,* 1918–1922); Count Hermann Keyserling (1880–1946).

In Germany today, the prescribed truth is the nation, the race. The under-lying authority is party rule. Individuals, their liberties, their reason—that is, the principles that propelled Europe's humanism over the centuries since the Renaissance—are rejected.

It's not only Germany, which once created valuable monuments of hu-manism, that is moving in this direction. Italy, Russia, and probably others are, too. Various people have pointed out that it's hard to frame fundamental differences between contemporary Germany and Soviet Russia. If world history as a whole proceeds in this direction, we may have to say that the prophecy of "a new Middle Ages" is accurate.

# 3.

In fact, in the centuries since the Renaissance, the principles that propelled Europe's humanism may have exhausted their potential, played themselves out. The negation inherent in these principles has come to the fore and seems to have led in all aspects of society to dead end, deterioration, collapse. Like the sorcerer's apprentice, modern man seems unable now to control the spirit he himself called up and set to work; instead, controlled by it, he is being destroyed.

As Renaissance concepts (following Ōrui Noboru's *Studies in Renaissance Culture*) we can list (1) human liberation/freedom; (2) naturalism/realism; (3) the awakening of the masses; (4) nationalism; (5) perfection of the indi-vidual/critical spirit; (6) idealism. If we add the scientific spirit, rationalism, and the utilitarian control of reality, for modern Europeans these are self-evident, the basis of their psyche, their motive force; but the principles that created modern culture appear now old and tired, already changed so much they cannot function creatively. It stands to reason that this is why Europe has been driven, war after war, to the point of collapse.

In the first place, human liberation gradually lost its early bloom and degenerated ultimately in the modern age into the unlimited pursuit of desire. Man achieved a human existence that liberated his own humanity from medieval fetters, but now men are driven by excessive desire tran-scending human bounds. As individuals, as states, they have a greed that knows no bounds. Psychologically and materially, the phrases "denial of self," "the mean," "preserving one's station" have been erased. Individuals who try to *sich ausleben* (enjoy a full life), capitalism that pursues unlimited profit, unprincipled European states that seek insatiably for new territories to annex—these are all unforeseen outcomes of modern Europe's human liberation.

Moreover, liberty too bore very strange fruit. Modern history had been a process of liberation, but as a result of piling liberation on liberation, when finally liberty became a reality, its fundament—liberty for what?—had been lost. Free modern man stands in a void. He can reject and criticize. But as a result of severing his connection to society's fundamentals, he doesn't know what to create, what to assert. Because his goal lies in an infinite yonder, he hasn't time to achieve it.

Again, much doubt has arisen also about how free the various systems—parliaments, newspapers—that guarantee and underwrite freedom really are. They are formal freedom, freedom in name only, and the truth can't be published. Free competition gives rise to inequality, and inequality in turn limits liberty. Working in concert, "Liberty and Equality" once propelled liberation, but now the two have become mutually contradictory: those places that have liberty don't have equality, and those places that have equality don't have liberty.

Renaissance naturalism and realism caused man to turn his back on God. Medieval man fought with mankind; modern man fought with God. He achieved the aforementioned liberty and as a result discarded "reverence" toward what we might term an infinite absolute being. He pursued the natural reality that was most beyond doubt: his own desires. For him everything became simple, solved or solvable. Seeking utilitarian control of reality, he gave free rein to rationalism and the scientific spirit.

But these very accomplishments of the scientific spirit gave birth in turn to fearsome aspects of the modern age. The industry that should make life easier on the contrary enslaved people. The development of weapons facilitated wholesale slaughter. Population growth increased economic distress, and this economic distress forced man to jettison intellectual and personal independence. Modern man is man with too-great desires and too-small character. Distance and time have been shortened, but that has not broadened human life; the distance and time that have been shortened have possessed man, indeed, have made him rush wildly about to shorten them further. Modern speed has no substance. Doesn't the hectic life modern man leads stand atop a sort of illusion? For example, so many writers publish their ideas, and publishers, dazzled, turn them into newspapers, magazines, books; but how many of the thoughts are more splendid than those of the calm days of the past? And readers who read it all—how much substance do they reap? Modern man is busy but empty, without ideas, distracted, unable to concentrate.

Having performed a splendid role, the European nationalism that originated in the early days of the modern period turned into state absolutism; in Nazi Germany it became overwhelmingly the leading principle of the new age. There nationalism became racism, became the worship of *Blut und Boden* [blood and soil], and trampled all the other principles of the modern world. If, tentatively, we can use the phrase "a new Middle Ages," this is its new god. In the very recent past, and not only in Germany, there are signs that even religion has come to be controlled by the state; in Nazi Germany the movement to destroy Christianity and create a German religion has got the upper hand, and General Ludendorff and his wife are trying to create a religion of Wotan worship. In addition, it is well known how completely in Nazi Germany the state is absolute and how individuals, minorities, intellect, liberty, culture are secondary to it; one can fathom this in the above speech of the *Reichskulturminister.*

Much has already been written about the forms taken in their decline by the awakening of the masses at the beginning of the modern age and the democracy that resulted. When connected with those masses, the achievement of individuality gave rise to foolish and conceited masses. People who still hope to preserve true individuality are scattered and fearfully isolated, and most people, although resembling each other, lose their sense of connection; human contact between person and person is gradually disappearing. So people who have been turned into atoms have no connection to what is fundamental in humanity, and all their thinking is isolated, so that only propaganda brings them together. Truth recedes; propaganda is all. What determines modern man's thinking is ideology—pseudo-ideas, half-ideas; society's inhuman regimentation regimented unthinking men.

Having exhausted its potential, the modern spirit changed into something that functioned to destroy what it itself had built up; this dead end of modern European ideas can probably be argued from various angles. To list here only its most crucial points—the loosing of boundless desire, state absolutism, economic hardship, great technological weapons, the intellectual poverty of the men who wield them, shallowness, the demagogic nature of ideology: enumerating them like this, one has the feeling that Europe's current state is the quite natural end result. As in the last days of the Hellenic world, this condition of war after war is the end point of a historical epoch, and, alas, that ancient prophecy may be on the mark.

Moreover, there is a historical irony here. It was in the Enlightenment of the eighteenth century that these "Renaissance concepts"—modern humanism—took their clearest theoretical form, and England and France were the nations touched most deeply and permeated by the spirit of the Enlightenment and that took it as their guiding principle. As nations, Germany, Italy, and Russia were affected relatively little by the spirit of the Enlightenment, and their societies preserved many feudal remnants; Russia in particular hadn't really left the Middle Ages. It's only natural that intellectually these states were able to cast off the modern age fairly easily; moreover, in the seventeenth, eighteenth, and nineteenth centuries, using those enlightened, progressive ideas, England and France were very active as states. They expanded territorially, amassed riches, laid claim to resources. Now these countries are rich. These countries are "have countries," and their ambitions are pretty much satisfied. So modern humanism in these countries can still support the status quo; but Germany and Italy suffered deep wounds in World War I and sank into disorder and economic distress, so there the negative aspects of modern thought ran riot, and although fundamentally less modern than England and France, these states felt more strongly the impasse of the modern, jettisoned the modern earlier, and entered what may be "a new Middle Ages."

## 4.

Germans are by nature agnostic, irrational. They are fiercely subjective and idealistic. We Japanese are not used to idealism, so we like to think of the idealistic—that is, the logical, the rational—as precise; but Germans are idealistic and imprecise. They trace everything back to abstract inchoate ideas. The psyches of Germans don't include the tendency to precision about phenomena in the objective world. To empty oneself and think oneself into the reality of objects is alien to Germans; they impose themselves on all objects. Idealistic and irrational in their own hearts, they inhabit a subjective world that is difficult for us to enter. They live in an abstract twilight and are not adept at knowledge of the bright outer world; inside is a complicated and diverse subjective world. The subjective: that is the psychic keel of the Germans. Their lyricism, longing, creativity, irrationality, fanaticism and zeal, interiority, amorphousness, music—all originate here. They exhibit the extremes of the subjective, its strengths and its weaknesses. The strengths are philosophy that doesn't depend on phenomena, music, expressionism, *Tat* [deed], perseverance, ego. The weaknesses are a life that needs phenomena, the plastic arts, impressionism, contemplation, cooperation and harmony, forms.

In German literature the portrayal of objective nature and the acute dissection of human psychology are as good as nonexistent. Love of nature in German literature is normally longing for nature. The greatest realm of German literature is the confession of inner subjectivity. And a special sort of Romantic vision. Suffering almost always from irrational impulse and excessive strength, it longs for salvation and escape. *Drang* (emotion that wells up from within and cannot be controlled) powers the ship of the German psyche that is built on this keel of subjectivity. To Germans, demands we consider bizarre are natural desires: after experiencing all human experience, Faust wishes to sink in final tragedy. Again, the dying Zarathustra, that enigmatic giant who prophesies doom and destroys, is an apparition with inexhaustible allure for Germans. For Germans the tragic fall is a favorite theme. And its cause is not external but usually internal to the main character, lurking in desires that exceed human bounds.

Goethe's "spirit of magic" and "spirit of the earth" and Nietzsche's Dionysian—these fierce irrational forces have always entranced the traditional German-like German. Germany today, we can say, is governed by irrational, elemental force. A Bach, a Burckhardt,[6] the facet of Goethe that yearned for clear-cut modeling—the German would say they are too cosmopolitan, too human, too broad. Heightened passion, darkness, a certain narrowness, and a yearning for fall and sense of tragedy seem to be essential elements of the true German character.

The literary works that express this spirit most straightforwardly include Goethe's *Faust*, Hölderlin's *Hyperion*, Nietzsche's *Zarathustra*. Further, there are Novalis's *Heinrich von Ofterdingen* and other tales we might call emblematic. These take no specific form; rather, they are hazily gloomy and filled with idealistic allegories. As for the general German concept of art, the very term "realism" denotes low value. Japanese artists desire harmony; German artists, restlessness.

When they are being German, Germans always react against an objectivity that takes clear form. The upsurge of the modern German psyche starts from a reaction against Western Europe's rationalism and Enlightenment thought. The German psyche always returns to the infinite, the dark, the irregular, the impulsive. Wagner's music is "music without a goal"; it has no melody, and just when it seems that something formful is about to float up out of the raging sea of sound, it sinks again. Moreover, Schopenhauer's philosophy takes blind will, will without either foundation or goal, as the essence of things. It was Nietzsche who saw the internal similarity between these two: "The startling unity of Wagner and Schopenhauer! Both of them start from the same impulse. The deepest roots of the German spirit gird themselves for battle."[7]

> In the rapturous swell,
> In the turbulent spell,
> In the welcoming wave,
> Holding all.

---

6. Johann Wolfgang von Goethe (1749–1832); Jakob Burckhardt (1818–1897).
7. Friedrich Hölderlin (1770–1843; *Hyperion*, 1797–1799). Takeyama translated *Also sprach Zarathustra* into Japanese (*Tsuaratōsutora kaku katariki*, 1943). Richard Wagner (1813–1883); Arthur Schopenhauer (1788–1860).

I'm sinking,
I'm drowning,
Unaware,
Highest love!

This passage from Wagner's *Tristan and Isolde*[8] expresses well the inchoate, infinite, irrational worldview in which the German spirit floats.

Germans are fundamentally mystics. In the depths of their souls they find it distasteful to recognize and respect the control of the objective world by laws of reason. Romanticism is a most German tendency; overwhelming the rationalism of Enlightenment thought, this romanticism proclaimed the "new Middle Ages." In Germany medieval emotions never died out completely. Modern characteristics—the individual, liberty, knowledge—never became the flesh and bones of their psychic life. In Germany personhood through individualism was only academic theory; it was the Anglo-Saxons who gave it reality.

Their noble achievements to the contrary notwithstanding, I sense that the spirit of investigation of those Germans engaged in the natural sciences does not arise from love of nature. German "hearts turn east; only their heads turn west." Their European intelligence is a means to conquer the objective world. Germans turn their backs on nature, so when they do face it, they know no way to treat it except to turn it into abstraction and, using scientific method, dissect it and conquer it. The natural sciences are probably not too faithful to nature. Love of nature does not give rise to science and engineering. Germans idealize everything and see objectivity as an abstraction. For that very reason they mastered the external world; the German attitude toward nature is utilitarian. Seek the rules of nature in order to conquer nature, not in order to follow nature.

Germans say, "We love nature," and they have a penchant for *Wandervögel* [outing clubs for boys] and the like. But that nature is something that emerges as a projection of the human spirit or of the mystic mind; it is not something that emerges itself, apart from mankind, the nature of the old pond and the frog jumping in. It is something controlled by man, so the hand of man reaches into its every cranny. With pet dogs, too, there are some that at first glance you can't tell are dogs: the head is a lion's head, but the rear end is shorn.

The extremely powerful weapons and organization at the disposal of today's Germans are the fruit of this utilitarian abstraction. Organization is a

---

8. These are the closing lines of the opera: "(Isolde sighs in ecstasy, held in Brangäne's arms, and sinks upon Tristan's body. Profound emotion and grief of the bystanders. Mark calls down a blessing on the dead.) Curtain." The translation is Andrew Porter's: *English National Opera Guide 6: Tristan and Isolde* (London: John Calder, 1981), 92. This translation suppresses some of Wagner's romanticism: "*in des Welt-Athems / wehendem All—*" (lines three and four here) is, more literally, "in the drifting universe / of the world-breath." Takeyama's Japanese (he cites no translator) is close to the original.

most powerful method for the human spirit to gain utilitarian control of the outside world. Precisely because they are subjective, remote from the world, Germans discovered these effective positivistic methods for conquering the outside world. In contemporary Germany, not only nature but society, psyche, ethics, truth—all are organized thoroughly. This net of organization stretches into every corner. To try to convey some idea of that society, let me give just one example. It's something I read in a newspaper. A primary school teacher asked his students, "Did you listen yesterday to the broadcast of the speech of the *Reichskulturminister*?" All raised their hands, except for one girl. When asked why not, this little girl replied, "Daddy said he didn't want to." The following day this girl's father was arrested.

The state takes the place God occupied in the Middle Ages; organization takes the place of the church; propaganda, the place of missions. The younger generations are all educated as the authorities wish, to become human beings of the exact same type. And the development of communications and technology and other cultural tools makes resistance on the part of the ruled completely impossible. That those leaders are always asserting and proclaiming that this is a turning point in history—this too is not without reason.

# 5.

The dead end of modern thought and the pathological symptoms of modern society predicted sixty or seventy years ago by Nietzsche and warned of by many other thinkers are today everywhere visible and have taken new forms. They have emerged most clearly and deeply in Germany. That is, Germany was not fully modernized via Enlightenment thinking, and in that age state activity had no material, existing rights, and Germans still retained much of their medieval character; in addition, the German people had lost their psychic balance from the deep wounds they suffered in the recent Great War, so the negative aspects of the modern world wielded here their greatest force. We can't know whether this is in fact "a new Middle Ages," whether there is a rhythm in history and it proceeds inevitably in this direction, or whether this is only a temporary epiphenomenon, and modern thought, having made good its shortcomings, will continue to develop with personal liberty as its base, a personal liberty it had achieved and then had become disillusioned with. However, we can say this clearly. As far as concerns this single issue of "freedom of thought," if the British and French win, it will be possible to preserve it in some form or other, at least for our lifetimes. If Germany wins, it will be wrested from us, fundamentally and instantly.

~

# The Younger Generation

"The Younger Generation" is a speech to an Ichikō convocation on July 22, 1945, less than three months after the German defeat in Europe and less than one month before Japan's surrender. Just turned forty-two, Takeyama remarks, "I don't think I myself belong to the 'old generation.' But it's certain I'm not one of the younger generation." He had been on the Ichikō faculty since 1926, teaching German language and literature. For some months during the war he had been the resident manager of one of the three large dormitories on the Komaba campus.

The address came amid the disruptions and deprivations of 1945: students working in factories or sent off to war, food shortages, frequent air raid alerts. But this speech is scholarly, asking a very great deal of its young and exhausted audience: considerable background in the contemporary literature of both France and Germany and a willingness to engage in serious intellectual endeavor when Japan was at—beyond—the point of collapse. Takeyama offers a serious analysis of Japan's intellectual dilemma, an analysis not all that different from those of other postwar critics with whom he would soon be at odds.

Here again Takeyama distinguishes Japan from Germany: "People often say Japan and Germany are similar, though I think there are more differences between them." Takeyama was a critic of the military and the wartime government, yet at a time when it might have been tempting to disparage all things Japanese, he chooses instead to remind his charges that "In the blood of us Japanese, there have long been very good things. We have noble, splendid virtues."

The wartime headmaster was Abe Yoshishige, whom Takeyama mentioned in "Ichikō in 1944."

115

～

A moment ago Headmaster Abe wondered, "What will become of the younger generation?" From time to time I too have thought about this question. Living on the third floor of Middle Dorm and listening to the sound of trashings, I've thought a lot about it.[1]

"Younger generation"—a generation ago the phrase was on everyone's lips, and it had a specific meaning. After the first great European war, Europe's young people had thoughts and feelings quite different from those of the older generation and began a new way of life that the older generation was at a loss to understand; this became a major social problem. During the war young people had either gone to the front and fought or worked in factories and on farms, and when they were demobilized and returned home, they had earned an important say in society. Then in the chaos of the postwar years, the authorities that till then had maintained order were toppled, and the livelihoods of the steady classes were destroyed, too; so young people suffered—thrown into this state of confusion, they rebelled against the older generation and tried to make a completely new start and find new ideals. Thus both intellectually and in their lives, so much that was abnormal appeared, one thing after the other, that adults came to look with suspicion and aversion, virtually with fear, on the "younger generation" of the time.

The various elements of this "younger generation" issue were either resolved in some form or carried over unresolved into the current great war in Europe and gave shape to a large part of the new crisis. In thinking about our road ahead, this issue has great significance and is worth reflecting on.

What manner of men were they—this "younger generation"? I can't go into detail here, so I'll mention some literary works that depict them. That way it will be easier for you to understand, to say, "Ah, *that* kind of person."

This younger generation was reflected, of course, in literature. Indeed, we can almost say that the literature of the day dealt *only* with this issue. This was true in both France and Germany. In France, for example, there were Romain Rolland's *The Soul Enchanted*, Martin Du Gard's *The Thibaults*, Gide's *The Counterfeiters*, also Cocteau's *Enfants Terribles*, Morand's *The Living Buddha*, and the like. In Germany, too, expressionist works treated this issue occasionally, and with neo-Kantianism, Remarque's works were virtually all in that vein. Ernst Glaeser is a Jew and so isn't translated much in Japan, but from first to last he depicted the younger generation exclusively, and his

---

1. The Japanese word, *su-tō-mu* [a phonetic representation of the English word "storm"], refers to organized trashings that were a hazing inflicted on younger students by older students: windows were broken, belongings tossed out, rooms left a watery mess (see Roden, *Schooldays*, 105–10).

depiction is fascinating on this point. Hesse's *Demian*, which you Ichikō students are always reading, is perhaps the prototypical portrayal of this issue.[2] What do the main characters of these works have in common? In a word, they are smart delinquents. Their thinking is destructive and rebellious. They live lives of instinct and impulse, and they pride themselves on amoral acts. These smart young people look at Nietzsche with new eyes and criticize society bitterly. Serving a bold life-first philosophy—in terms of the old morality it can only be termed delinquent—they plunge into lives this philosophy dictates.

Utitz's book *Die Überwindung des Expressionismus* is considered a classic in dissecting the tides of thought of this era.[3] According to it, we can list three characteristics of the feelings of the people of that generation.

The first is hate. Amid the suffering of the postwar era, young people embraced hate toward everything. It became one motive force behind their acts. They hated all old authority, old morality, old order. They hated capitalists, they hated other races, they hated Jews—in other words, they found enemies everywhere. Shaking their fists, they said to the older generation, "You created this mess!" As befits a "structure of hate," the Left filled its propaganda with words of hate; if you read the speeches of Hitler and Goebbels, the Right, too, competed with them in the use of invective and abuse.

The second is primitivism. The younger generation rose against anything governed by tradition, anything considered authoritative, and sought to destroy anything constructed rationally to regulate and constrain people. They sought out only that which connected most directly with life, which made them feel acutely, "Ah, I'm alive!" Savoring lives lived fully, sharply, certainly without doubt, they sought salvation in that ecstasy. They ran to emotions, instincts, violence rather than reason. Irrationalism became the tenor of society's consciousness. Evaluating this tendency, some said that the present world is all in flux. Absolutely all set forms were rejected; only the formless, primitive, still uncivilized had charm and attraction; people tried to escape from the old Europe and start over from totally bare life—that is, from the barbarous.

So in terms of time, people fled the contemporary and longed for primitive times or for the Middle Ages. In terms of space, they left Europe and

2. Romain Rolland (1866–1944; *L'âme enchantée*, 1922–1923). Roger Martin Du Gard (1881–1958; *Les Thibault*, 1929). André Gide (1869–1951; *Les faux-monnayeurs*, 1926). Jean Cocteau (1889–1963; *Les enfants terribles*, 1929). Paul Morand (1888–1976; *Bouddha vivant*, 1927). Erich Maria Remarque (1898–1970). Ernst Glaeser (1902–1963). Hermann Hesse (1877–1962; *Demian*, 1919).

3. Emil Utitz (1883–1956), *Die Überwindung des Expressionismus: Charakterologische Studien zur Kultur der Gegenwart* [The conquest of expressionism: Character studies of the culture of the present] (1927).

sought salvation in the East. But the East had in fact an older culture, so in the end they sought new light in the noncivilization of Africa. In the novels of Gide and elsewhere, the intellectuals and artists of the day who revered Africa are too numerous to list. Music adopted the rhythms of Negroes; painting searched there for new forms; in dance, too, jaded urbanites danced the dances of barbarians. There was even a weird practice called "*nackte Kultur*" [naked culture] in which these people stripped to the skin and lived in communes in the forest. Sports were praised, speed was revered, superstitions ran rampant—these phenomena were all related. As to morals, things we can't even imagine today were considered commonsensical, and middle schoolers—even middle-school girls—lived immoral lives, going so far as to inject each other with cocaine, and sometimes committing heinous crimes that caused a sensation.

The third characteristic is autointoxication via the mapping out of ludicrous megalomaniacal plans. The Nazis said, "Either we'll conquer the world, or we'll destroy it," and this tone appealed to the mood of the younger generation. But because this characteristic has no direct relation to what I want to say here, I won't address it.

Utitz's book was written before the rise of the Nazis, but precisely these three characteristics—hate, primitivism, megalomania—were also keynotes of Nazism. Subsequent history attests to the fact that this book offered clear insights into the age.

The younger generation of Europe after the first Great War had these characteristics and grew up amid chaos. But that doesn't mean that their way of doing things was only confused and decadent, far from it. They made strenuous efforts in the search for new morals, a new spirit, a new order, a new society. Along with reevaluating Nietzsche, they looked up to a number of living leaders. For example, Rolland and Gide and the brothers Mann, and for the more highbrow, Valéry and George, and social activists and politicians of various tendencies.

In France the social concern is so disconcertingly intense—in novels, fifteen- and sixteen-year-old children argue, "Next election Maurras will probably make it"—that the younger generation too, swinging back and forth between communism on the one hand, and the Right and Catholicism and the rest on the other, sought a new religion in vitalism.[4] There the issue of the younger generation remained unresolved right up to the current war. Unlike the French, Germans of the intellectual class had little social concern,

---

4. Thomas Mann (1875–1955); Heinrich Mann (1871–1950). Paul Valéry (1871–1945). Stefan George (1868–1933). Charles Maurras (1868–1952), right-wing writer and activist. Vitalism: the doctrine that organisms have a nonphysical (hence nonscientific) inner force that gives them life.

and the nation's way of doing things was extremely emotional. In a sense, you might term it religious. People often say Japan and Germany are similar, though I think there are more differences between them. But one trait they have in common is that neither country had a backbone class with sound political consciousness. Those with sound social judgment had no actual power. Both countries turned their backs on reality and evaded it. The tendency of the German younger generation reflected that characteristic. That problem of that country was solved by Hitler, and in the end, united by Nazi ideals, Germany plunged into the current war.

This has been a sketch of the problem of Europe's younger generation after the first Great War. It was transmitted to Japan, too, and for a time the phrase "younger generation" was a bit of a fad. But there was no taproot from which this problem could grow, so the fad soon died, and the phrase too disappeared. For a time there was the awful trend of the erotic, the grotesque, and the nonsensical; it may have been merely the Japanese version of this European trend as its influence spread to Japan.

But this time around, after the current war has ended, I think we'll face this problem. I don't know what form it will take, but the younger generation will surely think and live differently than the older generation, and friction and confusion will certainly arise. Japan's young people are well behaved, but when we think back a generation to the time when the Reds flourished, they were anything but well behaved. In that day the younger generation was either erotic/grotesque or Red, and the difference with older generations was very pronounced; but this time around, if the problem once gets started, it will be incomparably greater.

No, this "younger generation" is already becoming a problem. After Admiral Yamamoto said, "Talk about 'young people' today," the issue became much more prominent. The other day in the *Asahi* newspaper there was this statement: "When the Sino-Japanese Incident began, Prime Minister Konoe declared, 'If we don't solve this dispute now ourselves, it will be the cause of trouble for our children and grandchildren.' The war started with this intent but did not go as planned, and now people who were then about ten years old are fighting on all fronts."[5]

Who will dedicate himself to solve the coming issue of this "younger generation"? Who will search out a new morality for a new age and shine a light amid the chaos? It goes without saying that it will be someone who

---

5. Admiral Yamamoto Isoroku (1884–1943), architect of the attack on Pearl Harbor, said that the performance of the younger generation in the war was such that deprecating talk should cease. Konoe Fumimarō (1891–1946) was prime minister from 1937 to 1939. The "Sino-Japanese Incident"—war with China—began in 1937.

has already seen many friends off for the front, who realizes that the time will come when he too heads in that direction, who is now working in some factory or on some farm, who is among the Ichikō students gathered here tonight. This person will emerge from among you, or not at all. I hope and believe he will emerge.

Today's young people are always having tasks laid on them—"That's your responsibility." "This is your duty"—and you must get tired of it; but this task cannot be shirked.

I don't think I myself belong to the "old generation." But it's certain I'm not one of the younger generation. It's irresponsible simply to tell young people, "This is your task," "You have to do this." The question they ask in return is this: "Assuming the locus of the problem is as you say, then what should we do about it?" But I don't know how to answer this question. I've thought about it, but it's too difficult, and I don't have an answer.

What I want to say is merely this.

In the blood of us Japanese, there have long been very good things. We have noble, splendid virtues. But they haven't yet undergone careful reflection. We don't realize fully just what our own virtues are. What their meaning is and in what connection, on what basis they have value—that hasn't been verified. The result is that the special virtues can be abused and misused. Moreover, even such splendid virtues as self-sacrifice and love and duty aren't grounded in self-awareness, so if they should be attacked by others with assertions that have some logic to them, they get mowed down easily. That's because we don't have our own independent judgment with strong logical roots, and the virtues don't stand atop that judgment. It's like healthy bodies that haven't been inoculated. They're vulnerable to illnesses that attack from outside. To weigh things carefully and root things in self-awareness—that's the most important single thing in dealing with the coming chaos and building anew.

The West once experienced an era focused entirely on reason. It was only to be expected that when that age ran into a dead end, voices that rejected rationalism arose; but it's very strange that in Japan, which up till now hasn't had rationalism or had it only very weakly, the rejection of rationalism has been popular.

They say this war is a war of spirit against matériel. That may be the case, but it's also accurate to call it a war of emotions against reason. Frankly, it's undeniable that our side incurred a great disadvantage by ignoring rational thought. Moreover, no matter how this war ends, afterwards, in rubbing shoulders with other countries, we will not be able to survive bare-handed, without the weapon of reason.

In closing I want to introduce you to the following words. They are the words of Albert Schweitzer. This is what he says:

In a period that ridicules as antiquated and without value whatever seems akin to rational or independent thought, and which even mocks the inalienable human rights proclaimed in the eighteenth century, I declare myself to be one who places all his confidence in rational thinking. I venture to tell our generation that it is not at the end of rationalism just because past rationalism first gave way to romanticism and later to a pretended realism that reigned in intellectual as well as in material life. When we have passed through all the follies of the so-called universal realpolitik, and because of it suffered spiritual misery, there will be no other choice but to turn to a new rationalism more profound and more effective than that of the past.[6]

He wrote this in 1931, when Germany was in deep, deep chaos; they are words worth pondering deeply.

---

6. Albert Schweitzer, *Out of My Life and Thought: An Autobiography*, trans. Antje Bultmann Lemke (Baltimore: Johns Hopkins University Press, 1998), 226.

# Part III

# THE TOKYO TRIAL

~

# The Trial of Mr. Hyde

*The International Military Tribunal for the Far East (Tokyo trial) was the Pacific counterpart of the first Nuremberg trial. A panel of eleven judges, one each from the victor nations and from the Philippines and India (neither gained its independence until after the war), heard evidence against twenty-eight Japanese prominent during the period from 1928 to 1945, sixteen of them generals and admirals. The trial lasted two and a half years. The verdicts: seven death sentences, sixteen life sentences, two shorter sentences. Unlike Nuremberg, the Tokyo tribunal found no defendants innocent (two defendants had died, and one—the ideologue Ōkawa Shūmei, whom Takeyama mentions in passing—had been declared insane.)*

*The trial itself, I have argued elsewhere,[1] was a farce. Its law was new and applied ex post facto. Its judges were biased (e.g., the Filipino judge was a survivor of the Bataan Death March), its procedures flawed, its judgment faulty. It failed to indict the emperor or even to have him testify; it gave relatively little attention to Japan's colonialism (Taiwan, Korea) or to its slaughter of Chinese civilians or to its bacteriological warfare. It ignored the war crimes of the Allies (firebombing and atomic bombing by the United States, the Soviet Union's attack on Japan at the end of the war and its treatment of Japanese POWs). In retrospect it was—as wartime Prime Minister General Tōjō Hideki stated at the time—"victor's justice." Whether it established useful legal precedent, placing governments on notice that they must obey the laws of war, including the prohibition on aggression, is a matter of opinion. The UN trials of war criminals in The Hague and the Iraqi trial of Saddam Hussein indicate some of the difficulties in prosecuting defeated enemies;*

---

1. Richard H. Minear, *Victors' Justice: The Tokyo War Crimes Trial* (Princeton: Princeton University Press, 1971; Ann Arbor: Center for Japanese Studies, 2001).

the fact that prosecutors invoke Nuremberg but not Tokyo is evidence that Tokyo has little standing as precedent.

In addition to Ōkawa Shūmei and Tōjō Hideki, Takeyama mentions only one other Tokyo defendant by name: General Araki Sadao, army minister between 1931 and 1933 and education minister from 1938 to 1939. On votes of seven to four, the eleven Tokyo judges found both Tōjō and Araki guilty. The tribunal sentenced Tōjō to death, and he was executed in December 1948. Araki received a life sentence; paroled in the mid-1950s, he and all other surviving Tokyo trial convicts were released unconditionally in 1958.

But these specific legal flaws of the Tokyo trial were not Takeyama's concerns in 1946, when, in the early stages of the trial, he was a spectator. His concern was more literary, more imaginative, more profound. He argued that the small men in the dock at Tokyo were not the prime architects of Japan's tragedy. It was not that they were innocent; rather, it was that there were larger forces at work. Japan owed its fate primarily to being a "have-not country" and to being late to "Modern Civilization." In the second essay in Part III, "Letter to Judge Röling," Takeyama endorses the findings of the Dutch judge, B. V. A. Röling, including his suggestion that several defendants who were given life sentences should have been condemned to death, so he was not unwilling to accept important aspects of the Tokyo verdict.[2]

For Takeyama the Tokyo trial became an important continuing concern. In 1947 he met Röling, and a friendship developed. In 1949, soon after the trial ended, he published "Letter to Judge Röling." In 1956 he published Shōwa no seishinshi (Showa: Psychology of an Era; my translation is forthcoming, but not in this volume), which features the trial prominently. Takeyama traveled to Holland and spent several days with Röling ("Visit to Holland," 1957). Among his last essays (1982) was "The Tokyo Trial and Shōwa History."

In 1946 Takeyama drew on The Strange Case of Dr. Jekyll and Mr. Hyde, Robert Louis Stevenson's story of 1886. Stevenson's tale depicts a respectable doctor, Dr. Jekyll, whose experimental potion turned him—at first temporarily, then irreversibly—into a fiend, Mr. Hyde. Dr. Jekyll lived in affluence; Mr. Hyde cruised the slums in search of victims. Readers in 1886 took the tale as Stevenson intended: as an exploration of the dual aspects of every human being. In early 1886 John Addington Symonds had written Stevenson: "At last I have read Dr. Jekyll. It makes me wonder whether a man has the right so to scrutinize 'the abysmal deeps of personality.' It is indeed a dreadful book, most dreadful because of a certain moral callousness." Stevenson replied: "Jekyll is a dreadful thing, I own; but the only thing I feel dreadful about is that damned old business of the war in the members." "The members" is a reference to James 4:1, which in the Revised Standard Version reads: "What causes wars, and what causes fighting among you? Is it not your passions that

---

2. See Ushimura Kei, Beyond the "Judgment of Civilization," trans. Steven J. Ericson (Tokyo: LTCB International Library Selection No. 14, 2001), especially Ushimura's Chapter 5, "Takeyama Michio and the Tokyo Trial."

*are at war in your members?"*[3] *But 125 years after Stevenson wrote it, the tale has other resonances, among them a questioning of modern science.*

In the mid-twentieth century *The Strange Case* was likely as familiar to educated Japanese as to their European or American counterparts. In the 1930s alone, three translations of Stevenson's tale appeared or reappeared in Tokyo. But Japanese readers would have understood it in its original acceptation. Though Stevenson's tale implies a questioning of modern science, Takeyama's adaptation of the story is, I believe, original. Takeyama must have Stevenson among others in mind when he comments that "at the end of the last century" some people began to question—if "only in poetic form"—the pretensions of modern science.

Between 1945 and 1952 Japan was under American Occupation. Criticism of Occupation policy was not permitted. Occupation censorship was objectively less rigorous than the prewar and wartime Japanese censorship, but it was perhaps more insidious in that it left no traces. Under the wartime system, newspapers and journals indicated where censors had struck words or sentences or paragraphs: they left space blank or inserted circles or crosses in the place of the deleted characters. But the Occupation forbade that practice. Though written in 1946, "The Trial of Mr. Hyde" appeared in print only five years later, in 1951, when the censors had become less vigilant.

Writing in 1981 of "The Trial of Mr. Hyde," the literary scholar Etō Jun suggested that in Takeyama's mind the Occupation itself, with control of both organization and weapons, was "Hyde's doing." He wrote (the words in single quotation marks are from "The Trial of Mr. Hyde"): "Indeed, 'the German, Italian, and Japanese rulers' took Nietzsche's insight and 'put it into action.' But the American Occupationaires, too, brandishing the 'slender whip' of the 'idea' of 'democratization' at the 'elephant' that was the Japanese people— weren't they too actually 'putting it into action'? In fact, it is precisely they, is it not, who are 'fearsome modern men' neither more nor less than the Nazis?" So—in Etō's strained reading—the Tokyo trial becomes Mr. Hyde trying Mr. Hyde.[4] In 1946 Takeyama was certainly critical of the Tokyo trial, but in 1981 Etō misread Takeyama's essay for Etō's own ends.

In the early years of the twenty-first century "The Trial of Mr. Hyde" resonates for an American reader in a way Takeyama could not have anticipated. Takeyama stresses the overwhelming force of "Modern Civilization" and the resulting powerlessness of the individual in "have-not countries," where Dr. Jekyll turns into Mr. Hyde. In today's world the United States is of all "have countries" the richest, yet some of its intellectuals know now the powerlessness of which Takeyama wrote.

---

3. For the letters, see *The Letters of Robert Louis Stevenson,* eds. Bradford A. Booth and Ernest Mehew (8 vols., New Haven: Yale University Press, 1994–1995), 5:220–21. At the start of "Henry Jekyll's Full Statement of the Case," the final chapter of *The Strange Case,* Stevenson writes: "It was thus rather the exacting nature of my aspirations than any particular degradation in my faults, that made me what I was and, with even a deeper trench than in the majority of men, severed in me those provinces of good and ill which divide and compound man's dual nature. . . . And it chanced that the direction of my scientific studies, which led wholly towards the mystic and the transcendental, reacted and shed a strong light on this consciousness of the perennial war among my members."

4. Etō Jun, "'Haido-shi no sabaki' ni tsuite," *Bungakkai,* June 1981, 181.

～

One day I went to observe the war crimes trial.

On this day they were holding a special hearing, so tickets weren't necessary, and they didn't examine personal effects, either. The courtroom setup was complicated; for me, there for the first time, it wasn't easy to figure out. The judges sitting on a high dais, the prosecutors and defense attorneys speaking by turns as they stood at a podium in the trough below the judges, the interpreters in a glass box up near the ceiling: the words these people spoke came via earphones in two languages, and it took a while for things to come into focus. Into the courtroom came the rays of the late-autumn sun on a day of broken clouds, at times too bright for my eyes, then dark once more.

As I looked down from the visitors' section, I saw ruddy MPs standing in front of an array of flags, at attention like mannequins. Some thirty former generals and senior statesmen sat in the dock, their faces strangely glossy, pale and dark. Here and there electric lights, red and white, were doing their best to illuminate the dark. Typewriters sounded incessantly, like bees buzzing. Via a web of electric wires, messages were flowing back and forth. All this made me think I was dreaming . . .

The defendant being examined this day had not yet been reported about even in the press. There had been no photos of his face. He sat immediately behind General Tōjō, in the seat left vacant when Dr. Ōkawa exhibited signs of madness, and glared about haughtily.

He looked fearsome. He dominated the dock. The other defendants were all calm and had something of the dignity of small-minded people, and all of them exhibited a certain grimness, but they paled in comparison with this unknown defendant. His sharp and evil eye was the very image of the eye of the Mr. Hyde I had seen at the movies.

Talking wasn't permitted, but I whispered to the person beside me: "Who is that new defendant?"

My neighbor informed me: "Modern Civilization."

The prosecutor continued his sober and impassioned address. His main points follow.

## 2.

". . . This defendant, who appears in court today for the first time, bears a truly fearsome war guilt. His guilt isn't yet generally acknowledged, and it is utterly puzzling that now, when people rush to call down curses on various individuals—'*He's* guilty!' 'No, *he's* one of the gang, too!'—taunting them, lashing them, I haven't heard this defendant's name once.

"Behind the scenes of this recent tragic cataclysm in human history, out of view, this defendant set the stage for it and manipulated it. His demonic influence extended like a spider's web to every corner of society; its effects penetrated every person's mind. Compared with the power of this defendant, the scattered, desperate acts of Tōjō and Araki and their ilk are not worth mentioning; they were mere factors in this defendant's determined and fundamentally destructive power, and I'll even go so far as to say they danced unawares to his tune.

"The acts of this defendant were evil in the extreme. Why is it that in 'have-not countries' he appears as Mr. Hyde? Once he makes his appearance in countries with dense populations and scant resources, the people of these countries exhibit truly weird symptoms. In no time at all these nations lose the 'moderation and values' they've had since olden times and in the end go crazy. Even if that people once had many great virtues, it turns into a herd of sheep possessed by demons and, aiming for the depths, plunges over the cliff.

"This is Mr. Hyde. As in the tale, when he's at home in his luxurious living room, he's the fine, praiseworthy Dr. Jekyll; but when he wanders in the slums, this is what he turns into. In a rich country, Modern Civilization accomplishes sublime things, but in unfortunate countries with their various constraints, he takes this surprising form and works his evil in the places one least expects.

"Like ordinary people, this defendant was fundamentally not evil. Indeed, at his birth, he had a beautiful temperament and held promise of a brilliant future. However, as he matured, there came a time when, all of a sudden, he took on this demonic side. Even today, as Dr. Jekyll, he accomplishes astonishing achievements and maintains his noble character. But when he sets foot in the slums of the international community, he becomes inevitably this black demon.

"This important fact is still not well known.

"Even the people of 'have-not countries' still had in their mind's eye only this defendant's bright youth. So they relied on young Dr. Jekyll for their salvation. But quite unexpectedly, in such places Modern Civilization was old Mr. Hyde. People were much too naïve about this. It was only at the end of the last century and after the first Great War that some people became aware something was suspicious, but that was too general a feeling, and it was expressed only in poetic form.

"When this defendant sets foot in a 'have-not country,' he always turns into Mr. Hyde: that is truly a grave matter. For the sake of the future, too, it's something we must investigate thoroughly. The features of this late tragedy must not be forgotten, and its causes must be studied in detail. Likewise, when did the defendant come to experience this split personality? and under what condition does he take this form?—these are questions to which future scholars must devote their study.

"Here I don't propose to speak to these fundamental issues. I limit myself in today's examination to the defendant's responsibility for this recent tragedy."

## 3.

The prosecutor turned to face the dock. He continued: "I turn now to the war guilt of this defendant, and I shall begin, as Stage One, with his participation in the preparations for war, in particular his cooperation in unifying the nation ideologically."

So saying, he indicated the other thirty defendants in the dock. "As human beings, the generals and politicians sitting here do not measure up to the acts they carried out. As individuals they all are small-minded and lacking in insight—that is to say, ordinary. How could such people have become major actors in so great a human tragedy?—it's truly amazing. These men prosecuted a war that covered virtually half the earth, caused losses beyond the power of speech to say, yet stayed in power for many years and right up to the very end did not get one finger bloodied by their own countrymen. There have been far greater figures in history. But what those people did was a mere fraction of what these defendants did. The reason lies solely in the fact that they had this defendant abetting them. He lent them his great and limitless power.

"Indeed, this defendant had fearsome power.

"There are various reasons why this defendant was able to gain such power. At the moment I mention only one. That is, that the defendant took for himself all the wisdom of the ages.

"What do I mean?

"For example, consider here the telegraph, one of the weapons this defendant most prided himself on. For this machine to wield the power it does today, many people had to pour their best effort into its development. They focused their individual wisdom to produce this invention. Volta died, and Franklin, and Bell, and so did all the other inventors and developers. But their invention survived and sucked up all the wisdom of hundreds of extraordinary people and grew and continues to grow. This defendant put it at the service of generals and politicians.

"By contrast, what of normal human beings? They were not able to master their forefathers' experience. Some were able to accumulate experience by trial and error and finally attain a certain intellectual maturity, and some were not;

then they died. Each person had to begin all over again from the start. All the areas of human intellectual activity—ideas, ethics, the arts—those individuals studied and mastered in one lifetime, and then they died, and their wisdom died with them. Ordinary human beings were able, from infancy to youth, little by little, to gain or not gain a certain discrimination, and at that point they came into contact with people who wielded the awful capability that this defendant offers. So it was only natural that ordinary people lost out.

"In fact, using terms from the earliest Japanese chronicles, one defendant here, Araki, defined Japan once in a speech as 'in industry, the Land of Abundant Reed Plains and Rice Fields, in foreign policy, the Land of Peace of Mind, and in military matters, the Land of Many Beautiful Spears'; it isn't at all strange that someone might use this crude thinking to ridicule the defendants. Indeed, with minds that came from the distant past, Araki and his ilk used the weapons this defendant made available. The proof is that they saw no difference between these weapons and bamboo spears.

"In declaring his innocence at the outset of this trial, he said, 'In my seventy years of life, I have no such memory,' and he was indeed expressing his true feelings. Give Araki a Japanese sword and nothing more, and his 'faith' would be in its element and have considerable moral value. But he didn't have only the famous ancient blade he never let out of his grasp, so his faith wasn't in its element. Instead it brought about corruption on a huge scale. If you were to tell Araki himself that there was a connection between his own faith and the corruption it caused, he probably wouldn't have any idea what you were talking about.

"Thus, by offering these simple and naïve generals and politicians fearsome things, this defendant abetted them. Now to keep things simple, I'll speak about only two. They are, first, organization, and, second, weapons.

"By taking what this defendant offered, the other defendants became all powerful. Through this process these human beings came here at home to have the omnipotence of gods. They blocked the eyes and ears of the people and were able to have things completely their way.

"Those being ruled didn't have such weapons. As in olden times, they were individuals. The past had never seen such oppression of the ruled by the ruler. That the ruled were no longer able to resist the rulers is one major facet of this recent tragedy, one of its fundamental causes."

## 4.

As I listened to this examination by the prosecutor, I looked over at General Araki. Tall and erect, he sat there, unmoving as a statue. His triangular, deep-set eyes and his wedge-shaped protruding moustache were just as I had been used to seeing them in photographs. Back then throughout the land this man had stirred up such demonic force, and thanks to this Mr. Hyde, the demons he loosed had been recast in unexpected shapes and caused fearsome destruction. That's what the prosecutor was arguing.

The prosecutor continued: "First, what was this organization this defendant offered?

"Modern organization uses all the latest science. What even the ten best spies couldn't accomplish in the past can be accomplished today with a few yards of electric cord and one microscope. So even the most independent, hardiest person cannot escape modern organization's net. In ancient East Asia, sages who refused to submit to a new government could flee to the hills and survive by eating bracken. In the early modern West, Voltaire lived in Ferney near the Swiss border; when agents of the French government came, he fled to Switzerland, and when they left, he returned to Ferney, continuing his criticism of the ancien régime. But today such easy flight is no longer possible. No matter where you go, organization's net extends to all corners, and communication is by telegraph and wireless. No matter how fast you run, you can't outrun electricity. One notice goes out, and you're hauled straight before the ruler.

"The second thing the defendant offered was high-powered weapons.

"In the past, the ruler's weapons were crude. If a ruler brought virgin land under cultivation or, better, raised his flag, some opposition was possible. The citizens of Paris dug up cobblestones and piled up chairs and beds to make barricades and used hunting rifles to shoot it out with the ruler's army. Fighting for liberty and human rights, they achieved glory and honor. They shouted, "Aux armes citoyens!" and those weapons did the job. But since the February Revolution of 1848, there haven't been any such revolutions, even in Europe. They're no longer possible. The government's weapons are strong; against them there's simply no recourse. After that rulers became corrupt and collapsed from within, or they lost foreign wars, or armies that had organization and weapons equally as powerful joined the rebellion—unless it's one of those cases, no people has overthrown an oppressor and seized its freedom with its own hands. Today the fact that the Japanese people on their own didn't rise up and seize liberty and human rights is cited as proof of their inferiority, but that is not necessarily the whole truth. Such is the fate that this defendant has decreed for all oppressed peoples in modern times. In Germany, in Italy, in Japan—in all, alike, it took all the power of the Allies to overthrow their rulers. Tied up in the net of organization, without weapons to resist, these peoples didn't have enough power, and that isn't reason to fault them.

"The provision of organization and weapons: among the many crimes of this defendant, this is still relatively insignificant. But even with this alone, this defendant rendered decisive assistance to the crimes of the other defendants."

## 5.

"Moreover, the fact that modern rulers like these could strip the humanity from their people and have their way with them is not merely due to making them submit by force alone. Rather, it's because they could get the people to follow them voluntarily, with enthusiasm, actively. Rulers could now act precisely like hypnotists who put ideas into their subjects' heads and make them act as if voluntarily. This is a major difference between today's tyranny and the tyrannies of old.

"Toward this end this defendant offered them that most splendid possession of his—scholarship. He lent them political science, sociology, all the natural sciences, and even philosophy, psychology, and the rest. In accordance with the pedagogical methods these disciplines teach, organization and weapons could be deployed to greatest effect and achieved awesome efficiency. Thus the people being ruled were transformed even in the depths of their psychology and believed the prescribed worldview, either painting illusions that had no conceivable vestige of sanity, or thinking nihilism to be the way 'to live in the great and eternal principle'; it even got to the point that the people being ruled took satisfaction in jettisoning voluntarily their own humanity.

"Nietzsche says something to this effect: to rule humans is to make them enthusiastic about an idea. Isn't that a fearsome insight? The rulers of Germany, Italy, and Japan put that insight into effect. In these countries the people endorsed an idea passionately, just as their rulers wished. And in the end the people were made to dance, as if insane, to that tune. For example, here in Japan—it truly seems an illusion if you think about it—many young men didn't hesitate to insert themselves into the barrels of cannons and get shot out.

"The people, one might think, are like elephants. Elephants are large in body, strong, unmanageable if enraged; but they can be made to respond to the whim of a deft elephant trainer. So today, I think, the slender whip this elephant trainer uses is an 'idea'; does that make sense?

"This defendant taught the other defendants how to use this slender whip adroitly.

"As I mentioned before, this defendant—unlike an individual or the mass of people, who have a reputation for being even more naïve than individuals—possessed old wisdom. He realized that to the elephant trainer the ideas of individuals are an obstacle, so in order to eliminate that obstacle, he substituted ideology for thinking. Ideology is a substitute for thought. Ideology is ready-made and indoctrinated from without, but those who embrace it feel that it's very much their own thinking; moreover, they take comfort in the fact that many others share the same thinking. So it answers fundamental human needs: to think for oneself, asserting a dialectical egotism, but also to be safe—two birds killed with one stone. It is epoch-making, fanatical. It can even become a substitute for old religions. If used to praise an illusory ideal world and heap scorn on those who can be blamed for the shortcomings of the real world, it commands fearsome power.

"To instill this ideology in the elephant, the elephant trainer uses various methods. Even these methods were this defendant's doing.

"A moment ago I stated that this defendant made all fields of learning available to the rulers; I can't treat each field separately, so I mention here only one example, biology, and one principle. That is the principle of stimulus and response.

"This principle, I need hardly say, is one of the discoveries of modern biology. By and large, in the other Axis countries, biology itself contributed greatly to establishing their ideological bases, but I'll not speak about that issue. Here I wish to draw your attention to how this principle of biology was used as a method of unifying the popular mind.

"This principle teaches that in order to implant a psychological tendency in beings that learn through experience, repetition is necessary. And during that repetition, you need to accompany it with stimuli. Today's rulers knew this principle, and when they instilled ideology in the elephant, they did so always and ever with the same words. Simultaneously, they accompanied the repetition with other stimuli—privileges and fears.

"Dogs subjected to stimulus-response experiments are made to hear a certain sound at mealtime. When this sound is repeated, the dogs start to secrete gastric juices—soon even without seeing the food, merely by hearing the sound. So dogs inevitably connect a stimulus with a response that at first had no connection to it, and thus they expand their experiential knowledge.

"By the same method, a certain idea was preached to the people over and over again. And they learned that power accompanied the idea indoctrinated into them and that fear accompanied forbidden ideas. At length, when the people caught the whiff of power, that stimulus alone sufficed for them to secrete the indoctrinated idea. The more they embraced the idea, the greater the power given them, so anyone desirous of high status secreted the idea—for example, '*Blut und Boden*' [blood and land] or 'Absolute faith in victory.' And the converse—when they experience fear, it was the fault of all forbidden ideas, so they came to revile and shun them.

"Utilizing this method and mobilizing all cultural advances, the ruler waved his slender whip. How on earth could the poor elephant have resisted?"

## 6.

"However, some of the people cannot be domesticated so easily. Germany had some of these. So, too, did Japan.

"In recent years Germany sank to the very depths spiritually, but Germany being the country it is, a few people conducted themselves honorably. In Japan, even though individualism still hadn't put down strong roots, such nobility of spirit was not missing: that wasn't the case at all. And contrary to what one might expect, that nobility was exhibited by people who had acquired an old-style education. Those who had received the new *liberal* education knuckled under early for the most part, but some of the old men, on the contrary, were resolute. This was a nobility of that 'feudal character' which is bad-mouthed today. In Japan several examples allow us to say this feudal character saved liberal thought, or kept it alive. But even these individuals could not help submitting to modern organization and weapons. If they did not submit, they died meaningless deaths.

"On this point, too, this defendant bears heavy guilt. In the past, great personalities were able to hold their own against entire countries. That such people have gradually died out, that there's no way such individuals can arise today: Defendant Hyde has brought this about.

"Of course, in earlier times Germany and Italy both produced great individuals. In particular, the latter was at the forefront in awakening individuals. But the process didn't extend to the entire people. That's because they suffered the constraint of being 'have-not countries.' Not all persons could develop to their fullest: Germany and Italy ran into that constraint. People say: 'The people in these countries are still immature and don't understand the value of human life.' As a matter of fact, that's true. However, all the people were once immature. In some countries, the people enjoyed all the benefits of Modern Civilization; there Modern Civilization didn't turn into Mr. Hyde. That's because they did not experience the constraint I've just mentioned. This defendant was then still a bright young man, and when he first set foot in these countries, those peoples used this defendant's help to improve their conditions, so these countries still have leeway. There this defendant remains, as before, the respectable Dr. Jekyll.

"If in a 'have-not country' an individual human being wished to develop to the fullest, he had to fight Mr. Hyde bare-fisted. He had to reject over and over again the enticements of the ideology that pressed on his eyes and ears, not fear the threat of weapons and organization, find a way to earn his living, and keep his focus in a hectic life fixed on the human. If this person wished to be a person aware of his social responsibilities, what sort of situation was he placed in?

"The only time the ruled can resist is right at the start, when the powers of the ruler are still on the upswing. Once the ruler is in control and avails himself of what Mr. Hyde offers, it's too late. Moreover, should they be blamed all that much even if they didn't resist in this initial upsurge of power? Individuals don't have accurate information. They don't understand what's afoot at the moment. Things become known to them usually after the fact. One morning, suddenly, they read, 'Our military has been dispatched somewhere-or-other. Because of such-and-such reasons this measure is natural for national defense.' They feel a vague sense that something's wrong, but they can't tell whether that premonition is accurate or know how to protest to whom. Moreover, when it comes to their adversary's violence, political activity is precisely their adversary's profession and his vital interest. The individual is immersed in his work.

"If under these conditions one individual should decide to resist and his voice is stifled, then that's that; so in order actually to have effective resistance he must form an organization, get hold of weapons, collect information, raise money—that is, he has to become a politician. To the extent intellectuals are intellectuals, in politics they are impotent: that's a matter of course. And I can't think that all people must become politicians.

"They can't resist; they don't have information. They have no freedom of expression. This is the situation of intellectuals. In the final analysis, the ethical yardstick by which to measure intellectuals under the threat of Mr. Hyde is this: did they betray themselves?

"In fact, in places to which the evil influence of this defendant extends, the very concept of personality decays at its roots.

"In peacetime, the economy takes precedence; in wartime, politics is all. Seeing this, Mr. Hyde chuckles to himself.

"Let me add one thing here. As I said earlier, Japan's rulers had minds of the distant past. For this reason they were unable to use to good effect the weapons Mr. Hyde put at their disposal. The Japanese people were fortunate that that was the case.

"However, the Nazis were fearsome modern men. They knew to tie themselves completely to Mr. Hyde. Earlier in Germany there had been an age of neo-Kantianism. Consciously it purged all human elements and viewed everything solely in terms of a mental calculus. That's why Germany before the Great War was able to escape danger to its economic livelihood. But the other side of the coin was that it produced an inhumanity that was dangerous in the extreme. Indeed, Mr. Hyde availed himself of it. So the Nazi leaders accomplished demonic deeds much vaster than those of the Japanese."

## 7.

"Gentlemen of the Court, in this court we pass judgment in the name of civilization. We take this as an honor, as a point of pride.

"We revere civilization and worship its noble side. And we believe that this civilization of ours is pure in every respect, that its light will guide humanity forever.

"We embrace civilization in the form of Dr. Jekyll. We lament the fact that in several countries of the world it has taken the form of Mr. Hyde. To destroy its curse for the sake of the future is a great task assigned all humankind. To that end we must investigate civilization's Mr. Hyde exhaustively.

"Thus far I've argued as follows: if we set him for a moment in the ranks of the other defendants, this defendant offered them advantages, so he's guilty. Even in this context, the defendant's guilt, I have argued, is large. But the matter isn't so simple that this concludes it. The above is indeed only the very first stage of the accusation.

"When I think of it, I can't help lamenting, but indeed, the very fact that rulers like the thirty defendants before this court sprang up is itself the defendant Mr. Hyde's doing. He is not on the same level as they; he is their birth parent. When he appears in 'have-not countries' as Mr. Hyde, people of this ilk always spring up: the most recent history of the world attests this.

"Why, when Modern Civilization appears in 'have-not countries,' does he metamorphose into Mr. Hyde? When, under what conditions, does this metamorphosis take place? Does it give birth to rulers like these? At least, did it give birth? These are not just questions of morality, that people in some countries had bad attitudes and refused to obey what, in 'have countries,' Dr. Jekyll said. It is, I believe, a fundamental problem, and people in more fortunate countries, who have been spared Mr. Hyde, must also join in giving it thought."

The prosecutor made to continue his summation, but time had come for a break. Together with the other defendants, Mr. Hyde stood at his seat and turned away into the narrow hall leading to the holding cell.

It was so extraordinary a trial I left the courtroom in a daze, as if I'd been dreaming.

—October 1946

# Letter to Judge Röling

*Takeyama wrote "The Trial of Mr. Hyde" in the early days of the trial. "Letter to Judge Röling" followed the verdicts. B. V. A. Röling was the Dutch representative on the Tokyo bench. Takeyama had come to know him during the trial and maintained contact with him thereafter. This essay lays out some of the themes Takeyama pursued later in* Showa: Psychology of An Era *(1956), but unlike that quite scholarly work, this essay addresses the issue of war guilt in very personal terms.*

*When this essay appeared in the August 1949 issue of the national magazine* Shinchō, *its title was "Dirty Hands: Letter to Judge Röling."*

Mr. Röling, the Dutch judge at the Tokyo trial, was a man of simple scholarly mien, a "European" one respected on first contact. Koeber[1] gives the characteristics of the personality he favors: "simple, good, calm, quiet, educated . . . and a bit old-fashioned in both living and thinking." Röling fit this image to a tee. He was also a competent violinist and enjoyed playing trios almost weekly at the home of an acquaintance of mine. Though not technically all that good, his playing had a true musicality that came straight from the heart.

He and I talked to each other of our wartime experiences in our respective countries. I said, "I think some of those now on trial are scapegoats," and he

---

1. Raphael Koeber (1848–1923), a German, was professor of philosophy at Tokyo Imperial University beginning in 1893.

listened calmly, not voicing his own opinion. But he did talk about the situation of the Dutch under German occupation.

When the trial judgment was handed down, as reported in the press, he was in the minority and issued a dissent. The verdict was appealed to the U.S. Supreme Court. That happened just as he was very busy with departure, about to return to the Netherlands, and he said, "I think they'll not hear the appeal, but if they do, I'll be back. I want to know what the Japanese think, so please write me your thoughts." And he gave me a copy of the 249-page opinion he'd submitted to the supreme commander for the Allied Powers, General Douglas MacArthur.

The appeal was not heard,[2] nor did I send him my thoughts. What I'm writing here is the draft I wrote then, shortened in parts and lengthened in others.

Honored Judge,

You asked me for my reflections as a Japanese on the outcome of the Tokyo trial, so I'm writing these thoughts.

Indeed, after reading your Opinion, I have virtually nothing to say. About some events I had thought, "Wasn't such-and-such likely the case?" and in your Opinion it was all argued out with evidence and clear analysis and reasoning. That being so, let me set down some more general reflections. I have neither qualification nor knowledge to discuss the judgment in legal terms. But as a human being, I can't repress the following reflections.

During those years everything happened behind heavy doors, out of our sight. What's become clear now was wholly unclear then. Day after day we simply trembled in fear, struck dumb with astonishment at incomprehensible developments. Still, I experienced that history from start to finish, pursuing it or being pursued by it. With each separate development we reasoned back from results, imagining causes. Asking about the situation from "those in the know," we compared observations with friends. Above all, we pondered the meaning of what happened in our vicinity. And we built up our own—vague—ideas about the whole process.

Working from these ideas, I couldn't help having misgivings about views on several points that of late have circulated among the public at large. But lacking any concrete basis for my assertions, I could only embrace my doubts in silence. In particular, given the outcome of the trial, I had no way of resolving doubts I'd held all along.

The Opinion you gave me resolved all those doubts. It was a true pleasure to read.

---

2. The U.S. Supreme Court ruled that it lacked jurisdiction.

To mention the points in your Opinion that interest me in particular, you divide the era leading up to the war into three stages. The first is the period in which, via threats and assassinations at home and uncontrolled independent action abroad, one part of the military advanced its aims. The second is the period in which the state as a whole was united finally in pursuit of the goal of controlling East Asia and was divided, as to means to that end, into those who would rely on military might and those who would rely on peaceful methods. The third is the period in which military force was decided on as government policy (initially as a last resort, should the government conclude that peaceful means had no prospect of success). You study each person's actions and intent in each of these stages, adding three defendants to the list of those who should be condemned to death and concluding that five were innocent.

Throughout this era (I'm speaking as simply and schematically as possible) Japanese politicians faced the threat of assassination and domestic insurrection. Even short of coup d'état or revolution, to be "cold-shouldered" by the "will of the military" was a grave matter for the country. Without the agreement or permission of that part of the military, they couldn't reach any decision at all. Even if they weren't afraid of being assassinated, they had no hope of success; they might stake all, but their all was the only thing at stake. In fact, many people lacked sufficient courage, but it was not a situation that can be wrapped up morally by saying, "They lacked sufficient courage." If domestic insurrection did occur, those forces would surely emerge victorious, and there was no doubt that should that happen, foreign war would result. The categorical imperative was to avoid domestic insurrection. Operating within the constraints of this imperative, those in responsible positions had to find some means of escaping the dilemma.

The only way to prevent domestic insurrection was a policy of appeasement. It was just like what Chamberlain did with Hitler. Until England armed itself, the British prime minister made concession after concession. Having no way of arming themselves against the military, the Japanese politicians made concession after concession. They chose the lesser evil. So they assuaged the military, granting its wishes to a degree and satisfying it, and in return requested that military discipline be reestablished; bought time; and waited for likely changes in the situation . . . that was the only course open to them. They accepted the military's demand—control of East Asia—and made its goal their own, but how to achieve that goal was a different matter, and please have patience: they took this course, yet in the end it was the road to war that they made possible, and in hindsight, that's what in fact happened. But it was certain that if domestic rebellion arose, the upshot would be war, and this way war was still no more than a possibility, might even be prevented. Strengthening the power of the prime minister by creating one consolidated political party: this method, too, wound up on the contrary with the consolidated party swallowed up by the military. Putting key military men in positions of authority and having them keep the military in check, this led on the contrary to the opening of hostilities. All these were fruitless attempts by the powerless to restrain the powerful.

I lived through that era, and I have to think that these were counsels of desperation to prevent domestic insurrection on the one hand, and avoid war on the other.

What's more, the force that really counted did not show itself openly. Apart from the final scene—the opening of hostilities—it refused throughout. At first, it was an anonymous force with a strength that was hard to grasp clearly, and even after that force finally assumed shape, this "driving force" hid in the shadows and forced others to take responsibility. All decisions were issued in the name of the government; at home and abroad the appeasers made the will of the "driving force" known as their own will.

At the time those who truly thought responsibly couldn't say, "That's not the kind of role I want to play" and run away. They had to avoid dividing the country at a time it faced tensions with foreign countries, and they worried about what would happen if incompetent men of ambition occupied those positions. Above all, they had to preserve peace and order. The military, too, wanted for its puppets men as skilled as possible, with a sense of responsibility, credibility abroad, and the ability to sway the nation.

This happened in many arenas. On a very small scale I observed it myself close to home. The headmaster of the school at which I taught was a known opponent of the ultranationalists, and when he let slip word of his intention to resign, people said: "If you resign now, opportunists who have been aiming for this post will succeed you. Please do stay and protect what can be protected." Preserving one's purity by giving up the post, while perhaps not quite egotistical, was hardly the most honorable course.

Nor was that all. At the time the more appropriate manly attitude was rather to plunge into the ranks of the adversary and work from within. "Today Japan has gone off the tracks and is a runaway train. If we can't stop it, rather than sit in a passenger car, complaining and backbiting, we should climb up into the engine, stay the reckless hand of the engineer, and try to get the train back on track." This was the only road still open that might achieve results. Men of the greatest conscience had to cooperate with the bad guys to save the day. For a while, the outbreak of war was blocked, and it was only because of what these people did; one couldn't have asked that of men with clean hands.

Under such conditions, those most free of guilt joined in the crime. They became accomplices.

The people I'm talking of were never many in number, but they did exist.

In order somehow to save the peace, one man joined the cabinet when the specter of war loomed on condition that negotiations continue. For a while he thought about resigning but held off upon being warned, "If you resign, your successor as foreign minister will be someone who favors the immediate opening of hostilities." And in order to stay in that post and pursue his ends, he had to concede the principle, "If I see that peaceful methods show no prospect of success, I'll agree to war." . . . Again, one man joined a wartime cabinet in order to bring speedy peace. . . . Such acts were in fact attempts to fulfill international duties, not infractions against international duties: I can't thank you enough for perceiving this.

It's truly astonishing how intricately responsibility and guilt entwine. These men all atoned for their offenses, and one went silently to his death. Facing death, he said, "Since I was young I have devoted myself to the tasks of the day, taking things as they come. Dying, too, I shall take as it comes." People say he gained this peace of mind from the Eastern practice of Zen; as a Japanese, I take quiet pride in him.[3]

Such people have probably always existed in the world of men. Isaiah 53 writes of a man "wounded for our transgressions": "But he was wounded for our transgressions, he was bruised for our iniquities; upon him was the chastisement that made us whole, and with his stripes we are healed. . . . He was oppressed, and he was afflicted, yet he opened not his mouth; like a lamb that is led to the slaughter, and like a sheep that before its shearers is dumb, so he opened not his mouth. By oppression and judgment he was taken away; and as for his generation, who considered that he was cut off out of the land of the living?"

I had long thought that guilt and retribution were matters solely of the individual's conscience. Unless on examining his own conscience the individual blamed himself, guilt and retribution should be disallowed. But the war taught me that isn't so. One atones for the sins of others, and those others don't recognize his tribulations: when a person acts with great sincerity, this is sometimes unavoidable.

Again, the war made me sense acutely that there are realities that can't be worked out in terms of individual conscience.

---

3. The unnamed men described in these two paragraphs are, respectively, Tōgō Shigenori, Shigemitsu Mamoru, and Hirota Kōki. For Röling's comments on these men, all of whom Röling argued were innocent, see Röling's opinion in *Tokyo Major War Crimes Trial: The Records of the International Military Tribunal for the Far East*, ed. R. John Pritchard (124 vols., Lewiston, NY: Edwin Mellen, 1999): Tōgō (109:244–49), Shigemitsu (109:234–37), Hirota (109:192–93).

We cannot escape collective indictment. We have to accept as our own the crimes committed by the group—nation, race—to which we belong. None of us can escape this restraint, not even those who opposed mistaken national policy, not even children. It is terrible to see many children today going hungry, sick, homeless. There are many ways in which we atone for the sins of our parents, our children, our brothers and sisters, our husbands, our wives, and that's natural; but we must atone also for the sins of those more distant from us. There is no limit to our responsibility. It seems to inhere in our very existence. The Nazis practiced collective indictment—"Jews deserve to be punished because they are Jews." This, it need hardly be said, is utterly unjust and unfair. But in fact this is something wrapped up inescapably in the human condition. We should exert every effort to do away with it, but no matter how rational the world becomes, man can't escape from this issue of the relation between "individual and society," a relation set out insistently in totalitarian state thinking.

In order to live and work, we must accept what from the standpoint of reason and the individual conscience is unacceptable. We must reconcile ourselves to the fact that our very existence and actions themselves already involve guilt. Moreover, we are involved all our lives in relations with authority, and we are at the mercy of its will. Recognizing that this enigma is a fact, we must shape our own meaningful acts in this world atop this irrationality, despite it.

Urgent voices clamor, rushing to rational explanations: "It's not enigmatic. It's not irrational. It's because you people were obsequious! Because you were cowardly, supine! Because, on account of these accursed national characteristics, you made your peace with it, cooperated with it, didn't act!"

Sometimes I ask myself: "Am I guilty? Not guilty?"

I respond: "I'm a nobody, and I had little responsibility; I watched from the sidelines how those with great responsibility agonized, but I myself escaped that burden."

A voice inside me speaks: "That's your accidental good fortune. Such self-denigration is a moral evasion. Answer in terms of yourself as an individual."

I: "I was a bystander. I didn't cooperate; I didn't resist. Even now, thinking in terms of results, it would have made no sense to cooperate in a war that was doomed to defeat, and it would have been senseless to resist when resistance would have been hushed up. So what should I have done? Did I have any alternative to watching from the sidelines? In groups, I went along meekly, but that was mere gesture, like donning an army cap. In the company of a few friends I said very critical things. And inside, I continued to agonize."

The voice: "It's clearly a sin that you didn't express those views publicly."

I: "I couldn't go public. Open criticism wasn't permitted. At the time I didn't write, but had I written, I couldn't have published. And I couldn't have spoken out. If in fact publication had been possible, there would surely have been a great many voices out there. And as a people as a whole, we expressed our opinion. When one judges the Japanese, it makes no sense, it's wrong, to judge according to attitudes once the fascist system had come into being, as happens all the time these days. One should judge according to the attitudes before the transition to fascism. Seen from that standpoint, the Japanese didn't submit all that easily. In the general election at the time of the Okada cabinet, the antimilitarist factions won overwhelmingly. As a result, it was overturned by coup d'état. In the case of the unrest at the time of the Saitō speech and the aborting of the Ugaki cabinet, or public opinion at the time of the resignation of the Hayashi cabinet, had the two sides been of equal power, it would have been fully effective. At the time of the Yokusan election, knowing full well that it would be useless, I voted for Saitō Takao, in another voting district.[4] I thought that if there were many such votes, that too would be a statement of opinion. At the time this was the only way—perhaps not legal but not prohibited—to express an opinion. To choose illegal means was to take action not as a single citizen but as a politician; to what degree, I ask you, were we duty-bound to become politicians? I fulfilled my duty as one member of civil society, held a professional job, had a family; I had no talents in that direction, and I got no accurate news. They undertook political activity as their sole passion; they had organization and weapons and propaganda. Moreover, if what people are saying now is true, much illegal opposition did take place at the time.

"Above all, we were told nothing! What we were told was no more than explanations of faits accomplis, with reasons appended. At the Tokyo trial, a decision was made not to recognize the credibility of the proclamations of the Japanese government to its own people and to foreign countries, but those proclamations were all we had to go on. We couldn't form an opinion about anything. Usually we were driven forward, ever forward, in a vague, dense cloud of doubt. Get up in the morning; read the newspaper. There in large print: 'Our forces seized such-and-such place. . . . This was an unavoidable preventive measure. Had we not done so, our forces might have been wiped out.' Or 'The new prime minister hopes single-mindedly for peace. Toward that end the nation must muster its total strength. In this crisis, this is

---

4. Okada was prime minister 1934 to 1936; Hirota was prime minister 1936 to 1937; Ugaki was nominated to be prime minister in January 1937; Hayashi was prime minister in 1937. In a Diet speech Saitō Takao criticized the military immediately after the February 26 Incident; the Yokusan (Imperial Rule Assistance Association) election was in 1942.

the only way to maintain peace.' That's the kind of stuff we were told—about things abroad and things at home. Until after the defeat, we thought the Imperial Japanese Navy was in good shape.

"As a rule our judgments could not go beyond abstract conjecture. Through the whole period, the only concrete facts I myself knew firsthand were these: I had traveled to North China and been to Yungang. A small detachment of troops was stationed there, and an old woman worked in the canteen. At the time of the Marco Polo Bridge Incident, she had been in Chengdu as a volunteer nurse, and she told me what happened: 'Beginning two days before the incident, the Japanese army in Chengdu began to move, loaded rice onto many camels, cut through the detached palace that normally was out of bounds, and in the middle of the night advanced ever southward. The large numbers were surprising, and I thought to myself—Japan, too, has all this machinery.' On hearing this, I concluded for the first time that the incident had been the work of the Japanese side.[5]

"When over a long period of time a nation has been under the influence of managed public opinion, one-sided and stripped of all basis for judgment, how can any nation—not only Japan—continue to have sound judgment? Is it possible to sit in judgment on a people governed by totalitarian systems of the modern type? Where fundamental human rights are not recognized, does moral responsibility arise? Where there is only the freedom to go to jail and the freedom to die?"

The voice: "That may be so for ordinary people. But weren't you an intellectual of a sort? Weren't you 'wrapped in deep skepticism'? And isn't it the case that beyond being skeptical you did nothing, attempted nothing? Intellectuals in other countries did more."

I: "What shaped our fate was something truly strange. It was like the 'wriggling demons' of the old tales, something we couldn't get a firm grip on. It was not like the clear-cut situation in other countries.

"Our government was legitimate to the end; foreign countries recognized it and negotiated with it. Until the war all disputes were settled through formal government-to-government negotiations. Foreign countries knew the facts far better than we did, and they had power. They weren't controlled as we were. And even those other countries expected, as did we, that sooner or later Japan would come to its senses. In fact, such efforts were undertaken in Japan. If we were to resist, the target should have been not the government but those operating behind the scenes, and the issue of power aside, they didn't show their faces, and we had no way of knowing what decisions were being made where.

---

5. Marco Polo Bridge Incident: on July 7, 1937, fighting broke out between Chinese and Japanese forces just outside Beijing. The incident escalated into all-out war.

"What does it mean to blame a person retroactively, after the fact, for not having been able to know at the time how the forces governing him would change in the future? The future is truly a sealed book. (At that time, if there were discussions, in particular about the future, between those who relied on spirit and those who relied on matériel, the former always triumphed.) If we had known then what we know now, when all that transpired has become known, all of us would have taken a different attitude. But is a people to be blamed for not having that insight? 'Even the prime minister didn't know how the military planned to act or with what aim. Even the Army Minister couldn't guess.'" (Konoe diary.)

Voice: "Don't you admit your own lack of courage?"

I: "I admit it. But when a person knows that sacrificing himself will have absolutely no effect, does he have a moral duty to do so anyway? I think one has a duty to fight violence, but must he fight violence no matter what the conditions? Isn't it rather our moral duty to work not on something completely hopeless but to save and protect what little is still within our power to save and protect? I'm not saying I did that. But I can't believe that under such conditions, the absence of foolhardy bravery automatically constitutes positive guilt."

Voice: "So you think you're innocent?"

I: "Yes, rationally."

Voice: "What about your countrymen's atrocities? Don't you feel somehow complicit in that crime?"

I: . . .

Voice: "During those difficult days you thought only of yourself. When others—young men—were called up and departed, you were glad, somehow, that it wasn't you. And you did nothing that was doomed to fail. Are you entirely at peace with that? Don't you have even a bad aftertaste?"

I: . . .

Voice: "One more key point. Through accidental good fortune, you were a nobody, without status, someone utterly beneath notice. But if you had been in a position of responsibility, in those conditions would you have entered the other camp and worked with it to steer things in the proper direction? Would you have climbed up into the cab of the runaway train to stay the hand of the engineer? As a result of choosing between two evils, would you have become a confederate in the crime, realizing the guilt that inheres inescapably in existing and acting, and afterwards, cursed and scorned, gone silently to your death? A friend you respect wrote, 'Intellectuals are people resigned to their own meaningless deaths,' that is, to martyrdom. It's certainly true that man fulfills himself by atoning for the sins of others. Did you do that?"

I: "No, I didn't."

Voice: "If in the future you are in that situation, will you?"

I: "I'd want to try. But I don't know if I could. Frankly, I have my doubts."

Voice: "I hand down my judgment. Rationally, you're indeed innocent. But according to another code of laws, I pronounce you guilty."

Honored Judge,

We committed many crimes. In order to start over, Japanese must atone and be cleansed.

But come to think of it, this guilt is complicated, difficult to pin down—in its essence, in its reach, in the locus of responsibility. As one who lived through that era, I think it goes without saying that those representatives of the military condemned to death were guilty (going by your evidence, all but one general), but I can't help feeling that in the last analysis anonymous, amorphous forces were responsible. The young officers in the grip of a paranoid ideology. The ideologues who stirred them up. These are all parts of an intangible social mood. Unfortunately, those people had weapons. And the preceding era's corruption, its dead end, and such factors as the prohibition on emigration, the threat and attraction of communism, the bloc economies internationally—these offered fertile soil for their passions.

The fact that Japanese in general obeyed the orders of the state, submitted, and so became the cause of much guilt—that's very bitter, but it goes back, after all, to this. Japanese were not able to awake to the fact that "when one's country loses its true spirit, it is no longer one's country. The country itself is not the ultimate goal; when it destroys your humanity, it should be disavowed." Told the "country is at stake," they banded together—that, too, played its part; but they didn't consider that even should the country go under, they'd save their humanity. They did not discern with sound judgment the true nature of the ideas indoctrinated into them by all methods, one-sidedly, nor did they have the courage to resist overwhelming, modern power.

We can't escape this indictment, and it's a severe one. We weren't occupied, like France, by a foreign country. Nor, like Germany and Italy, were we subject over a distinct period to the despotism of a force that published its platform. It was carried out with methods that on their face were entirely legitimate, with window dressing; it established itself over many years through complicated struggles and very gradually, as irreversible faits accomplis, and we became aware of its true nature only after the cataclysm. Now, thinking back, we can say, "It shouldn't have happened," but at the time all these things were unknowns, things that might or might not happen. Yes, we weren't brave, but to say that in the latter half of the period there was no resistance—there are many extenuating circumstances.

Japanese committed so many crimes they shocked themselves. We even had a predisposition to guilt. Knowing this, we can only be ashamed and have no words to apologize. The abuse of the freedom we still had in a free era, the corruption, the reaction that arose against them, excessive trust in the military, then flattery and opportunism, then knuckling under, chauvinism latent everywhere, a voluntarism bordering on dementia, torture long practiced domestically, unspeakably atrocious behavior abroad . . . these things are all targeted for blame now and ridiculed as national characteristics, as the consequence of the congenital inferiority of the Japanese.

These things are indisputably both Japanese weaknesses and weaknesses of humanity itself, laid particularly and painfully bare under those conditions. They are probably far more universal than is currently being said. I hope the present Japanese self-hatred contributes to a true cleansing.

Dying to atone for the guilt of others, that's what young men sentenced to death as war criminals did overseas and what aged politicians did at home; they must become a valuable sacrificial offering for this cleansing.

You came to Japan and recognized—even admired—our virtues. Seeing the Japanese, you said, "Such a people will surely pick themselves up again." But you wondered, "How could these Japanese have committed such atrocities?" I want to reflect further on the Japanese, who, like all peoples, have their virtues and their failings. For the many kind intentions you showed us, I express deep appreciation and respect.

—June 1949

Part IV

# TURN TO THE RIGHT

~

# The Student Incident:
# Observations and Reflections

*Until 1950 Komaba, just west of Tokyo's Shibuya Station, was the site of Ichikō. Takeyama had taught there since 1926. But the postwar reorganization of Japanese education turned Ichikō into the General Studies Division (the first two years) of the new Tokyo University, formerly Tokyo Imperial University. Takeyama taught there for one year, retiring in 1951 in his mid-forties.*

*This essay describes the student boycott at the Komaba campus in September 1950. The events Takeyama describes here contributed to his turn to the right. The essay appeared first in the December 1950 issue of one of the most influential journals of the day, Chūō kōron, so Takeyama must have written it virtually overnight.*

*World events had a direct influence on this essay. The "incident" took place in late September and early October of 1950. In late June of that year the Korean War broke out; in November President Harry S Truman made it known he was consider-ing the use of atomic bombs in that war. And in Japan, the American Occupation was far into its "reverse course," the move to the right that undid many early reforms and antagonized much of the Japanese Left. The Red Purge Takeyama mentions was the second of two major Occupation purges. The first, in early 1946, barred some 200,000 people from public office—for example, school principals—on the assump-tion that they had been part of the wartime establishment. The second, in 1950, targeted leftists, particularly members of the Communist Party.*

*Tokyo University was not Takeyama's beloved Ichikō. The student body was larger and less inclined to revere the faculty; it did not carry forward the traditions of Ichikō. And if this essay is any indication, Takeyama's attitude toward the students had changed dramatically. Here we find a real contempt for the student agitators. Not only contempt, but also fear: Takeyama sees the student boycott as "one manifesta-tion of the international revolutionary movement" and the student leaders as "petty*

*Hitlers." Within months, in "Those Who Refuse to Enter the Gate" (the next and final translation in this volume), Takeyama will conclude that students who refuse to cross the picket line are siding with the Soviet Union in the Cold War. Freedom is at stake: "For the sake of freedom, adopt a certain intolerance, and for the sake of peace, discard nonresistance."*

⌒

What I myself observed of the student incident that began September 29 relates to the General Studies Division of Tokyo University, and it was a small coup d'état. The student "exam boycott" or "riot" shocked the public, but more important than the specific manifestation is its underlying meaning. This incident is the sum total of long years of effort the left wing has directed at students, and I think it may change our schools permanently.

In the past such incidents had prehistories lasting several months and reached their denouement only after many ups and downs, but this time the prehistory lasted only a few days. The incident was planned in great detail and in secret, and once it erupted, for several days the organization and power of the left-wing students ruled a substantial portion of the campus. Four days earlier, in protest against the Red Purge the student general assembly had approved a boycott of the exams. The next day the dean summoned the student government chair and warned him that a boycott was illegal. There is a handbill from the student side reporting these events; it depicts well the overall atmosphere of this incident, so let me reproduce it in full.

### The Dean Has Decided on Punishment!

At 12:30 p.m. on the twenty-sixth Dean Yanaihara suddenly demanded a meeting with the chair of the student government, and it was held in the dean's office. At the Administration Building, some 450 students listened to broadcast reports of the meeting.

The dean took up first the point that placards and notices on campus and elsewhere were put up without prior notice to school authorities and demanded to know who had posted them. The chair of the student government refused to respond but said the signs were legitimate since they were in accord with the student government's decision; as for the dean's statement on the issue of notification, that in terms of the college's bylaws the signs merited punishment, it was of course the chair's duty to carry out the decision of the student government not to obey bylaws that differed not at all from the Peace Preservation Law. In passing, the dean declared that the council of student governments of newly created universities that had convened on campus the previous day was a gathering without prior notice and a grave step, and that he would like to discuss the matter; the chair replied that he was under no obligation to respond to questioning that called to mind the behavior of the Thought Police.[1]

As far as concerns the core issue—the exam boycott—the dean said, "I won't postpone the exams, much less call a faculty meeting. If the boycott proceeds, I'll punish those responsible." With firm resolve, the chair said, "We'll boycott! In accordance with the student government decision, if you punish people, we'll call an indefinite general strike." Demand of this dean the following three things:

1. That he give his word not to conduct a Red Purge;
2. That he convene a democratic faculty body with decisions by secret ballot;
3. That he not punish the leaders of the just struggle!

Defend progressive faculty and the student government chair, and protest resolutely to the dean!

We did read this handbill, but none of us dreamed that these threats would become reality on such a scale three days later.

On that morning, when I got to Shibuya Station,[2] school employees were passing out handbills the school had printed to those headed for campus. These handbills carried a map and read, "Boycotting students have established a picket line at the main gate, and you can't get in that way, so enter via such-and-such gates." The broad campus has a number of gates, and the handbill indicated two. I transferred to the Inokashira Line and got off at the campus station; students were standing in a line shouting to those heading for school, "Go to the back gate! The back gate!" I thought these were antiboycott students leading us to the two gates the school had indicated. So I joined the line and shouted with them, "Go to the back gate! The back gate!" After a bit I decided to enter the campus myself and walked between the lines of students distributing handbills and shouting. To my surprise, the destination to which the lines smoothly channeled us was neither of the two gates the school had indicated. Those forming the lines were students in

---

1. Yanaihara Tadao (1893–1961), scholar of colonial politics and Christian pacifist, had been expelled from Tokyo Imperial University in 1937 for his antimilitarist stand. The Peace Preservation Law (1925) outlawed groups advocating change in the polity. The Thought Police were wartime Japan's agency charged with monitoring public (and private) attitudes.

2. Coming north by train from his home in Kamakura, Takeyama would have transferred at Shibuya to the Inokashira Line, which has a stop adjacent to the Komaba campus.

favor of the strike, not students against the strike. Those heading for school had been channeled between cleverly constructed dikes; though suspicious, we had no way to resist, and all of us were led into the large cafeteria.

Here there were already several hundred students who had been lured in. In front of the cafeteria a firm picket line was set up, and access from the cafeteria to the school was cut off. Those heading for school had been neatly interned. Moreover, the road leading off campus from the cafeteria was open, so there could be no charge of illegal confinement.

Realizing my egregious mistake, I tried to squeeze between the pickets and get to school. The students who had linked arms averted their eyes, shook their heads from side to side silently, and wouldn't let me through; but one student who appeared to be the leader for this sector saw the situation and came running up. Very courteously, he said, "We're to let in teachers who don't actively oppose us," and he opened a gap in the human fence. I was surprised too by the relation of command and obedience that obtained at this spot between sector leader and foot soldiers; according to what I heard later, the logic was that this picket line let teachers through even as it kept students out, so it didn't obstruct the official duty of administering the exams.[3]

In times of revolution and coups d'état, is there always a curious confusion about who is on which side? In articles about the French Revolution, I've read that such was the case, and I recalled my own experience a dozen years earlier. At the time of the February 26 Incident, a friend and I had walked about Nagata-chō.[4] As we hung about with the curious onlookers in the menacing atmosphere, I realized I was quite at sea: I couldn't tell which of the soldiers standing about all over were rebels and which were loyal troops. Even the detachment camped outside the prime minister's residence, I couldn't tell whether they were occupying it or defending it. At one place they said, "We're not here just for show!" so we realized for the first time that they were rebels. Here and there on the snow-covered roads machine guns were emplaced, and we didn't know how to get through, so we asked an infantry scout standing there. He belonged to the rebels, and he had probably been ordered, "Treat people with courtesy." Polite in the extreme, he told us, "Over by Metropolitan Police Headquarters it's dangerous. Please go via Akasaka Mitsuke."

In the cafeteria the several hundred interned students were raising loud, unhappy voices. They had numbers but no organization, so they were completely under control. This was the meeting site for all-student assem-

---

3. Professors at Japan's state universities (as in France and Italy) were—are—public officials.
4. Tokyo's Nagata-chō, site then and now of government offices, was the scene of the army revolt in February 1936.

blies—that was the rationale for leading the students here. Activists were giving stirring harangues. "The campus demonstration yesterday at Waseda University ended in suppression by armed police, and several dozen students were arrested. The sacrosanct campus was trampled on by police whose muddy boots were made in America. This repression means that the Red Purge is the enemy's final assault. On-campus assemblies should be immune to police interference. Why in the world can't students sing songs and march on campus? Friends! Remember that the suppression of the student movement was the last step leading to war! If we're defeated now, the tragedy of the student-soldiers who died in the Pacific War will be repeated . . . " The huge cafeteria, with concrete floor below and steel beams above, resounded to applause and shouts.

Later, several professors went to the cafeteria in an attempt to bring out the interned exam takers. From cafeteria windows behind the picket line, interned students leaned out and seemed to be awaiting us. But then the leader of the picket line confronted us, pointed to the ground under our feet, and said in angry tones: "There's no crossing this line!"

It's no tale of courage, but addressed in this manner, I stopped. At such times a language professor who had never fought anyone face-to-face was quite at a loss. A young man, naïve and forlorn barely a year earlier, now had grasped the authority to direct several hundred people, blocked our way with menacing looks, ordered us about in a threatening manner, and we quailed before him.

When in the midst of the heated give-and-take the time came for decisions, this leader always sent a runner asking "headquarters" for directions. Somewhere they had a hidden government, probably outsiders to the university, and their orders had absolute authority over the students.

A student came by. One of those who favored taking the exam, he had got onto campus by slipping through a fence somewhere. The leader challenged him and, looking back at his underlings, yelled: "He's one of them. Follow him!"

I scolded him, saying students shouldn't spy on students. In response, he asserted forcefully the justice of their resistance to the state. These were his firm views: Everything the state does is by coercion. Extreme steps are necessary against it. The people to blame are those who made it necessary to take these steps. Then he added: What we're doing isn't violence. Only those in authority can wield violence; we who are oppressed can't wield violence. What's more, if the majority decision of the student government isn't permitted, doesn't that mean the authorities no longer recognize any student freedom at all?

We didn't succeed in freeing the students.

Somehow or other, a good many students have come to believe they are constantly persecuted. Their harangues are in part an admission of this sense of threat. Instilling in the masses the illusion that they are victims is said to be a contemporary political art, so it may be effective for student politicians to instill that sense. At school, unless the acts are absolutely intolerable (even if they are), punishment or prohibition can't be carried out, yet the students think the school always manipulates all policies and restricts their freedom. Therein lies a completely baseless illusion. "By these unjust means the enemy takes revenge for our actions in fighting official oppression"—this assertion is repeated constantly. "The enemy has already taken aim. Now he has only to pull the trigger"—such words are highly effective.

This time around, improper demands were rejected and illegal assemblies forbidden. These acts were promptly perceived as oppression. The prehistory—why had things turned out this way?—was not an issue. So the upshot was, "If we're not allowed an absolutely free hand, we're being persecuted." Their concept of freedom is a particular one: freedom usually takes the form of resistance, and freedom cannot be regulated by law. "All law is created unilaterally and applied unilaterally by those in authority": they assert this as social science theory, but I have the sense it is first and foremost the Oedipus complex that young men of this age have. And politicians take advantage of these adolescent emotions.

Of the victimhood they mouth, the only part that sounds sincere and deserves sympathy is that they may be drawn into war.

Forming the other side of this coin of sense of oppression is their overweening confidence, which is shocking. It may have something to do with the bold front they put up to hide their sense of powerlessness. They have an exalted sense that they know everything and can—should—decide everything. Seen through their eyes, what pitiful creatures the school authorities are! "We ourselves know better about peace and freedom. It's not an issue of the petty regulations the school is a stickler for; with an exam boycott of the sort Prague students and Chinese students carried out to good effect earlier, we're out ultimately to paralyze the state, starting with a nationwide boycott and sabotage. And we've got a broader international consciousness. With links to the student international, National Federation[5] has rich data and resources. It's riding a more inevitable wave of history. Adults don't accept the ideal society of a certain foreign country we know of, even as a castle in

---

5. *Zengakuren* (National Federation of Students' Self-Government Associations) is the Japanese association of student organizations; it had links to the pro-Soviet International Union of Students that had its base in Prague. The "take-the-exam" faction Takeyama mentioned earlier was the Democratic Union, an anticommunist group.

the air; but how greatly our trust in it inspires us! Above all, we've got real power. On this campus, we're the only power. The school doesn't lift a finger against us. We can mobilize all the students!"

At the beginning of summer, I had heard one of the influential politicized students say, "According to reports now reaching us, the world situation is becoming very tense." He wasn't speaking nonchalantly, as a teacher might, and indeed, several days later the Korean War broke out. Afterward someone remarked, "Sure, they understand better—their side started it."

This student played up the fact that they had to set the exam boycott for that date because the Red Purge was to be carried out beginning in early October. But the Red Purge could not be carried out then. Complaints arose from students who had been stirred up for the boycott. So he claimed, "We boycotted, and the enemy chickened out and postponed it."

When he demands a meeting with the dean, he takes many other students with him, and to the official in charge of student affairs who says he "cannot accept the decision of an illegal meeting," he declares angrily, "If you say we can't meet, we'll meet through the power of the 3,800 students who support me and show you! We'll force the dean to answer!"

Ordinarily it would be unthinkable for students to threaten the school in this way, but now such things happen.

This student incident had two highly conspicuous features. First, the exam boycott was decided on by majority vote; second, the action corps made their debut.

September 29 as exam date was set on April 17 by the academic calendar, established then at the beginning of the school year. Even simply as a bureaucratic matter, administering an exam to four thousand people is no easy affair, and preparations were already in train. But on September 20 a postponement was suddenly requested on the grounds that the exam inconvenienced demonstrations against the Red Purge; in denying the request, according to the students' terms, the school "launched a preemptive strike."

These were truly outrageous words, and a resolution was attached: "If people are punished for this, we'll protest by going on indefinite strike."

How such a resolution became a majority decision and governed the whole is an issue of major significance. They did seize cleverly on the exams, which absolutely everyone hates, and it's also true that most students are apathetic— in contrast to the political discipline of some students; but we have to recognize that the situation is the result above all of the fact that for many long years left-wing forces, using every organizational means, have propagandized and fought tenaciously. The logic of the Left became common coin among the students; perhaps the strength to rebut it effectively did not emerge.

One analogy has become potent: "Back around 1935, following on the heels of the suppression of communism, pressure on liberals rose, and thereby the way to war was paved. People of goodwill who tried to defend liberty were scattered and isolated. They didn't combine forces and act. By the time they realized what was happening, it was too late. And what about now? Isn't it that time again? Don't many signs indicate 'Now or never?' The Police Reserves have come into existence, the purge of those considered part of the wartime establishment has been lifted for the most part, Communist Party members are being purged from the media, judo is being revived, the *Kimigayo* resounds, Professor Harada dies, the Ministry of Education calls our movement a disgrace.[6] Isn't it all too clear in the present situation that the evil of the warmongers is heading our way?"

The film *Listen to the Voices from the Sea*[7] was successful propaganda. Showing all too clearly the cruelty of war, it caused this analogy to gain acceptance far and wide.

Young people have no sense of reality. Reality is something they reorganize conceptually, so by instilling that concept, it's relatively easy to implant in them a specific vision of reality and make them act accordingly.

Left-wing students have created a sturdy organization, they have acted energetically under the guidance of outside experts, and they have lots of money. Virtually every day for months, they distributed handbills. Liberal students distributed handbills, too, but they seemed to have less money and distributed small sheets only a few times. Important posts in student organizations were held for the most part by the left wing, and its tangible and intangible pressure penetrated far and wide. It took advantage of the impact of the words "Red Purge," and it also used kangaroo court methods: Do you oppose the Red Purge? No? If not, you're an imperialist. As with intellectuals in general, so with students—it's terrible to be seen as "nonprogressive," and now they say there's even dread: "Unless you're with us, when the revolution comes, you're dead." The power of organization is indeed great. Other people, even if numerous, aren't organized and can't take action. Organization is like Gulliver in Lilliput: when, inspired by a certain idea, this Gulliver rampages, the Lilliputians can only watch.

Still, it is both lamentable and shocking how easily all the students got dragged along. Scattered calls to "Oppose the Red Purge" sounded begin-

---

6. *Kimigayo*, the "national anthem" by custom throughout the twentieth century, was not made the official national anthem until the twenty-first century. Harada Tatsuyoshi (1903–1950) was a Tokyo University professor (Roman law); he committed suicide on September 1.

7. *Kike wadatsumi no koe* was a collection of writings (Tokyo: Tokyo Daigaku Shuppankai, 1949; *Listen to the Voices from the Sea: Writings of the Fallen Japanese Students*, trans. Midori Yamanouchi and Joseph L. Quinn [Scranton: University of Scranton Press, 2000]) left by former students who died in the war; the editors eliminated some patriotic writings. A film of the same name, directed by Sekikawa Hideo, had its premiere in 1950.

ning fairly early, and even such figures as Nakano Yoshio and Mori Arimasa were said to be candidates for the purge. Convinced, on the basis of such nonsense, that to defend liberalism, "We students have no alternative," the students turned to violent boycott. There is no connection at all between opposition to the Red Purge and exam boycott; if a connection exists, it's that the boycott steadily weakened the position of President Nambara,[8] who opposed the purge, and proved a handicap to the opposition to the purge. If the causes of the current incident had somewhat more basis, the school could have been somewhat better prepared!

The greatest eye-opener was the sudden appearance of the action corps. With military-style formations, it dominated campus. Its numbers decreased little by little because many had joined by being stampeded or out of a sense of duty, but at the start it was said to number six hundred, and it acted in well-ordered fashion with frightening discipline; it was virtually a private army. It was probably of the same order as in Nazi Germany. Indoctrinate ideology into young men, stir them up, organize them, make them march, make them sing, and use them to move the world—I couldn't repress the fear that this modern political style might finally be beginning in earnest now in Japan, too.

Several hundred students lined up in four lines and marched, linking arms four abreast. In the vanguard waved an antiwar banner—its ground dyed in two colors, blue and red, and against that ground a painted dove in flight. Placards with slogans in huge letters also kept pace. The whole seethed with energy. Songs of the International Union of Students, with stirring and youthful melodies, made one think it had the encouragement of sympathizers worldwide. The leaders stood up front or walked alongside. This action corps formed a scrum at the gate of the school, stormed its way to demand meetings, sang loudly at the exam site, and sometimes destroyed the blue books of those taking the exam; several officials administering the exam suffered minor injuries from being kicked.

The action corps occupied the tall clock tower, too. Here flags were raised, and slogans were hung. At the signal of those standing watch atop the tower, the corps down on the ground ran here, ran there. Messengers raced about on bicycle. They say that for two weeks outsiders had been spending the nights in a dorm room and that everything proceeded on orders from that room.

When meetings were held and decisions taken, when representatives and the school were negotiating, the action corps mounted demonstra-

---

8. Nakano Yoshio (1903–1985), professor of English literature; Mori Arimasa (1911–1976), professor of French. Nambara Shigeru (1889–1974), law professor, president of Tokyo University after World War II, and leading liberal.

tions. Including a girl or two in its ranks, it formed a scrum. Singing, it circled the building where the dean was, then stopped in front of the building and this time began to quickstep. Shouting, "*Wasshoi, wasshoi!*" the long line moved slowly left and right, as the leader directed, undulating like a snake. Then they lined up in front of the building and began to shout in unison so as to make themselves heard inside. The demonstrations always follow this pattern.

The leader shouts, "Purge Minister of Education Amano, cat's-paw of imperialism!"

The corps chants it back in unison.

Then, "We hate war!" "To expel those who fight for peace and freedom is to destroy order!" " . . . to destroy reason!" " . . . to destroy morality!"

The corps chants it back.

Corps members stay at their posts, accepting orders from above and never acting on their own. The military training received several years ago must be useful—the group actions on command of the leader are crisp. In addition to the headquarters cadre, members of struggle committees are active, and who they are is kept secret. Even if you ask, they don't tell. Apart from the dozen who take very open leadership, you don't know who the main activists are. Everything is anonymous group action; with little power of its own, the school faces an elusive group whose identity is secret.

The school is in a bind. University self-government means handling campus affairs on campus, but no one foresaw that a situation such as this might arise. In order to preserve self-government, the school has to deal with force without force of its own. For revolutionary movements it's the place in today's society with the least resistance.

The school doesn't use spies or the like, so of course its hands are tied; its current opposite numbers are people from the same world as the eight or nine men whom the government, with all its resources, can't nab;[9] moreover, the school doesn't even have administrative authority it can bring to bear.

The academy should be a place of reason and persuasion, and it takes unwavering pride in the fact that academic self-government doesn't allow outside interference. So the concept is firmly entrenched that allowing police onto campus—no matter what the cause—is bad, inauspicious. Bringing in the police means jettisoning self-government; it's very hard to think of it as the use of official force to restore an order destroyed by violence that has rendered official duties impossible. The academy should police itself with its own power; still, the academy must avoid violent confrontations among stu-

---

9. After being purged by the Occupation on June 6, 1950, the top nine leaders of the Japan Communist Party went underground.

dents. Above all, now it has to let as many would-be students as possible take the exams. The academy can't allow students to get into political fights. So in order to keep pep squads from other schools out, teachers have to become gate watchers and sometimes night watchmen.

Once the police squads came onto campus, the commotion was terrible.

At the gate pickets were stationed several deep, the student scrum facing in both directions, out and in. Already agitated, they sang antiwar songs and moved rhythmically left and right. The chair climbed up on the gate and gave a speech. A loudspeaker boomed from the eaves of the guard's hut beside the gate. Professor Ide's message was read out over and over.[10] Applause rose, and the students shouted out the messages the chorus chanted.

Several hundred examinees had gathered in the open area outside the gate. Blocked from entering the campus, they had been standing there since morning; proboycott students mixed in with them, carrying placards with the message, "À nous la liberté!" and arguing.

For hours now, standing between these two opposing forces, the dean had been persuading and scolding. He wanted to lead the examinees somehow or other onto campus; but no matter how fiercely he argued, he wasn't succeeding.

Meanwhile, sirens sounded on the far side of the open area. An eerie cry arose from the mass of students. At long last a detachment of police appeared, riding in white trucks.

With the backing of the police, the dean continued his persuasion, but the situation didn't improve. On the contrary, the mood hardened. The best possible issue had been added to the harangues of the agitators. As time passed, the maelstrom of angry voices grew. The scrum swayed left and right, and just as when water is about to boil, something invisible to the eye seethed above the crowd. Shouting and moving about in confusion, onlooking students joined the scrum.

Thinking that if the students coalesced behind the boycott, I simply had to do something, I too was surrounded by several hundred students. One shouted, "Professor, I voted against the boycott, but with things as they are, can't you call off the exam? This is too much. If things go on like this, something bad will happen. Please do something. Hasn't the faculty stood on the sidelines for too long?" Excited, face pale, jaw trembling, running his hands through his long hair, he pointed toward the gate, where already events were coming to a head.

---

10. Ide Takashi (1892–1980) was a much published philosopher and Communist Party member beginning in 1948; the party later expelled him. Among his books is *Shijin tetsugakusha* [The poet philosopher] (Tokyo: Koyama Shoten, 1944).

The scrum had been broken, and carried forward by their own momentum, two dozen policemen tumbled onto campus. Those fleeing in all directions and those giving chase crossed paths. Arms outstretched, several professors pleaded with the students not to resist the police. Fortunately, the collision of forces didn't escalate further.

The loudspeaker blared constantly. I remember hearing the words, "Extraterritoriality has been breached."[11]

The dean's attempt to escort the examinees through the picket line had been rebuffed, so the police had charged to get them onto campus. They had opened a breach, and it became possible at last for examinees to come in. But now an unexpected thing occurred, causing consternation for the school. Having waited till now outside the gates for the chance to enter, the examinees said, "We refuse to enter under police escort."

Without the power of the police, the school couldn't administer the exam; even with it, it couldn't. To save the situation, the school got the police to withdraw and cancelled the day's exam.

The day ended in victory for the boycott faction.

A student assembly was convened immediately, and it added impetus to the cause. Even neutral students felt aggrieved. That's what a shock it was to see the police up close.

On the pretext of resolving the situation from now on, the chair of the student government asked for a meeting with the school authorities. Among the conditions the students put forward at this time were the following: "Express the responsibility of the dean and the faculty for calling in the police in the form of the dean's apology or resignation." And "Nullify this exam because so few examinees took it."

The school took the position that this exam was absolutely legitimate but that on account of the obstruction many would-be exam takers hadn't been able to take it; so it would let those students submit petitions for a second exam and then would give the exam over. The response: "The National Federation's struggle schedule is set. The proposed second exam obstructs us in carrying out that schedule, so put off the exam until after October 23. If you postpone it as per this request, we'll collect all the petitions and hand them over to you. This way the school will be able to administer the exam without disruption."

In other words, they would collect all the applications themselves, grasp total power, and run the second exam under their own authority.

The school rejected all these demands, but the conditions showed clearly what the students had in mind for the school: complete control of the school. If the school knuckled under to this high-handedness, soon not only student

---

11. "Extraterritoriality" refers to the quasi-independence of the campus from police.

affairs, but also educational affairs would all be theirs to direct, jurisdiction over the school would belong not to the dean but to the student government chair, and the school would wind up a sort of institute under the control of one group of political students. What they especially wanted to control was personnel. According to a rumor—I don't know how accurate it is— the University of Pisa operates in this fashion, and for the progressives that has become an ideal.

Even as Dean Yanaihara was carrying on the arduous negotiations with the students, Professor Ide's message was broadcast repeatedly, and as I listened to it, emotion welled up. I thought: "You never can tell who will become the hero of the day."

Yanaihara had once sacrificed his job to the cause of peace, and for eight years he'd been out of work and not knuckled under. He'd staked his all on not making people hear the "voices from beyond." When during the war he gave speeches, students flocked to hear him. Right up to the end of the war, his was the only such voice. No one could fault his devotion to peace and freedom. But now the politicized students spoke of him as their enemy. They knew little about the events of several years ago. They didn't know who they were dealing with, what they were saying, what they were doing. They even passed out handbills, "Dean Yanaihara fears peace." Just before he departed for the United States, they posted signs, "Don't come back."

I had been acquainted with Ide and knew he was truly good-natured; I also saw that though appearing offhand, he was very sensitive. I don't doubt that subjectively he was always sincere. But seeing the seething tumult into which his message flowed over the loudspeakers, I couldn't suppress this very impolitic thought. His book *The Poet Philosopher*, published during the war, carries in place of a foreword an essay: "A cup of cool water for the student-soldiers going to war." I won't cite it at length, but in essence it told the students to sacrifice themselves: "Friends, may you die beautiful deaths. That is my only wish." One can't conclude from this that it was he who caused them to hear the "voices from beyond," but the new edition of this book that came out after the war omitted this passage. If his purpose was simply that deletion, he shouldn't have issued a new edition, and if it was a reprint, it should have kept this preface and elucidated his position. Hearing the voice now repeating his message—"Friends! I don't want you to have to 'Listen to the voices from beyond' once more. Once war begins, it's too late."—had a different effect on me than on the student "friends." Hearing this message while witnessing Yanaihara's labors, I couldn't keep my temper in check. It was sad to see a person of goodwill being used in such fashion.

The boycotting students used every trick in the book. Political haggling wasn't the only thing. They cut the school's phone lines and wiretapped the school's contacts with the outside. Science majors know how to do that.

At the school, we teach everything. A law professor is said to have taught that in a riot if you hit someone with your fist, you're likely to be caught on film, but if you kick, you're not. "I taught them outrageous stuff . . . " Hearing that, everyone laughed.

Watching the action corps marching, a physical education teacher said, "If they do that every day, they won't need physical education."

Up till now the school had communicated with the students through representatives of the students, but they misrepresented the school's message, so the school was unable to communicate its true intent to students at large. At last, the school started printing and distributing handbills giving the school's views and the actual state of affairs. (The students blocked the handing out, too, so the school mailed them out individually.) This method began to have its effect. So the student government passed this resolution: "It's not right that the school spend our tax money on such handbills." When someone asked where they got the idea, the answer was, "The minister of education. He said it was outrageous that the boycotting students wasted tax money."

One student's assertion: "The Nambara Declaration is vague. It's meaningless to say it's OK to embrace communist ideas but not OK to manifest them in action. If you embrace a political philosophy, it's only natural that you want to propagate it and act in order to realize it. If you don't permit that, freedom of thought is a lie. If such action is inconvenient for the present order, it can't be helped. History shows that since ancient times there's been no progress without revolution, that at their start all revolutions are always illegal and that they become legitimate after the fact. The freedom of thought we demand is a larger freedom. If, in the name of order, you suppress justice . . . "

For politicized students, this is classic logic. The great majority of students have been propagandized, drawn in, and have come to follow along without all that much awareness and without giving serious thought to the issues, but a few leaders are true revolutionaries. Because it's students doing it, we call it a student movement and tend to regard it as something distinct, but in essence it's one manifestation of the international revolutionary movement.

During the several days of disorder, there was frequent discussion at school of the relation between thought and action.

One professor's skepticism: "What does it mean?—You're free to embrace any ideas you wish, and we won't expel you for belonging to a certain political party, but actions are a different matter. If you simply embrace an idea or, what is more, are studying it, there's no need to belong to a party. If you join a party, it's to do political work. People joining a political party have declared their intent to act in accordance with that party's policies. If they haven't acted yet, it's merely a matter of tactical judgment, that the time isn't ripe; but such people surely have a latent predisposition to act. When the time comes, they'll act. Think of what will happen when the revolution succeeds: will those who were members of the Communist Party hold back to the same extent as nonparty members on the grounds that they only embraced the ideas but took no action?

"Even should people with this latent disposition to act be considered unfit to be professors, how does that violate their constitutionally guaranteed human rights? Not everyone can become a professor. Not making someone who can't do math a math professor doesn't infringe on his fundamental human rights; in the same way, I don't think it's particularly illogical to consider people unfit to be professors who've expressed the intent to overthrow the constitution when the time comes. The university doesn't transcend the constitution."

A rejoinder: "That's Eells's argument.[12] The Communist Party is a legal political party recognized by the constitution. If at one point we say that Communist Party members should not be allowed in the university, then at some other point it will be Liberal Party members who shouldn't be allowed in the university. That politicizes the university. The school must be politically neutral to the end. The university, too, must recognize political parties the constitution recognizes. The university doesn't transcend the constitution." The very same words get bounced back.

Rejoinder: "That's the problem. Isn't it a mistake to make it a choice between Communist Party and Liberal Party? It should be between Communist Party and constitution. In the context of respect for the constitution, it won't do for the school to politicize or join the Liberal Party or Socialist Party, but it's only natural that the university reject anyone who would destroy the constitution itself—indeed, isn't that its duty? To reject people who would overthrow the parliamentary system and institute a dictatorial regime is not the simple politicizing of the academy. We have to defend freedom in every sense. In the first place, aren't we seeing every day close up that these people are carrying out an extreme politicization of the school? Just as the Korean War demonstrates that a military vacuum can't exist, so this student incident demonstrates that there can be no neutrality toward communist forces

12. Walter Crosby Eells (1886–1962) was an adviser on higher education in the Civil Information and Education Section of the Occupation and a prominent anticommunist campaigner in 1949. In 1954 he published *Communism in Education in Asia, Africa, and the Far Pacific* (Washington, D.C.: American Council on Education).

in the academy. Because they are infringing on neutrality relentlessly. One can't say that freedom mustn't defend itself against dictatorship. Although the students call that turning fascist. Still, members of the Communist Party get elected to the Diet. Today's constitution itself embraces those who would reject it and destroy it. In the name of liberty it recognizes the liberty to destroy liberty. No matter how it rates as political calculation, it's surely strange as principle."

Rejoinder: "Good heavens! Has 'defend the constitution' become 'reject the constitution'? If so, we can't scold the students!"

This amateurish debate went on endlessly. After all, each and every one of the rampaging students and of the faculty who tried to pacify them mouthed liberty and peace and wished devoutly for them. For liberty and peace the students boycotted, set up their picket line, shouted themselves hoarse, turned red in the face. For liberty and peace the faculty got cramps from endless meetings and functioned as watchmen. What A thought of as liberty and peace, B saw as iron chains and violence; what B thought of as liberty and peace, A saw as exploitation and treason. Thus liberty and peace displayed completely contradictory aspects, so there was no way within the academy to carry on rational persuasion.

Politically gifted young leaders are sometimes given to trickery. This is both because they are narcissistically self-absorbed and because they take the existing order as their formidable enemy. The vast ambition of the leaders among them, their keen intrigue, flashy gestures, adroit harangues, threatening style of bargaining backed up by anonymous mass force—it's a strange connection, but they made me think of petty Hitlers. At the start of the incident they rejected all talks with the school and tried to get their way by bullying. It wasn't a matter of the pros and cons of the case.

The school too took a hard line this time and in the end expelled a dozen students. It's not an easy thing to expel people for their ideas, and up to now common sense has held that "punishment administered clumsily is always a defeat." All students sympathize with those expelled, no matter what the cause, and their side has a national student organization to use for its counterpropaganda. This time public opinion was against the students, so it was possible to expel the leaders. Had the National Association this time too used tactics tailored specifically to each of the schools, it wouldn't have incurred so totally negative a reaction, things might have ended without the mobilization of government force, and each school might have been in deeper trouble. The students expelled this time not only stayed away from the factual investigation of the case but also refuse to accept the notices of expulsion. They assert that they are still students. They feel the glory of having done battle; they haven't the slightest sense of crime. For revolutionaries, *not* to trample on existing law is the crime. Until quite lately, there were stories that the expelled students were getting protection and compensation from another quarter. The student government resolved to continue to recognize them as officers and the dorm, to treat them as dorm students (this resolution was soon withdrawn). That is, even expulsion, the most severe penalty the school can impose, has no practical effect on students as they're currently organized. So far as concerns fundamental solutions from here on out, one foresees many difficulties still.

As I witness these things, I remember again something from fifteen years ago. When Lieutenant Colonel Aizawa murdered the chief of the Bureau of Military Affairs, he hadn't the slightest awareness of having broken the law and simply reported to his new assignment. The public was skeptical, wondering at his sanity, but many young officers stormed into the courtroom and declared their approval of what he had done.[13] Confronted with something more intense, awareness of the law doesn't last long.

Still, it is frightening how little the average student heeds school regulations. For young men brought up in an age of black market purchasing and illegal sales, regulations carry virtually no weight. Speaking to students about school regulations is like talking to a wall. Majority decision is what now carries the most weight with them. Once decided, "the will of the majority" overrides all else.

But if you stand on the side of the core political students, this sort of lawlessness has a consistent logic. It is as follows: "In the final analysis, what we have in mind is not such trivia as academic self-government (we speak of it merely for tactical reasons) or whether this movement is procedurally legal, much less whether the boycott is wasting the nation's tax dollars. It's Japan as a whole; it's humanity. Should the country be engulfed in war, willy-nilly the schools will become slaves. If society as a whole has its freedom stolen away, all assemblies will be illegal. Once that happens, it's too late. We must fight right now, while there's still time. 'Illegality' is illegality merely in terms of laws made by those who spur us on to war. We want freedom and peace! For the sake of freedom, we must obey absolutely the orders of a superior in some unknown location. To achieve peace, we must start riots. This obedience is freedom; this war is peace. 'Against the conspiracy of the provocateurs who tirelessly light the fires of war, peace-loving forces of the entire world are applying decisive force and fighting in order to preserve at all cost our right to life and our freedom—in France, Italy, Vietnam, South Korea, and elsewhere.' We rise up as one link in this international chain.

---

13. On August 12, 1935, Aizawa Saburō murdered Major General Nagata Tetsuzan.

Look! We've received a message from Prague headquarters in support of this action . . . "

They serve "Soviet-style freedom and peace." Take that position, and countries under dictators are enviably free, and the attack across the thirty-eighth parallel was not aggression but liberation, even peace of a sort. Very active at one time, the "Committee to Defend Peace"[14] disappeared with the Korean War, but the movement to gather signatures to the Stockholm Appeal still continues. It will probably continue until the Soviet Union has its own store of nuclear weapons. What they desire most is liberation and inclusion behind the iron curtain; they assert "freedom of speech and thought" vociferously now, with their end goal losing "freedom of speech and thought."

Talk with firmly convinced politicized students and criticize them on this point, and they'll flash a superior smile, look you in the eye, and say, as if pitying you, "Professor, you're still reading only the commercial press . . . "

For people with views like theirs, the current incident is the opposite of what it really is. That there should be no punishment at all for that seditious riot is a shocking assertion, but even some university professors express that opinion: that's because in today's world two completely irreconcilable positions coexist.

The left-wing students who seem to obey no law at all are actually obeying an extremely strict law, self-sacrificingly, in very sincere allegiance. Late one night I listened to a Japanese-language broadcast from Moscow. A gentle female voice enunciating slowly told listeners to write down what she said. The announcer claimed to be Okada Yoshiko,[15] but was it in fact she? In this hour of dictation broadcast nightly, many young men write down their political instructions eagerly. Then the voice instructed them to collect signatures on the Stockholm Appeal. "Those who refuse to sign—how cold-blooded they are! Don't they care if the cruelty of Hiroshima happens again? If people refuse to sign, remember their faces . . . "

A broadcast at the beginning of October praised the heroic struggle of the Tokyo University students.

Five years after the war, the issue of young people that always arises after a war has become really serious. The school too has already become a different place from the school some of us had grown attached to. With the current incident, I think, the old-time camaraderie has finally been wiped out.

---

14. *Heiwa o mamoru kai* was founded in April 1949 and devoted itself to collecting signatures for the Stockholm Appeal and to opposing the Korean War. The Stockholm Appeal was a petition drive the World Peace Council initiated in March 1950 calling for an absolute ban on nuclear weapons.

15. Actress Okada Yoshiko (1903–1992) and her lover, Sugimoto Ryōkichi (1907–1939), sought political exile in Russia in 1938; Sugimoto was liquidated, and Okada became a propagandist.

The students who caused the current incident danced to the policy of inciting domestic unrest before 1952 and creating a "revolutionary situation in Japan." In spring and fall, there's always trouble. This year's fall "grand strategy" succeeded at the sacrifice of the students who were made to dance. The students who were made to dance, one imagines, had thought of it easily to themselves as a simple affair. I asked one activist, "What was your plan for after this incident? It's one thing if the revolution as a whole succeeds, but if not, doesn't it stand to reason that even if you controlled the schools for a time, you'd be done for afterwards?" He replied, "The attack on the government is the task of another section of the party."

Meanwhile a faction arose that favored taking the exam. We rejoiced greatly, but in fact this was the mainstream faction of the Communist Party; there had been friction earlier between it and the international faction that started things. Had we relied on it, the school would have driven the tiger from the front gate only to welcome the wolf at the back.

Some people say that the Communist Party is the only party seeking to make good the shortcomings of today's society. Some say, let's get reformed first by Soviet-style popular democracy, then advance to European-style democracy. Many are irresolute and follow where the masses lead. Some confess their antipathy to the fact that they were unable to resist manipulation by the left-wing students. Most people are lost and adrift, bewildered. What the future holds is not easy to decipher.

Today's student problem arises not because students have some specific grievance against the school; it takes its direction from outside in the light of international conditions and other issues and is a show of force to the nation and a training ground for the future. So it is a mistake to think of it as being only school versus students. This incident was the work of forces with those goals who under the pretense of defending liberalism took advantage of the liberal ideas of average students.

The current incident was an epoch-making event and offered clear lessons for both school and students. It brought a new political and tactical awareness even to those who till then had been daydreaming, unrealistic, naïve. The most important among those lessons is this: if uncritical trust in "Soviet-style freedom and peace" continues unchanged into the future, then there can be no solution to the ideological problem of the students.

~

# Those Who Refuse to Enter the Gate: Thoughts on One Contemporary Frame of Mind

*This is one of the most sweeping and dogmatic essays Takeyama ever wrote; he fin-ished it in April 1951, six months after the boycotting students refused to enter the Tōdai gate.[1] Takeyama rewrites recent Japanese history, sets current events in Japan into the world context of the Cold War and the Korean War, and makes statements about the United States that will surprise many American readers.*

*This essay is a major first step toward Shōwa: Psychology of an Era (1956), the longer work that covers the prewar and war years.[2] Takeyama traces Japan's ills back not to 1930 and the hijacking of the Japanese government by the military, as American scholars in particular were wont to do, but to 1920 and Japan's relatively brief and limited flirtation with Marxism; that's why he speaks of "Japan's thirty years of travail." And he calls the young officers, who were insubordinate and rebellious in the 1930s, "anticommunist Bolsheviks." In this way, the issue is from the first the communist threat and communist totalitarianism, not domestic ultranationalism. So his "dark valley," the term Japanese often used and still use to describe the wartime years, has a different reach from that of other commentators.*

*Perhaps most important, Takeyama refuses to treat Japan as a special case, as uniquely weak and flawed. In 1946 Ruth Benedict published* Chrysanthemum and the Sword, *an analysis she had written during the war for the Office of Strategic Ser-vices, predecessor to the CIA. She did not speak Japanese and had not been to Japan; her sources were limited to what was available to her in the United States during the war. Nevertheless, the book had an enormous impact, both in the United States and*

---

1. The version of this essay in Takeyama Michio, Mite, kanjite, kangaeru (Tokyo: Sōbunsha, 1953) differs slightly from the one in the Collected Works [in Japanese]. The latter omits brief passages (at most, a couple of lines at a time) and makes minor additions.
2. My translation of Takeyama's Shōwa no seishinshi is forthcoming.

in Japan; it reinforced the arguments of scholars who focused on Japan's psychological backwardness. But Takeyama attacks both Benedict's argument and its reception in Japan. There is a "Japanese pattern," but it does not explain the war.

His image of the Soviet Union is uniformly hostile. The Soviet Union attacked Japan on August 8, despite the nonaggression pact still in force at the time; the Soviet Union is to blame for the Iron Curtain. Freedom does not exist in the Soviet Union; the Japanese prisoners of war held for many years after the war and sent back to Japan (from Nakhodka, the port just north of Vladivostok in Siberia) had been brainwashed. He refers approvingly to Arthur Koestler's Darkness at Noon (1941) and to The God That Failed (1949), both anti-Soviet books. In these ways this essay prefigures Takeyama's involvement later in the decade with the Congress for Cultural Freedom, which enjoyed secret CIA funding.

Takeyama never traveled to the United States, and as a consequence he never wrote at length about the United States. His statements here are fascinating and contradictory. On the one hand, the United States is magnanimous Occupier, with General Douglas A. MacArthur as "the man who combined in himself both [Dostoevsky's] Jesus and the Grand Inquisitor." President Truman's firing of MacArthur in April 1951—the month Takeyama finished this essay—provides an object lesson in the openness of U.S. society. On the other hand, the United States is a "backward twentieth-century nation," catching up only in the 1950s with the laudable anticommunism that had swept other countries, including Japan, much earlier. And were the United States to leave Japan, he suggests, it might destroy Japan on the way out the door, rendering Japan of no "use value" to a presumably communist successor. He sees no wrong in the Occupation's "reverse course," during which it undid many of its early, liberal reforms. He even calls for the revision of the constitution the United States wrote for Japan: "Clinging to absolute pacifism . . . is likely to be the road to war." Here Takeyama's course is strikingly different from that of many postwar intellectuals: he becomes more committed to the United States as the Cold War deepens, while they endorse the Occupation's early reforms and attack the "reverse course" and American policy in, for example, Vietnam. As for so many American commentators during the Cold War, so with Takeyama: there's no room for neutrality. Japan's students and intellectuals should see the light, stop shilly-shallying, and "enter the gate."

This essay appeared first in the June 1951 issue of Shinchō.

The exam boycott last fall is important for several reasons and included one highly emblematic incident. To wit, the boycotting students set up a tight picket line at the gate of the university and wouldn't let students who wanted to take the exam through, so the school couldn't administer the exam. Finally, on the second day, having exhausted all options, the school called in the police to break through the line. So a breach was opened, and it was possible finally for the examinees to enter the campus. But now a strange thing happened, causing the school consternation. The examinees who had been waiting outside the gate for the chance to enter now said, "We refuse to enter via the path the police opened up."

Without police power, the school couldn't administer the exam; even with it, it couldn't. To save the situation, the school got the police to withdraw and cancelled the exam. The shock of seeing the police close-up offended all the students; it was almost as if the charge had been proven that the school exercised arbitrary coercion. So the day ended in victory for the boycott faction.

To me this incident exemplifies in point-blank fashion both the mood, difficult to grasp clearly, that prevails among both students and the intellectual class in general and also the effects this mood generates. It illustrates concretely, I think, a psychological dilemma that now weighs heavily on us.

The examinees had to make up their minds on the spot, and they made their decision. The reason they didn't take "the path the police opened up" was their unhappiness that the campus had been trampled on by what they took to be violence restraining freedom. They wanted a more ideal solution for taking the exam. They didn't like so ugly a fact. *No matter what the circumstances, compulsion is bad. Violence is Step One in the destruction of liberty and peace. The turn to fascism opens the road to war. So we refuse to enter the gate.*

So the school couldn't administer the exam, and emboldened, the left-wing students accused the university authorities of suppression—calling in the police—and demanded of the dean either his apology or his resignation. At least for that day, the students who had set up the picket line were victorious and controlled the campus. To be sure, only the school was involved, so order was soon restored and the school even gave the exam; but were society as a whole to go down this path, it would be ruled forever by the victorious side.

This refusal to enter the gate out of love of freedom and peace poses a major problem for us today. Addressing specific concrete facts with vague and absolute concepts of liberty and peace likely produces unforeseen results. The conditions under which we are operating now are tough, and if we hope within these constraints to achieve absolute demands instantaneously, the result may be the opposite of what we seek: this is the worry I can't rid myself of.

Normally, for the most part, I'm in contact with young people, and they are all extremely anxious and angry about today's world tension and the direction Japan is taking amid that tension. They despair over the apparent return of the "dark valley" and think they must resist it. That they can't do so gives rise to today's guilty conscience. The boycott was a manifestation less of communism than of liberalism. Apart from the puppeteers pulling the strings in the background, the students—even the radicals—hoped this boycott would protect freedom of speech and prevent fascist war. But I think things are more complicated than that, and it's critical that we see things as they really are; as one ordinary citizen, I want to offer my opinion. What I write here I'm not at all happy writing, and I know I'll incur the displeasure of many, so if I could, I'd leave this issue untouched and persuade myself that we're in better shape than this analysis indicates; but in our current situation I think my conclusion is logically unavoidable.

## On Freedom

If we are to achieve freedom and peace, can freedom and peace in the real world be absolute and unlimited? If there are limits, what are they?

"At least half of human happiness depends on whether one recognizes the freedoms of thought, belief, expression. . . . The clearest method of proving the correctness of thought and belief is to set all ideas and beliefs out in the free market and see which has the greatest persuasiveness, which is supported by the most people. . . .What is most important for us is to testify to just how correct our own assertions are, not by protecting the freedom of the thoughts we ourselves like, but by protecting the freedom of the thoughts we most detest." I agree wholeheartedly. I aim to make freedom of thought a reality, and I want to contribute in any way I can to that end. I'm taking it upon myself to respond to those voices calling for resistance, who would obstruct it.

We cannot be nonresistant no matter what the situation. We must be intolerant of intolerance. Modern freedom was achieved gradually, through fierce struggle. Protest against restraint of speech is an expression of this intolerance. The advocates of freedom naturally include this intolerance in their advocacy. We blame ourselves and fault others for negligence in the face of the suppression of speech and ideas fifteen years ago. We must be tolerant of speech we dislike merely emotionally or out of some particular interest, and of course there should be freedom to study even intolerance; but we must be rigorous in defending freedom itself. This intolerance is one property of tolerance and is indispensable in establishing it. The intolerant steps we take to achieve it are legitimate exercises on behalf of freedom. Perhaps this is because freedom is something we have to struggle to achieve; freedom is not utter and boundless passivity. Should intolerance use authority to suppress tolerance, people have a duty to resist, and if people seek to destroy tolerance by taking advantage of tolerance, by organizing, and by taking action, forbidding such action cannot be said to deny the fundamental human rights of those whose acts are forbidden. That's because such people themselves would deny the fundamental human rights of the whole group. This prohibition is not suppression. It's the legitimate defense of freedom. Still, it is a prohibition, so an unpleasant taste inevitably accompanies it, but in fact it paves the road to freedom.

We hope for a world in which the powerless and the few can protest against power. So we have to oppose views that deny the powerless and the few and create a world in which only one official view can exist. We reject these views because of their content, not because of the numbers of those who voice them. We must reject such minority views out of respect for minority views. But if in the final analysis a minority view would create a totalitarian police state and lead to a world that does not recognize fundamental human rights, we cannot tolerate it simply because it's a minority view. The "freedom of thought and speech" that asserts that we should entrust "freedom of thought and speech" to a dictator is fundamentally intolerant. Those advocating it fight for it by advocating "freedom of thought and speech" zealously now in order to forfeit "freedom of thought and speech" later. On its face it's a call for tolerance, but in fact it's an assertion of intolerance. It's mere camouflage. Freedom to reject freedom isn't a property of freedom.

Not to resist acts that lead to intolerance, to abstain from using force against such acts simply because force is force, that is the suicide of tolerance. Or it is the acceptance of homicide. This is what results when our concept of freedom is still unexamined and vague, virtually esthetic. Of course, discrimination against an article of faith isn't desirable, but if that article of faith would create a world of "discrimination against articles of faith," one can't be nondiscriminatory toward it.

This is a matter of principle. It goes without saying that it's wrong to attempt to take advantage of principle. Nor can we reject principle merely because it's abused. I've read that it's not good to overvalue freedom, that traffic controls are necessary, and that the Communist Party is the salt of the earth, that it's the only force able to correct Japan's long-standing evils. Prestigious specialists say these things, so hearing them, the perplexed man in the street has no alternative but, like men in the street, to think, "Gee, I wouldn't have thought so, but . . . " Traffic controls are important, and we obey willingly, but totalitarianism isn't traffic control; it says, "You there: don't take this road. Take that one. We'll decide your destination. It's for the good of you, the masses." Even if the Communist Party acts at present very often like the salt of the earth, once it gains control, there can be no salt in a world of power that brooks no criticism; moreover, it's not possible to believe that modern totalitarianism, once it is established, will evolve into a democracy with respect for human rights. It's a dangerous gamble to believe an untrustworthy absolute promise for the future. Because those doing the promising are human beings, not gods.

In a more positive vein, people assert that it's precisely in communist countries that freedom exists. This seems to come down to the issue, "Freedom for whom?" There are far more proletarians than bourgeois, so dictatorship of the proletariat offers democracy for more of the people doing the dictating than does bourgeois dictatorship. But this logic holds only if we presuppose that the two political structures are the same. Guided elections among the proletariat are considered formal freedom, and for those who truly believe in that principle and don't try to go beyond it, that too is freedom; that freedom existed in Nazi Germany, too.

"In bourgeois dictatorships, one is free only on election day to vote for someone, but on normal days one isn't free from starvation or free from unemployment. In proletarian dictatorships, it's the opposite. Which freedom is preferable?" This argument is utterly unpersuasive, but it's the conclusion of theorists writing in the best journals of opinion.

In essence, if it's for the sake of the people, it's OK to disregard the people, and form suffices; this is a separate topic from freedom, and its introduction into the debate on freedom only renders the argument circular.

No matter what the goal, the free demand for totalitarianism is an intolerant demand. As for those now trembling in fear because "the repression has begun"—strip away the opportunistic elements, and it's not repression but defense. One can't think otherwise. Yet our constitution seems tolerant even of intolerance. Is that because it was written in the immediate postwar years, before freedom had split? If we hold to its clauses now, we jeopardize its spirit. In terms of its clauses, it makes sense to weigh Liberal Party against Communist Party; but in terms of its spirit, that choice is strange, and we should weigh liberal constitutionalism against totalitarianism.

The boycotting students believed that what they were doing was a means to the end of freedom. If I could have shared that belief, I too would surely have had no choice but to join the picket line. I too believe that society's freedom takes precedence over the school's freedom; that if society's freedom is lost, freedom of thought too is lost; and that if necessary to save society's freedom, it's unavoidable that we sacrifice temporarily the school's freedom and thus save the school's freedom, too. On this logic I agree with the boycotting students. But I can't agree that there is "freedom of thought and speech" in universities in the Soviet Union or that there is any guarantee of such freedom in the future. Again, I must oppose the argument of the examinees that "police power is fascism"; I have to think the police power of totalitarian states and the police power that breached the picket line at the gate operate according to different principles. In the current case, crossing the picket line saves freedom, and not crossing the line loses it.

## On Peace

On peace, too, the outlook is extremely limited.

Even for communist countries, peace is not the last and highest goal. Communists are not simple pacifists. That's only natural, in some cases legitimate. When Hitler attacked, the Soviet Union fought bravely, and despite the huge loss of life, one can't fault it for not being pacifist. Communist China, too, when it thought its borders threatened, sent troops even though there was a chance atomic bombs would be used. One can't use nuclear weapons, but the use of human wave tactics is unavoidable. For reasons we don't know, China also went into Tibet. Even should a civil war develop, it was maintained, this was absolutely just. What was explained first as counterattack against invasion then became liberation; finally they said it's a civil war that doesn't permit outside interference. The Committee to Defend Peace didn't criticize putting matches next to the powder keg under conditions that might spark worldwide conflagration. Peace is not the highest principle; it ranks below defense, liberation, and the like; even should Japan, a country without arms, be the target, in time of crisis there's only the Sino-Soviet alliance to do battle with. They say that the people of communist countries too fear war, and that's probably true; but if a foreign country were to take advantage of a whole nation's fear of war to pursue its ambitions unresisted, people who preach "peace at all costs" in the face of such a development would undoubtedly be guilty of great crime and be punished.[3]

Japan has use value, so if we were to lose all defenses, we'd surely be absorbed, directly or indirectly, by one method or another, into the Iron Curtain. The reason might be counterattack against invasion or liberation or civil war that foreign countries should not interfere in. What would happen then is my imagination, my nightmare.

In responding to a magazine's question, "What would you do if they attacked?" the majority of intellectuals said they wouldn't resist. What might happen if they stuck to that spirit of absolute peace? If Japan were taken behind the Iron Curtain, the constitution would be amended. Today's

---

3. The Committee to Defend Peace (*Heiwa o mamoru kai*) was founded in April 1949 and devoted itself to collecting signatures for the Stockholm Appeal and to opposing the Korean War.

peace constitution would be abolished, and a bellicose anti-American, anti-imperialist document would govern us. We'd have to act in accordance with that new constitution. We would already have become totalitarian, so criticism and protest would be crimes. Nor could we say, "I absolutely won't fight." The young people of Communist China would be fighting, so could the young people of Communist Japan get by without doing likewise? Liberation and other goals take precedence over peace, so I don't think they could. Martial valor would be drummed up, the country as a whole would become a great military goods factory, and we would go either to fight the French in Vietnam or to make a forced landing on Taiwan: this conjecture isn't far off the mark. Clinging to absolute pacifism, as people now advocate, is likely to be the road to war. At least in terms of the odds, it's the more likely; if you bet on peace, absolute peace will be the price of the bet.

Should that happen, even if it were a matter of defending peace by passive resistance, the present peace constitution would have disappeared, so there would be no basis for the people to act in the spirit of the current constitution. Gandhi's name is too easy to invoke. The enemy wouldn't be Anglo-Saxons who respect human life, nor are we a country that can be self-sufficient spinning thread on a wheel. Even risking your life to defend peace, you'd be risking only death; you couldn't advance your cause. Rather than dream empty dreams of passive resistance after the event, isn't it better to act now, while there's still time, to defend the spirit of the present peace constitution? And in order to defend its spirit, doesn't it make sense to amend, when necessary, some of its provisions?

If the current instance were a choice of either/or—that is, either peace or freedom—and if we could have peace only by discarding freedom and putting up with a totalitarian system, and the young people wouldn't have to go off to war, then discarding freedom might have its reward. But the examples of North Korea and Communist China teach otherwise. Moreover, the history we've experienced teaches us there can't be an either/or choice between freedom and peace, that to jettison the former is in the end to lose the latter, too.

Suppose that the Japanese stick to abstract principle and are nonresistant to absolutely everything, so Japan has no future prospects and the Occupation army withdraws. At such a time, in order to render Japan of no use to its successors, the Occupation army would destroy everything of use value. In worse shape than right after the war, we'd wander starving among the ruins. Because there'd be little use value left, we might not get absorbed into the Iron Curtain, but so long as we had use value, we'd be absorbed. Afterwards, again, another country might come and liberate us. But since Japanese didn't resist in defense of freedom earlier, it would be unthinkable that a second Occupation would be as magnanimous as the first. In the end, it would be total national ruin.

Whichever the case, get this far, and alas, those dreams of absolute peace would be betrayed by reality. All one can do is choose the side that offers the best odds for peace. So long as there are forces that take advantage of "peace at any cost" to advance their ambitions, this emotion is not right even for peace. This fact is attested to by the Europe of the earlier Great War. Talk like this, and you'll immediately be called a war lover or be told, "You go first," so no doubt the wiser course is to stay silent. But this isn't something that can be resolved as an issue of the emotions. We truly are in a tight spot.

There is a counterargument based not on emotions but on fact: Even if you've resolved on nonresistance to defend peace, is resistance feasible economically? Won't you simply antagonize and anger the other party? If you jettison absolute peace, are you ready for the misery of the next war? They won't attack.

Actual methods of resistance should receive the careful attention of specialists; that's not for us to speak of. But in debate among the citizenry, it's OK for nonexperts to speak.

No country anywhere is powerful enough to defend itself single-handedly. There is no alternative but to be covered by collective defense in some form or other and in turn to assist that group of states. States behave now differently from the old days. Even when it's a matter of defense, no country can dream of taking on the world alone; it's not a revival of the old militarism, but action via resolutions of the United Nations, as countries are doing now. These countries can't be thought of as being colonized; their level of independence is higher than if they were to join the Iron Curtain and abandon their autonomy. Economically they'll get by, and it's undoubtedly cheaper than if they were less independent.

"We can't antagonize them!" It's one thing if they get angry only if you anger them, but they get angry even without being angered. Earlier, the Soviet Union attacked in revenge when the neutrality pact was in force,[4] and distrust on this score is wholly ineradicable. It's not a matter of angering them but of offering them a pretext. If it's a matter of pretexts, there are a whole lot of other ones, so it amounts to the same thing. In order to antagonize them as little as possible, be as nonantagonistic as possible. If you are nonantagonistic, they won't get angry. There is no other dependable ethic.

---

4. The Soviet Union attacked Japan in August 1945; though denounced earlier that year by the Soviet Union, the Japan-Soviet neutrality pact still had most of a year to run.

"The misery of the next war will be beyond all imagining." But for the reasons I've already given, even if you try to avoid this wretchedness via nonresistance, you won't be able to. At best, you won't be used like North Korea to attack others. Peace involves other parties, and you can't accomplish anything by your own mind-set alone; you can't restrict pacifism, as people do, merely to your own mind-set. Not only is internal subversion taking place before our eyes, but the Soviet bloc's expansionist ambition, much in evidence in the postwar era, undoubtedly continues, and one can't think moral appeals will persuade Stalin. He's probably hoping for peace. But it's the peace of peaceful invasion. And then?

"They won't attack. That's an illusion; it's a tactic of the imperialists who want to pursue their ambitions by instilling a sense of fear." When I hear this argument, I'm relieved. I cling to this peace of mind. However, if it's possible at all, it's not possible between country and country as we think of them. It may begin by creating an alibi for oneself: foreign countries shouldn't interfere. Internally there are many such elements, and they can get sucked into the enigma that is peace and freedom. We had our fill of seeing this in these last years, and in many other countries it's actually happened. Moreover, implanting this illusion of fear, on the contrary, seems like an ambitious stratagem of the other side—you come to think that unless you submit right away, you'll be sorry later. If that's not the case, it would be nice if the Soviet Union, since it has joined the UN, cooperated more for peace with the UN as a whole. But if, as the Soviet Union's apologists say, the UN is being manipulated for the unilateral advantage of the United States, then Soviet Union secession from the United Nations would be more persuasive . . .

## Confusing Liberty and Peace

Come to think of it, the Japanese since the defeat have been the most fortunate people in human history.

The story of the Grand Inquisitor in *The Brothers Karamazov* is well known. In ancient times Jesus sought to teach man freedom. Then the devil appeared and said: "Anything so troublesome cannot make man happy. Man will be happy only when instead of freedom, he is given bread, given a worldview, and bound by absolute authority." Jesus rejected the offer and gave mankind only the freedom that is a sign of mankind's nobility of spirit. So then mankind fell into fearsome wretchedness.

In postwar Japan we were granted all three of these. Jesus and the devil cooperated in planning for us. The liberty-expounding evangelist imported food, rescuing us from starvation, gave us a democratic worldview and set up the system, and ruled with absolute authority. Because we were trained in this fashion, the road to the broad outside world seems now to be opening up.

Fortunately, the freedom we were taught was dictated; we didn't have the freedom to choose between freedom and unfreedom. And for a time there were no doubts about this freedom. But soon this happy condition came to an end, and the meaning of these grand terms—"freedom," "democracy"—began to shift. I'd almost say this was because the cooperation between Jesus and the devil ended and the two began to oppose each other. Those who returned from Nakhodka with heavy burdens on their backs came ashore with a different conception in their heads, and freedom and democracy began to splinter. Those who emerged from prison right after the end of the war and went straight to GHQ to express their gratitude soon turned traitor to GHQ,[5] and peace too broke into pieces. A great conceptual confusion arose; no one knew what was what. The meaning of terms changed, and some came to have precisely the opposite meaning.

It was in the spring of last year that in our neighborhood this strange confusion became intense. What until then had been liberation came to be termed colonization; democracy came to be termed imperialism; aid, exploitation. The commotion called the "peace offensive" arose, too, and events happened where it was hard to tell whether they constituted liberation or invasion. Some people had already said that freedom is putting up with dictatorship, that the totalitarian police state is the goal of progress, and that those protesting the suppression of minority views are singing the praises of the single-party state; and their counter—"What about you?"—seemed almost to be borne out. Suddenly many people came to use the word "freedom" in a changed sense. The tempo of contemporary life is fast, of course, but those who outlawed armed forces barely five years ago urged armed forces, and just when all restraints on speech might have ended, restrictions began. What had been encouragement for any movement "for the people" turned into the prohibition of the February 1 General Strike, and Communist Party members went underground. Seeing this, people agonized: what they had experienced before was happening once more. They were understandably shocked to learn that signing the prohibition on nuclear weapons in fact increased one country's military might, that this meant war rather than peace; none of the beautiful terms stood on its own, and they all had some hidden meaning.

---

5. Japanese POWs from the Soviet Far East returned after heavy indoctrination. In its early days the Occupation emptied Japan's prisons of political prisoners, most notably the communists Tokuda Kyūichi and Shiga Yoshio, who stopped at General Douglas A. MacArthur's headquarters (GHQ) to offer their thanks.

As, exhibiting this confusion, freedom and peace splintered ever further, two completely contradictory positions came in the end to coexist; freedom and peace—no matter which one it was—collided with another freedom and peace. The third position disappeared, so it was no more than a vain dream to cling to the pre-split situation, when the concepts meant only one thing. A choice presented itself to us, our first in a long time. "The Japanese people are free to accept this offer or not to accept it"—so it was said. We had to choose one or the other.

(To put it this way may still shock some people. The man who combined in himself Jesus and the Grand Inquisitor was suddenly dismissed.[6] Then, the Republican Policy Committee of the U.S. House of Representatives asked four questions of the administration. One of them was this: "Is it inevitable that Japan become a communist state?" We may still be unable to determine our own fate.)

But this conceptual confusion is not in fact something that first arose in contemporary Japan. It had already caused the world suffering earlier. In the age of the Yalta accords and the Potsdam Proclamation, there was a temporary unity, and for a while there was no split; but now for a second time, in one sense in simplified form, it appeared before us.

It's deeply significant, the process whereby before World War II France suffered with that tripartite situation and thereby lost its standing. The liberty that had long shown signs of deterioration, the Nazi sympathizers who hated that deterioration, the Soviet sympathizers who believed in the expansion of freedom—intertwined, these three were major reasons leading to France's collapse.

The confusion in those days was so extreme that even the best minds of Europe couldn't grasp it clearly. Communism was still considered to belong to the lineage of freedom, indeed, to be at its head; poetic and idealistic, the Left's resistance in the Spanish civil war appealed to the conscience of all Europe. In the 1930s, France's great intellectuals outdid each other in their trust of it, praise for it. The Resistance in the last days of World War II confirmed it once again. But soon many of these people discovered that it was the antithesis of freedom and turned their backs on it. Before they turned away, the three strands of the European psyche were represented in the formulation: "Freedom/communism versus fascism." Today's Japanese intellectuals still largely conform to that formulation. It has become virtually received wisdom, self-evident and beyond doubt. Two further factors played a role: since that time and until just recently, news from Europe had been cut off, and fascism was still a latent possibility. Because of the code

---

6. In April 1951 President Harry S Truman relieved General MacArthur of his command.

word "progress," communism was believed to raise freedom to a higher plane.

In Europe today, the confusion of these three strands seems to have been resolved. It resolved itself into an opposition: freedom versus unfreedom. In terms of the three strands, the formulation became "freedom versus communism/fascism." Before, it was thought one looked forward and the other looked back; now both of them, as class or racial totalitarianism, have come to be seen as critical threats to civilization.

Moreover, a new dilemma emerged. In order to resist these totalitarianisms and defend peace and freedom, you can't adhere to liberty and peace on the surface or unconditionally; you must realize that there's another, unseen dimension. People learned from historical experience that brutal forces are at work in the world, so if out of national egotism you avert your eyes, you can't understand history. Now we here are being made to experience this, but we still haven't realized and understood clearly. It's difficult to grasp this complex situation consciously. Unconsciously, the Korean War provided a great shock.

## What Bewitches Intellectuals

The most significant historical event of the twentieth century is the establishment of the Soviet Union; it is a totalitarian country that uses modern tools and, with ideology as a weapon, encroaches on other countries via internal subversion. In order to oppose the assault of this totalitarian country, countries must assume totalitarian forms. Once the foundations of the Soviet Union became firm, countries in contact with the Soviet Union all confronted the issue, "collapse or defend," turned reactionary in accord with their individual characters, and soon went downhill. The countries near the Soviet Union all went fascist. For a while, the countries at a distance sensed only the danger posed by the countries between them and the Soviet Union that had become fascist. Those fascists were overthrown, but the main font and source of totalitarianism remained, and finally it collided with freedom. Once the collision took place, the threat of internal subversion was absolute, and freedom had to restrict freedom in order to defend freedom. A policy of appeasement only strengthened the opponent and left still greater difficulty for the future; so in order to preserve the peace, they had to arm themselves. The United States confronted the Soviet Union last, so it has been the last to take this path. Up till now America has preserved most of the heritage of the eighteenth and nineteenth centuries, but now finally it is in the process of entering the twentieth century. It's a "backward twentieth-century nation." There's a reason Americans say they understand now Japan's thirty years of travail.

The defenders of freedom assume forms that are one step closer to totalitarianism. At this stage, if you look only at surface manifestations, the basis for criticizing the other side disappears. Moreover, there's even a risk they will regress again into the degenerate state that fascism represents. This, I think, is the greatest cause of the difficulty in our current psychic state. People hate to acknowledge this cruel irony. They want freedom and peace to be freedom and peace, think that's what they ought to be. Not willing to put up with the contradictions forced on freedom and peace, they would rather cling to an "imagined void." With this as criterion, they feel acutely that surface manifestations that are unavoidable given the finite conditions mark the breakdown of freedom and peace.

Serving this "imagined void"—that is, measuring reality against absolutes—gives rise to discontents and denials in various forms. The forms range broadly: progressives, fellow travelers, party members.

When human beings face reality, their psychological tendency is not to want to think about the conditions that gave rise to that reality. Most people isolate single phenomena, compare those phenomena with others, and by doing so reach abstract judgments. They take into account only the immediate conditions, not the historical processes that led to those conditions. It's sometimes unfair to equate methods and actions taken at the beginning and methods and actions taken thereafter. Only force can oppose force. In the case of the Korean War, you can't take what happened by the deliberate and active initiation of the communist forces and, since we must judge from the course of events, the subsequent response that led to the carpet bombing of North Korea and the emiseration of the North Korean people and ask: "How can people who resort to such force criticize North Korea's initial use of force?" Still, people sometimes do so. The issue is this: which side attacked first? For people who saw how the Iron Curtain spread after the war, there is no room for doubt about which side is responsible for the tensions in today's world. The same holds true of religious discrimination. In the beginning there should have been tolerance even of intolerance, but because intolerance tried to use tolerance to destroy tolerance, tolerance gradually turned into intolerance against intolerance. This too we have experienced up close in the changes of these several years, so looking merely at current manifestations, I can't believe it represents intolerance for the sake of intolerance. Again, to equate the French under Nazi occupation and the Japanese under U.S. occupation is to fail to differentiate the processes that led to occupation and the future prospects. What they have in common is merely the word "resistance." Even if saying this seems to truckle to those now in control, it's a fact.

Most assertions arise not from a recognition of fact but from a sort of will to believe. Arising from dissatisfaction with reality and the illusions this dissatisfaction spawns, the will to believe has startling power and rules people's hearts.

"The reports in the commercial press are all lies. Because these are propaganda. The reports in the noncommercial press are all true. Because these aren't propaganda." Unwittingly, many people come to think this is true; wrapped in mystery, the unseen world has astonishing persuasive power. The fact that the Soviet Union seals itself off from view is important in generating beautiful illusions. So a good many people believe that "In the Soviet Union freedom of speech is guaranteed in the constitution, there's no censorship, and there are only regulations; in short, free speech prevails. Moreover, although Japanese laborers exhausted from working overtime barely earn enough to keep food on the table, in the Soviet Union 200 rubles of the monthly wage of 2,000 rubles suffices to pay for food. As in the film *Tales of Siberia*,[7] women who work in factories during the day don fine clothes at night and go to concerts." When there's a will to believe, adroit propaganda encounters no credibility check. The supreme commander of the Allied Powers is dismissed by the civilian president and, back in the United States, speaks his mind to Congress, and accounts are transmitted to Japan, too. In such a case in the other camp, it would be purge, courtroom repentance, firing squad, and only the party line. The facts make clear that the workings of the two sides are this different. To begin with, it's a strange government in which so many high officials are executed one after the other for "conspiring with foreign countries"; in 1939 Stalin too conspired with Hitler. Yet credibility is still given to the reports of this camp, and it's a step forward when reports from the two camps get equal treatment. The sentiment that it's unfair not to listen to what each side says is a factor, too, and it makes people think the reports of the two camps are of equal value; moreover, some people think reports from the suppressed, distributed clandestinely, are more reliable.

Exculpation, virtually automatic and blanket, for Soviet acts. That country is categorically incapable of evil, has no shortcomings of any kind. Even if shortcomings exist, these are because the present is a transitional phase and because the Soviet Union is surrounded by enemy countries with hostile intent, or these are the effects of capitalist remnants. Space doesn't permit listing examples of such automatic, reflexive exculpation,

---

7. A Soviet film directed by Ivan Pyryev (*Skazanie o zemle sibirskoy*, 1947) was shown in Japan with the title *Shiberiya monogatari*.

but for the young they are a seductive confusion. This arises in part from the fact that the Japanese have lived in peace since the days of national isolation[8] and haven't known the extremely cruel methods of Europe and are inexperienced and naïve, and also from the fact that at home they aren't suspicious but leave their houses open, unlocked. When the Korean War broke out, as one might expect, it caused the exculpators some confusion. Some sympathizers evaded the issue: "When fire breaks out, you don't look for the spark that started things. You put the fire out." But they soon recovered: "Newsreels just before the war showed U.S. troops, and the backdrop was North Korea, and *Stars and Stripes* reported that the U.S. Army had said, 'Our preparations are completed.' These things prove that the U.S. Army invaded first." Such arguments existed, and since people don't understand such events easily, they swallowed whole hog the logic put out from somewhere or other. One able young scientist believes even now that the United States was the attacker. If he thought otherwise, his entire psychic world would collapse, and in such situations people prefer to twist the facts.

As soon as war broke out, one group that had been zealously active on behalf of peace up to just before the war began to exculpate North Korea's action. Even though it's clear what that meant, neither those belonging to that group nor those who listen to its explanation attempted to judge according to the facts but, of course, simply carried on discussion of its theories.

How subjectively and abstractly man thinks! The human psyche searches for a framework and recognizes as real only those facts that fit that framework. Normally, abstract thinking is thought to be on a higher plane than empirical thinking, but beyond a certain stage, the former is easier and the latter tougher. Ask people back from a trip abroad about the state of affairs in that country, and few respond clearly and concretely. In most cases they'll simply report what they saw, with a specific verification. Ask repatriated people about their war experience, and they'll respond fuzzily and dreamily for the most part or speak of ideas they've read in magazines since their return. Man sees reality as illusion. The reality in which he lives is an illusion illuminated by the light of dark discontent; the reality of a distant country is a reality illuminated by the light of rose-colored ideals. I wish we had a major book on the role of wishful thinking in history!

Man can't stand not to have a psychic framework. I was touched reading the volume of the memoirs of intellectuals who became members of the Communist Party. Every account mentioned this fervent hope. As man's innate—metaphysical, virtually sacred—hope, it has an element of the reli-

---

8. The Tokugawa rulers, 1600–1868, enforced a policy of seclusion.

gious. Gaining such a framework, man can act for the first time with burning desire. Some examples: "Until then, I had been indecisive and gloomy; it clarified things for me. It burned my bridges, transfixed me, nailed me to the cross—brought a quick end to the opportunism of the intelligentsia, which up till then had been my condition." "I set myself in the movement and thereby denied my self. Doing so, I experienced a raising up and a true sense of life." "Submitting to party discipline, attempting to obey, accepting majority rule, acting organizationally, practicing self-criticism—this is to reform the old Adam and create a new man. I recovered gradually from detachment in word and deed and from egotism, characteristics both of me and of the intelligentsia in general. My short temper and peevishness learned patience. My nervous cry-baby-ism is turning gradually into stout-heartedness. The vigorous life of praxis guards my body against illness." We can take these to be the struggles of modern man who feels the burden of freedom and is tired of independence. The weakness of freedom—its inability to set concrete goals for people desperately in search of a framework—was the fundamental shortcoming of Japan in the past, and the fact that this movement provides such a framework is its strength. Freedom can be a goal precisely while it hasn't yet been attained; but once it has been attained, preserving it is difficult to turn into an object of passion. Indeed, the freedom to destroy it makes a more alluring impulse.

Even people who don't join the party yearn for that rose-colored "imagined void," and, with it as yardstick, despair over reality and find consolation and pleasure in speaking ill of their own country. Such uprooted, deracinated people make very good debaters. They ground themselves on a fanciful utopia, but the other side has to take upon itself the many shortcomings of reality. Fellow travelers who feel inferior to the movement become spokespeople against its opponents, sometimes with astonishingly rich resources and doctrinal catechisms learned by heart; debating with them, one gets the feeling one is debating the Soviet Union's propaganda bureau. Moreover, some people say, "I couldn't live in the Soviet Union," and "It rejects what I myself hold most dear, so I can't make common cause with it. But it represents progress, so I won't stand in its way." Among today's Japanese intelligentsia, "progress" and "the backwardness and feudal nature of Japanese society" have become dogma, and so long as one remains captive to this spell, one can't shed the intelligentsia's troubled conscience and inferiority complex. "Progress" is the Open Sesame, the key to everything. The minds of the intelligentsia are under the sway of these ideas, so communism, to them the pinnacle of progress, is above criticism, virtually sacred.

## Progress

Progressivism and its logical corollary, the assertion that all evil is attributable to Japan's backwardness, have dominated the postwar intelligentsia. (In fact, that was already the case twenty or thirty years ago, but the fascism and war of the intervening period are considered proof.) Considering this virtually self-evident, people think only, "Let's move forward!" and this becomes the framework that unifies the spirit of the intelligentsia, their conscience. Those who differ are conservative and reactionary, people who make common cause with evil.

However, this is too pat an explanation of too complicated an issue, too simple, too one-sided, too abstract. There's another way to look at it.

Children mature; living things evolve to a higher level; modern science and technology make astonishing progress and move steadily upward; the masses have been liberated from slavery by repeated revolutions: impressed by all this, people unconsciously take the concept of progress to be self-evident—that's not at all surprising. At one time the whole world believed that firmly.

But skepticism about this optimistic idea of progress was already quite strong in Europe at the end—no, the middle—of the last century. Except that it was still expressed in aesthetic or abstract terms . . .

"Time marches on; we'd like to believe that everything in it also marches on. . . . The most level-headed are led astray by this illusion. But the nineteenth century does not represent progress over the sixteenth; and the German spirit of 1888 represents a regress from the German spirit of 1788." These are the words of Nietzsche,[9] written fully sixty years ago; he scoffed at people who believed that history as a whole followed a natural upward path, called them "cultivated Philistines." Among a minority of intellectuals, skepticism grew steadily, and fin de siècle thinking spread. There were countless exemplars, but Hearn[10] was one such in our neighborhood: coming to Japan at the time of the Sino-Japanese War, he sensed salvation in the wholeness of a still-living past. But most people believed, as before, that civilization rested on a firm base and was progressing ever upward.

This belief was shaken and shattered by World War I. "What 1914 illuminated was a world hardened, stabilized, stationary, or moving in accord with slow evolution at a virtually undetectable pace. What 1918 suddenly showed everyone was the instability of that world. The instability of Western civilization, of all civilization, the instability of all collective systems, the role of violence, the contempt for human life damaged the roots of the

---

9. *The Will to Power*, trans. Walter Kaufmann and R. J. Hollingdale (New York: Vintage, 1968), 55.
10. Lafcadio Hearn (1850–1904).

psyche" (Crémieux, *Inquietude et reconstruction*).[11] This was France, and the mood in defeated Germany was gloomy; most people came to recognize with Spenglerian despair that the modern era is a degenerate era, and this was one cause of the sudden rise of the Nazis.

But belief in progress remained deeply rooted, and for a time it seemed to have the strength to surmount this breakdown. Wilson at Versailles and the success of the Soviet Five-Year Plan breathed new life into it. When the totalitarian nations split into two camps and fought in Spain, one totalitarianism was thought to face forward, and the other, backward (the Nazis abutted the countries of Western Europe, they were an immediate threat, and their methods were undisguised; the Soviet Union was still under construction and showed many indications of idealism), so French intellectuals, traditionally interested in progress, supported the Soviet Union. Among them were major figures who exemplified the modern psyche. But in many ways reality betrayed those ideals, and the cooperation of the two camps in 1939 came as a great shock,[12] and in the postwar era in particular, events like the Korean War occurred one after the other in Europe, so those gods stumbled and fell.[13]

What was believed to be a cure for the disease was in fact a manifestation of that disease. It's not a matter of which of the two is better. Totalitarianism itself, of whatever kind, is not progress but a symptom of the collapse that the modern age has brought on. It's already impossible to defend the belief, strong since the Enlightenment, that history moves in a straight line upward and if not, it's because some evil remnants of the old are blocking it—remove them, and the upward trend will resume. Progress is detectable only from a specific standpoint; from a different standpoint, things look different. Children do mature, but then they also grow old. Living things do evolve, but no living thing lives forever. Moreover, they are done in by their own strengths. Rhinoceroses die by the horn; humans, perhaps by machines . . . ? The masses carried liberation forward, and its zenith was dictatorship. Can we believe it's a one-time, transitional phenomenon? For the sake of an untrustworthy future promise, do we have to put up with so great a burden? Supposedly, dialectical development stops with the appearance of the ideal society, but what if it stops before the ideal society is realized?

Whether history has an overall goal was the issue in the debate between Jaspers and Lukacs[14] and so far as I know, at least among German intellectu-

---

11. Benjamin Crémieux (1888–1944), *Inquietude et reconstruction, Essai sur la litterature apres la guerre* (1930; *Fuan to saiken*, trans. Masuda Atsuo [Tokyo: Ōyama Shoten, 1951]).
12. In 1939 the Soviet Union and Nazi Germany signed a nonaggression pact.
13. R. H. S. Crossman, ed., *The God That Failed* (New York: Harper, 1949).
14. Karl Jaspers (1883–1969); Gyorgy Lukacs (1885–1971).

als the rejection of the idea of progress is common sense. It was before the war that Löwith[15] wrote, "Today people still believe in the ideal of progress only in America and Russia and Japan; old Europe began long since to doubt it"—and the thought of the common people is that "Progress is like covering yourself with a blanket: pull it up to your chin, and your feet stick out; cover your feet, and your shoulders are bare." There's no longer the idea that progress exists, with communism at its apex. Communism is mainly a practical movement of workers.

The maturation of society that Western Europeans now have in mind is something different from progress. It's more like a balance amid the conditions in which man is placed. It's something like the sum total of freedom and equality in finite circumstances, completion amid specific historical circumstances. Hope for a shining, universal salvation is now a distant memory. Reality has taught man that to apply absolute demands directly to reality gives birth on the contrary to unhappiness and suffering.

Koestler's novel *Darkness at Noon* expresses this way of thinking in the following terms:

> The political maturity of the masses cannot be measured by an absolute figure, but only relatively, i.e., in proportion to the stage of civilization at that moment. This process might be compared to the lifting of a ship through a lock with several chambers. The walls of the lock chambers represent the objective state of control of natural forces, of the technical civilization; the water level in the lock chamber represents the political maturity of the masses. It would be meaningless to measure the latter as an absolute height above sea level; what counts is the relative height of the level in the lock chamber. The discovery of the steam engine started a period of rapid objective progress, and, consequently, of equally rapid subjective political retrogression. The industrial era is still young in history, the discrepancy is still great between its extremely complicated economic structure and the masses' understanding of it. We believed that the adaptation of the masses' conception of the world to changed circumstances was a simple process, which one could measure in years; whereas, according to all historical experience, it would have been more suitable to measure it by centuries. They have reached the next higher lock chamber, but they are still on the lowest level of the new basin. Thus it is comprehensible that the relative political maturity of the nations in the first half of the twentieth century is less than it was in 200 BC or at the end of the feudal epoch.[16]

According to the earlier conception, there are advanced countries and backward countries, each containing within it progressive forces, and the

---

15. Karl Löwith (1897–1973).
16. The passage on which Takeyama draws is from protagonist Rubashov's prison diary (trans. Daphne Hardy, New York: MacMillan, 1963, 167–71). The order of the sentences is not Koestler's.

advanced countries take the lead, and the backward countries follow after them; united, mankind is pointed in a particular direction to fulfill overall goals. But now this overall scheme has collapsed: "All goals are particular, temporary, provisional. To formulate all of history as one-time, decisive history is possible only if you always ignore what is essential" (Jaspers).

The historical scheme in the consciousness of today's Europeans is in general the following: History as a whole isn't something that is first young, matures gradually, then gets old. It's large and complex, and any number of life processes intertwine, each rising and falling to its own pattern. The different strata mix and overlap. Every age has its youthful types; every age has its decadence. The passage from Nietzsche I quoted above continues: "When I observed humanity, the overall impression was of a giant laboratory." Over there, something works; over here, something doesn't.

In this complex lab, a common destiny came into existence only with World War II. History finally became truly world history. It is an era of fearsome cataclysm. No one knows whether history can be saved. That's because of civilization's dark side that mantles the whole. Contrary to expectation, "progress" brings destruction. Because a Rousseauian "nature is good" is rooted deeply in European consciousness, this cultural threat that outruns the capacity of the human spirit appeared much earlier in its literature and arts. (One recalls from some time ago the films *Metropolis* and Chaplin's *Modern Times*.)

Japan is no exception to this world history. Japanese think that with progress, all evil will disappear, that they can put to rest all problems by saying all evil has its roots in the static water level in the canal of the past. But gradually, very recently, literary works that take as their theme the tragedy of modern culture have been translated and introduced, and they shocked people, and right at that time, by coincidence, the Korean War broke out. This made people sense that there really are cold, unforgiving historical forces that defy solution by such phrases as the "saving grace of progress" or the "curse of feudalism" and that these forces advance to envelop us. In the face of these things, the opinions of practical politicians are far more rational and convincing than the opinions of the progressives; the latter float off into space. This is because progressives are fundamentally *déraciné*.

## On Judgments of Japanese Culture

In the army, the military men, and the attitude of the people who truckled to them, we had our fill of seeing how evil were the workings of historically backward vestiges of the past; these are things that permeate the Japanese character; they are the cataclysm's true perpetrators—thus the intellectual verdict of postwar Japanese.

But is it really so simple? I have to think that this verdict reverses cause and effect and exaggerates the memory of this war that was result, not cause, in particular the phenomena of its final days, and conflates Japanese particulars and human universals. It also neglects the historical processes that led to these phenomena.

To the extent we can know them, the essential threads of this impossibly complicated historical process are as follows. Beginning in the 1920s, the leftist movement swept all before it, and as was said at the start, it was utterly insufficient to "fight ideas with ideas"; so suppression and prohibition ensued. This was the general reaction against communism, and all the countries in the vicinity of the Soviet Union did likewise. Even America, far from the Soviet Union, comfortably off, and with the greatest tolerance for ideas, is now being driven in this direction. Australia and other countries suspended laws, or tried to. It's not anything attributable only to Japan's feudal nature. It's only that the threat arose early, so the reaction too arose early. Then cause became effect and effect, cause, and things developed in complicated ways. The forms the reaction took were more humane than in Germany, but because Japan was backward in terms of ideas of human rights, they were harsher. In fact, this was the only way to stop it. And even at this point, insubordination in the name of national reconstruction was a rising tide that finally swept the military. The young officers who were influenced by communism and called for the overthrow of the social structure might be termed anticommunist Bolsheviks. They did don ethno-mythical masks, but they hoped to solve overpopulation and economic distress and correct class injustice, and the solution was none other than violence. There was resistance. The general election during the Okada cabinet went overwhelmingly against the military cliques. The result was overturned by coup d'état. Insofar as the swings in popular mood at the time of the Saitō speech and the miscarriage of the Ugaki cabinet and public opinion at the time of the resignation of the Hayashi cabinet are concerned, had the opposition had equal power, it would have been fully effective. Up until then, aside from the ways power was exercised, feudal nature was not a major force. But the power of the military prevailed, and totalitarianism arose, then war. The entire nation was mobilized, life in all its aspects became difficult, and collapse appeared everywhere. Moreover, in Japan control was uniformly lenient, not so harsh as in Germany and Russia, a way of doing things not suitable to modern totalitarianism (in fact, it wasn't true totalitarianism—the seventieth Diet convened but couldn't decide on basic foreign policy, and General

Tōjō resigned in the middle of the war), and because individual desires were not suppressed, collapse amid extreme foolishness became unavoidable. This collapse took what are now called feudal forms. Human weakness appeared in Japanese patterns.

In the process leading to war, the prime mover was revolutionary insubordination, the diametrical opposite of a feudal remnant. The premodern was style, not substance. The crime of the people lay in knuckling under and submitting, but this was not necessarily simply the crime of servile psyches. Of course, there were many things to be ashamed of and blamed for, but one might even say it was a matter of course that the people were unable to offer any resistance to the military's plans. As things got worse, inauspicious phenomena became general, and because they are still fresh in memory, they came to be thought of as the cause of all the bad, and conditions at the end of the war were taken to represent Japanese character itself.

Here we come, I think, to an important matter. I mean the relation between those who shape an age and the society that is shaped by them. The former are usually a minority, a vanguard, a surface wave. Underneath is the deep and unchanging stratum left over from the previous age, and passive and indolent, it is sluggish. It does not understand the new age shaped by the activist minority but suspects, doubts, and scorns it; yet before long it gets dyed by it. This power to color others is what makes the new character new. What supports it is the active life sense unique to the age; the existing character of the majority has lost its power to infect others. It is neutral; it has no formative power. It can't function as prime mover but is dormant. Without power to create new forms, the submerged layer sleeps. (We can sense one example of this clearly in the relation between today's *après-guerre* generation and ordinary people.)

It's usually a minority of activists who determine an age, shape it. The communists and the young officers were like that. Ordinary citizens are not extremists, whether of left or right; in the face of social change they are merely colorless, passive. Even if its character was feudal, the deep stratum below the surface waves was not prime mover and could not determine the new historical direction.

Inhumanity within the military, boss relationships throughout society, and the like—they're often talked about, but had mobilization and total collapse not taken place, this latent character would have remained unchanged. However, total war mobilized even this deep, latent stratum. So when total collapse arrived, in this stratum it took unique forms. The latent became manifest. Those tragic phenomena of the last days of the war and of the postwar probably appear in any nation subjected to the same conditions; they were that agony's Japanese form. The behavior of Japanese when driven to the wall naturally took historically determined forms. One can't use that fact to say these forms were the cause of the crisis itself.

So no matter how much you try to document the inadequacies of Japanese modernization and the backwardness of national character, you can't make it the prime, substantive cause of the collapse. That cause was rather the young officers, inspired by communism and traitors to feudalism. If you say they fought as they did and rampaged with such cruelty because they were backward, the same character likely would have manifested itself even more clearly in the Sino-Japanese and Russo-Japanese wars, when in generational terms the officers were older and more feudal. But such was not the case. Japanese love moral interpretations, so they explained the cause of this latest great drama too in terms of feudal character or subservience—that is, in terms of human character. No one did this more than the progressives, who fault Japanese for having insufficient critical spirit.

After the war, everything about Japanese culture was judged from the point of view of progress. But this involved much nonsense. Cultural forms all have an internal logic, so when we judge individual cultural phenomena, we must think first of their meaning and value in terms of the logic internal to the culture to which they belong, then afterwards weigh them against universal standards. One can't judge Japan's traditional culture out of the blue, in terms of Europe of the eighteenth and nineteenth centuries. Today that painstaking process of judging cultural phenomena is being short-circuited, and Japanese culture is being judged mechanically against the set criteria of another model. This is like exhibiting a cow at a horse show—the cow has horns and can't run, so it's disqualified for not being a horse. What we should do is judge the merits of each—horses as horses, cows as cows, in this case choosing one or the other, horse or cow. You certainly shouldn't say this cow's horns are weapons, so it's bellicose, and it can't run, so it's backward. Moreover, we still have virtually no understanding or awareness of the logic internal to that special thing, culture's Japanese pattern (*The Chrysanthemum and the Sword* tried, but didn't succeed), and the intelligentsia adheres to abstract, universal principles and doesn't like to admit that such a thing exists; so the average Japanese will continue to move according to Japanese patterns, separate from the intellectual consciousness of the Japanese elite.

To apply set logic and make snap judgments about everything is a dereliction of the intellectual duty of the intelligentsia. If I may say so, lazy intellectuals should be very embarrassed to speak ill of a diligent people who are the world's best at making few demands and working away in silence.

## Conclusion

Facing grim reality and thinking factually, we can't save freedom and peace by hoping for them in some "imagined void." Faced with a fateful choice, we must recognize this. Given that human dignity—choice—has been restored, we must also accept the anguish that accompanies choice. And we must minimize the ills that accompany and take advantage of choice.

Liberalism used to be called the breeding ground of communism; now it's the tool of American imperialism. In both cases, incidental impurities are mistaken for an unexamined freedom. It's very difficult to get rid of the impurities and attain freedom in its true form. But this is the task.

If we say, "For the sake of freedom, adopt a certain intolerance and for the sake of peace, discard nonresistance," we must accept ridicule for a certain superficial similarity to the earlier age of fascism. Earlier, the reaction against communism was carried out with no self-awareness and gave way in the end to another totalitarianism. (At the time of the Saitō cabinet, there was about a year when the balance held.) This time we must defend ourselves against totalitarianism without letting ourselves fall prey to any totalitarianism. If people confuse this defense with totalitarianism itself, then it will be totalitarianism that takes advantage. It's on this tricky fine line that we stand.

Even though it shows signs of decline, the Soviet Union probably has much right to speak about equality. Or had much right, or wishes it had. And in order to further equality, this justice that has been left to the future, it is sacrificing both freedom and peace. Moreover, using freedom and peace as means, it presumes on the feelings of people in other countries, people who want to believe in freedom and peace. But freedom is the foundation of everything. If freedom disappears, peace disappears—history attests to this beyond all doubt; and given that "absolute power corrupts absolutely" and that today totalitarian power cannot be overthrown from within, freedom is also essential for equality. Freedom can be placed in someone else's keeping only in very extraordinary situations and only temporarily; it can be entrusted for a long time without damaging equality and peace only to God, not to man. Freedom contains inequality; equality contains unfreedom; and peace, in maintaining the status quo, injustice. This is the lamentable condition of human existence. But at the present time, freedom is the prime issue.

I'm wary of such slogans as "To be neutral is to cooperate with aggression," and I hate seeing compulsion and its like before my very eyes; they have the smell of weapons. But now is not the time to linger outside the gate.

# Index

A., teacher of mathematics, 45
Abe Yoshishige, xx, xxi, 19, 35–36, 42, 115, 116, 142
Africa, 118
air raids, 37, 41, 42, 44–46, 61–62, 64–65, 115
Aizawa Saburō, 169, 169n13
Akatombo, 72
Allen, Louis, 16
Allies, the, 132
Amano Teiyū, 162
American Occupation. See Occupation of Japan
Anami Korechika, 50
Anglo-Saxons, 113, 180
Anti-Comintern Pact, 99
anticommunism, 23, 174, 194
Antigone, 60
appeasement, 185
Arabian Nights, 69, 79, 80
Araki Sadao, 126, 129, 131–32
Asahi, 119
assassination, 141
atomic bombs, 153, 170, 179, 183. See also Hiroshima

atrocities, 18, 71, 77, 147, 149
Augustine, Saint, 107
Axis, 134
Axis Alliance. See Tripartite Pact (Axis Alliance)

Baba Kimihiko, 3, 12, 18
Bach, Johann Sebastian, 47, 112
Bataan Death March, 125
Baudelaire, Charles, 44
Benedict, Ruth. See Chrysanthemum and the Sword, The
black market, 69, 79–80, 169
Brehm, Bruno, 101, 104–5
Britain. See Great Britain
Buddhism, 14
Burckhardt, Jacob Christoph, 112
Burma, 13–17

censorship, xxvii, xxviii, 1, 127
Central Intelligence Agency (CIA), 19, 21, 22, 173, 174
Chamberlain, Neville, 141
Chichibu, 46–48, 51
China, 4, 5, 15, 18–19, 125, 158; Harp

of *Burma* and, 13, 71; Communist, 179, 180; North, 71–78, 90–94, 146
*Chrysanthemum and the Sword, The,* 173–74, 196
*Chūō kōron,* 19, 153
Cocteau, Jean, 10, 116
Cold War, 2, 18, 19–21, 173, 174
Coleman, Peter, 26n40, 26n42
Committee to Defend Peace (*Heiwa o mamoru kai*), 170, 179, 179n3
communications, 59–60
communism, 166, 176, 179, 185, 192, 194, 197; and the Reds, 119; 1930s suppression of, 160; totalitarianism and, 18, 185. *See also* China; Soviet Union; and individual purges
Communist Japan, 180
Communist Party. *See* Japan Communist Party (JCP)
Congress for Cultural Freedom (CCF), 6, 19–20, 21–23, 26n40, 27n48, 27n50
Constitution (1946), 167, 168, 174, 178, 180
Crémieux, Benjamin, 190–91
crimes. *See* atrocities

"dark valley" (*kurai tanima*), 173, 176
delayed-action bombs, 55, 58
democracy, 19, 104, 110, 171, 182, 183
*Democracy* (magazine), 51
Democratic Union. *See* "take the exam" faction (Democratic Union)
dictatorship, 105, 106, 178, 183
DuBos, Charles, 66

East, the, 118
Eells, Walter, 167, 167n12
emperor, 50, 51, 62, 62n15, 120
England. *See* Great Britain
Enlightenment, the, 110, 112, 113, 191
Epstein, Jason, 21
erotic/grotesque, 119

Etō Jun, 127
Euripides, 69
Europe: after World War II, 185, 192, 193; before World War II, 54, 117, 118, 132, 181, 184, 188, 190; culture in, 16–17, 99, 105, 106, 107, 108; elite education in, 7; nationalism and, 109; Takeyama's travels in, 6, 17, 100, 106; writers in, 6, 9

fascism, 145, 175, 179, 184–85, 186, 190
fate, 16, 53, 55–69
*Faust,* 112
February 1 General Strike, 183
February Revolution (1848), 132
February 26 Incident (1936), 156
feudal character, 135, 193, 194, 195
first higher school. *See* Ichikō
food shortage: Ichikō students and, 32–33, 37, 38, 41, 42, 115, 182; in "Scars," 79–89; Takeyama family and, 48, 49, 53, 55, 68; force, 61
France: after World War II, 169, 180; before World War II, 111, 116, 118, 132, 184, 190–91; and the Enlightenment, 110; Takeyama's preference for, 9; in World War II, 114, 148, 186; writers of, 107, 115
France, Anatole, 106
Franklin, Benjamin, 130
freedom: defined, 109, 176–79, 182–85; Nazi Germany's rejection of, 106, 114; in the 1930s, 160; in postwar Japan, 154, 158, 166, 169, 175, 197; Soviets and, 170, 187, 197; Takeyama praised for, 22
French Revolution, 156
Fukuzawa Ichiro, 20

Gandhi, Mahatma, 180
George, Stefan, 18, 118
Germany: culture of, 100, 108–10,

136, 190; Goebbels's speech about, 101–5; Hitler's speech about, 105–6; national character of, 99, 111–14; and new Middle Ages, 106–7, 110–11, 114; Takeyama's travels in, *xviii*, 100; Weimar period, 100, 106–7, 116, 118–19, 121, 191; World War II and, 115, 127, 132, 135, 148, 194. *See also* Nazism

GHQ (General Headquarters, SCAP), 183, 183n5

Gide, André, 116, 118

Glaeser, Ernst, 116–17

*God That Failed, The*, 174, 191, 191n3

Goebbels, Joseph, 99, 100–5, 106, 107, 110, 114, 117

Goethe, Johann Wolfgang von, 13, 100, 112

Goldstein, D., 28n50

Grand Inquisitor (Dostoevsky), 174, 182, 184

Great Britain, 5, 7, 22; before World War II, 110, 111; in World War II, 15, 71, 114, 141

Great War. *See* World War I

Greek tragedies, 66

guilt. *See* war guilt

Hague, The, 125

Hall, Ivan P., 2, 18, 21, 23, 26n45, 28n51

Harada Tatsuyoshi, 160, 160n6

*Harp of Burma*, 2, 6, 10, 12–19, 28n50; film treatments of, 2, 6, 17; and Ichikō, 10, 18; "Mizushima" in, 4, 15, 25n31; translations of, 22, 25n31

Hayashi Kentarō, 99

Hayashi Senjūrō, 145, 145n4, 194

Hearn, Lafcadio, 190, 190n10

Hebbel, Christian Friedrich, 4

Hegel, Georg Wilhelm Friedrich, 55

Heraclitus, 62

Hesse, Hermann, 17, 117

Hibbett, Howard, 13–14

Hidaka (head teacher), 35–36

higher schools, 6–8, 17, 40, 40n17. *See also* Ichikō

Hirabayashi Taiko, 20

Hirakawa Sukehiro, xi, 16, 24n3, 100

Hiroshima, 43, 49, 125

Hirota Kōki, 143, 143n3, 145n4

Hitachi, 11, 31–34, 39

Hitler, Adolf, 119, 141, 179, 187; speech by, 99, 100, 105–6, 117; student leaders compared to, 154, 168. *See also* Nazism

Hölderlin, Friedrich, 112

humanism, 2, 11, 17–18, 22, 108

human liberation, 108

human rights, 121, 126, 167, 177, 178, 194

Hunt, John, 20, 21, 26nn46–47, 27n48

Hussein, Saddam, 125

Hutten, Ulrich von, 58

Ibsen, Henrik, 6

Ichikawa Kon, 2, 6

Ichiki Kitokurō, 4

Ichikō, *xiv*, *xv*, *xix*, 6–10, 17–18, 153; and capes, *xv*, 37; and "dorm rain," 8, 40, 40n17; faculty of, *xv*; graffiti at, 40; labor service and, *xxii*, 11, 31–39, 43, 45–47; military and, *xxiii*, 34, 39–41; non-Japanese students at, 9; send-offs for students bound for military service, *xxiv*, 38; Takeyama and, *xvi*, *xvii*, *xviii*, *xix*, *xxiii*, *xxiv*, 100, 115–16, 142; and townspeople, 31–33; wartime conditions at, *xxi*, *xxii*, *xxv*, *xxvi*, 31–42, 120. *See also Harp of Burma*; Komaba campus

ideology, 66, 105, 110, 133–34, 136

Ide Takashi, 163, 163n10, 165

Ienaga Saburō, 19

"imagined void," 186, 197

Imperial House. *See* emperor
imperialism, 183
Imperial Japanese Army, 146, 148
Imperial Japanese Navy, 146
individualism, 135
intellectuals, 136, 147, 175; of Europe, 118; postwar, 174, 184, 185–89; responsibility of, 146, 196
internal subversion, 182, 185
International Association for Cultural Freedom (IACF), 2, 22. *See also* Japan Cultural Forum (JCF)
International Military Tribunal for the Far East, 125–37, 139–40, 145
International Union of Students, 161
intolerance, 154, 176–77, 186, 197
Iron Curtain, 170, 174, 179–80, 181
Isaiah 53, 143
Ishihara Hōki, 20
isolation, 188, 188n8
Italy: and European culture, 110; postwar, 169; Takeyama and, 5; and war, 108, 111, 127, 132, 148

James 4:1, 126
Japan Communist Party (JCP): postwar, 19, 163n10, 167–68, 171, 177–78, 188–89; and purge, 153, 160, 162, 162n9; and war, 61, 61n14, 183, 183n5. *See also* communism; Marxism
Japan Cultural Forum (JCF), 20, 21, 23, 27n48. *See also* International Association for Cultural Freedom (IACF)
Japanese Diet, 3, 168
Japanese national character. *See* national character
Japanese surrender, 43, 62, 71, 90, 115
Jaspers, Karl, 191, 191n14, 193
Jelenski, K. A., 27n50
Jiang Kai-shek, 18, 92
*Jiyū*, 6, 19–23, 26n40, 26nn46–47, 27n48

Kamakura, 46, 48, 51, 64, 71, 155n2
*kamikaze*, 1, 38
Kanazawa Hakkei, 43–44
Katayama Toshihiko (T. K.), 53
Kats, Ivan, 22
Kawabata Yasunari, 24n10
Kawamura Minato, 17
Kawasaki, 36–37
Keene, Donald, 16
Keyserling, Hermann, 107
Kierkegaard, Søren, 63
*Kimigayo*, 160, 160n6
Kimura Kenkō, 36–37
Kimura (teacher), 42
Koeber, Raphael, 139
Koestler, Arthur, 174, 192
Koizumi Shinyo, 19
*Kokoro*, 71
Komaba campus, *xiv*, 31, 115, 153. *See also* Ichikō
Konoe Fumimarō, 119, 147
Korea, 4, 6, 9, 15, 125; North, 180, 182, 186, 188; South, 169
Korean War: lessons of, 167, 173, 185, 191; outbreak of, 153, 159, 186, 193

labor service. *See* Ichikō
Left, the Japanese, 6, 23, 153; and student boycott, 154, 159, 160, 175
liberal education, 135
liberalism, 2, 161, 176, 197; and prewar Japan, 32, 160; Thomas Mann on, 35
Liberal Party, 167, 178
liberals, 35, 160
liberty. *See* freedom
*Listen to the Voices from the Sea*, 160, 160n7, 165
Löwith, Karl, 192
Ludendorff, Erich, 110
Lukacs, Gyorgy, 191, 191n14
MacArthur, General Douglas A., 174,

184, 184n6. *See also* Occupation of
Japan
Maistre, Joseph de, 107
Manchukuo, 9, 15
Manchuria, 43
Mann, Heinrich, 106, 118
Mann, Thomas, 6, 9, 18, 32, 35, 118
Marco Polo Bridge, 146, 146n5
Maruyama Masao, 19
Marxism, 173
Maurras, Charles, 118
Mereon (Mereyon). *See* Woleai
(Mereon)
*Metropolis*, 193
Metropolitan Police Headquarters, 156
Middle Ages, 107, 111, 117
Middle Dorm. *See* Takeyama Michio
Military Affairs Bureau, 34, 39, 41
military (Japanese): in China, 72–78,
90–94; and militarism, 16, 181;
police, 38, 42; and politics, 59,
141–42, 147, 173, 193, 194; training,
*xxiii*, 31, 34; and war crimes trials,
148; and wartime inspections, 34,
39, 40–41; young officers, 148, 169,
173, 194. *See also* Imperial Japanese
Army; Imperial Japanese Navy
Ministry of Education, 160
Minobe Tatsukichi, 11
Mizuno Rentarō, *xviii*
"Modern Civilization," 126–27, 128–37
*Modern Times* (film), 193
Morand, Paul, 116
Mori Arimasa, 161, 161n8
Mörike, Eduard Friedrich, 53, 55–57
Mozart, Wolfgang Amadeus, 56–57, 67,
68
Mr. ____, 49–51

Nagasaki. *See* Hiroshima
Nagata Tetsuzan, 169, 169n13
Nagatoro, 46–47
Nakano Yoshio, 161, 161n8

Nakhodka, 183, 183n5
Nambara Declaration, 166
Nambara Shigeru, 161, 161n8
Napoleon, 59
Narita Ryūichi, 17
national character, 99, 149, 173, 193–
95, 196
National Federation (*Zengakuren*), 158,
158n5, 164, 168
Natsume Sōseki, 6
Nazism, 127, 191; culture of, 118–19;
Japan compared to, 119, 148,
161; and Jews, 105, 117, 144; and
modernity, 136–37; and repression,
114, 178; Takeyama's criticism of,
5, 23, 99–114. *See also* Germany;
Goebbels, Joseph; Hitler, Adolf
Negroes, 118
neo-Kantianism, 116, 136
Neutrality Pact (nonaggression pact,
USSR-Japan), 174, 181, 181n4
"New Middle Ages, A," 106, 107, 108,
110, 114
Nietzsche, Friedrich, 6, 112, 114, 117,
118; quotations from, 11, 58, 60,
127, 133, 190, 193
Nitobe Inazō, 6
Nogi Maresuke, 12
Novalis, Friedrich von Hardenberg,
107, 112
nuclear weapons. *See* atomic bombs;
Hiroshima
Nuremberg Trial, 125–26

*Oblomov*, 45, 45n4
Occupation of Japan, 19, 53, 127,
153, 174, 180, 186; and purge,
153; and Red Purge, 153, 154, 159;
reverse course of, 173, 174; second
Occupation, 181
Oedipus, 58, 158
Office of Strategic Services, 173. *See also*
Central Intelligence Agency (CIA)

Okada Cabinet, 145, 145n4, 194
Okada Ryōichirō, 3
Ōkawa Shūmei, 125, 126, 128
Okuizumi Hikaru, 17
oppression, 158
organization: and Germany, 113–14;
and Ichikō students, 39; and modern
state, 34, 58, 61, 131–33, 136; and
Tokyo University students, 156, 159,
160, 161
Ōrui Noboru, 108

pacifism, 174, 179
Pascal, Blaise, 61
Passin, Herbert, 19–20, 21, 23
peace: and communism, 179, 180, 185,
197; in left-wing propaganda, 169,
175, 181, 182, 183, 184, 186. See also
pacifism
Peace Preservation Law, 155, 155n1
PEN Club, 6
Petzold, Bruno, xix, 9, 24n20
police: Reserves, 160; and student
protests, 162–64, 175; thought
police, 155, 155n1. See also
Metropolitan Police Headquarters
Potsdam Conference and Proclamation,
43, 50, 184
POWs, Japanese, 125, 174, 183, 183n5
Prague, 158, 158n5, 170
progressivism, 3, 190–93
Prometheus, 61
propaganda: American, 49; communist,
187, 189; in general, 110, 166;
Japanese, 60; of the Left, 159, 166
Proust, Marcel, 66

rationalism, 120, 121
Reader's Digest, 69
reason, 110, 117, 120, 162
Red Purge. See Occupation of Japan
Remarque, Erich Maria, 10, 116
Renaissance, the, 108, 109, 110

revolutionary movement, 153, 162, 166,
169, 171
Rilke, Rainer Maria, 18
Roden, Donald, 7, 10
Röling, B. V. A., 126, 139–49
Rolland, Romain, 10, 53
romanticism, 107, 111, 113, 121
Rousseau, Jean Jacques, 193
Russia. See Soviet Union
Russo-Japanese War, 3, 196

Saitō Makoto, 197
Saitō Takao, 145, 145n4
"Scars," 18
scholarship, 133
Schopenhauer, Arthur, 112
Schweitzer, Albert, 5–6, 13
Security Treaty (U.S.-Japan), 27n48
Seidensticker, Edward, 19, 21, 22, 23,
25n39, 27n48
Sekai, 19, 72
Seki Yoshihiko, 21, 26n46
Shibuya, 35, 38, 43, 46, 153, 154
Shiga Yoshio, 183, 183n5
Shigemitsu Mamoru, 143, 143n3
Shinchō, 43, 53, 139, 174
Shisō, 99
Sino-Japanese Incident (1937–1945),
119
Sino-Japanese War (1894–1895), 3,
190, 196
Socialist Party, 167
Sophocles, 57
South Pacific, 13, 35, 47
Soviet Union: apologists for, 170, 187,
189, 191; before World War II,
108, 110, 170n15, 185, 191, 194;
and Cold War, 154, 182, 185, 197;
and democracy, 171; and freedom,
178–79; and Iron Curtain, 174, 179;
in World War II, 179, 187, 194;
World War II entry of, 49, 125, 174,
181, 181n4

Spanish Civil War, 184, 191
Spengler, Oswald, 107
Stalin, Joseph, 182, 187
*Stars and Stripes*, 188
Stevenson, Robert Louis, 126–27, 127n3
Stockholm Appeal, 170, 170n14
Stone, Shepard, 21
students: action corps of, 159, 161–62, 166; compared to Nazis, 153–54, 161; postwar protest movement of, 153, 154–71, 174–76, 178–79. *See also* Ichikō; Tokyo Imperial University; Tokyo University
Supreme Commander for the Allied Powers (SCAP), 140, 140n2, 187. *See also* MacArthur, General Douglas A.
surrender. *See* Japanese surrender.
Suzuki Kantarō, 50
Symonds, John Addington, 126

Tachikawa, 46–48, 51, 65
Taiwan, 4, 9, 125
Takada Rieko, 17–18
Takayanagi Kenzō, 20
"take the exam" faction (Democratic Union), 158, 158n5
Takeuchi Yoshimi, 16
Takeyama Michio: and Congress for Cultural Freedom, 2, 6, 19–23, 26nn46–47, 27n48, 27n50, 29n51; family background of, 3–4; foreign travels of, 4–5, 6, 13, 17, 100, 106; and Germany, *xviii*, 16–17; and Ichikō, *xvi*, *xix*, *xxiv*, 4, 6–7, 10–12; and labor service, 11, 31–34, 43–46; later life of, *xxix*, *xxx*; and Middle Dorm, 36, 37, 41, 116; and *Shōwa no seishinshi* (*Showa: Psychology of an Era*), 126, 139, 173; and Tokyo Imperial University, *xvii*, 4, 6; and Tokyo University, 4, 6, 153. See also *Harp of Burma*; "New Middle Ages,

A;" "Modern Civilization;" "Trial of Mr. Hyde"
*Tales of Siberia*, 187, 187n7
Tanaka Kōtarō, 20
telegraph, 130
T. K. *See* Katayama Toshihiko (T. K.)
Tōgō Shigenori, 50, 143, 143n3
Tōjō Hideki, 125, 126, 128, 129, 194–95
Tokuda Kyūichi, 183, 183n5
Tokyo Imperial University, *xvii*, 4, 100
Tokyo trial. *See* International Military Tribunal for the Far East
Tokyo University, 25n39; and Ichikō, 153; self-government at, 158, 162–63, 169; and student protests, 27n48, 154–71, 174–76; and Takeyama, 4, 6, 153; and Tokyo Imperial University, 11–12, 153
totalitarianism, 178, 180, 186, 191, 194, 197
total war, 195
"Trial of Mr. Hyde," *xxvii*, *xxviii*, 34n7, 125–37
Tripartite Pact (Axis Alliance), 99
Truman, Harry S., 153, 174, 184n6, 187
*24 Eyes*, 17

Uchida Shūhei, 4
Uchimura Kanzō, 4
Ugaki Kazushige, 59, 145, 145n4, 194
ultranationalism, 142, 173
United Nations, 125, 181, 182
United States, 7, 127, 157, 165, 192; Army, 51, 188; bombing of Japan, 1, 62, 64–65; and Cold War, 21, 27n48, 27n50, 182, 185, 194; Congress of, 187; imperialism of, 197; Supreme Court of, 140; Takeyama and, 173–74; in World War II, 32, 63–64. *See also* Central Intelligence Agency (CIA); Congress for Cultural Freedom (CFF); Occupation of Japan; Office of Strategic Services

USS *Enterprise*, 6
Utitz, Emil, 117, 118

Valéry, Paul, 118
Vietnam, 169, 174, 180
vitalism, 118
Volta, Alessandro, 130
Voltaire, François Marie Arouet de, 132

Wagner, Richard, 112–13
war guilt, 18, 130, 143, 144–48
Waseda University, 157
Washio (student), xxv, 38
weapons, 34, 58, 61, 109, 131, 132–33, 136
West, the, 120

Woleai (Mereon), 71–72, 79
World War I, 111, 114, 118, 119, 129, 136, 181, 190
World War II, 1, 184, 193

Y, Major General, 39, 41
Yalta accords, 184
Yamamoto Isoroku, 119
Yanagida (teacher), 38
Yanaihara Tadao, 6, 154–55, 155n1, 159, 163, 164, 165, 175
Yokusan election, 145, 145n4
Yonai Mitsumasa, 50

Ziegler, Leopold, 106–7

# About the Editor

Richard H. Minear is professor of history at the University of Massachusetts, Amherst. He is the author of *Victors' Justice: The Tokyo War Crimes Trial* (1971) and *Dr. Seuss Goes To War* (1999). His translations include *Requiem for Battleship Yamato* (1985), *Hiroshima: Three Witnesses* (1990), *Black Eggs* (1994), and the autobiography of historian Ienaga Saburō, *Japan's Past, Japan's Future: One Historian's Odyssey* (2001), for Rowman & Littlefield.